Early Enthusiasm for

David Garrison's

Church Planting Movements

"...an extraordinary and ground-breaking book. From now on it will not be possible to discuss evangelism and missions without considering Garrison's description of a church planting movement. Certainly, everyone who reads this book will deeply desire to see a church planting movement break out among his own community."

— Dr. Robert Garrett
Professor of Missions
Dallas Baptist University

"We need this book TODAY! Both laity and missionaries will mine the riches of this new resource of CPM best practices. CPM advocates enjoy!"

— Dr. Michael Barnett
Chair of Missionary Church Planting
Columbia International University

"David Garrison's Church Planting Movements is a powerful new strategy showing how God is working in the world today and demonstrating how He wants to work."

— Dr. Steve Wilkes
Professor of Missions
Mid-America Baptist Theological Seminary

"This informative and inspiring book will stir the souls and captivate the minds of lay people, pastors, missionaries and educators."

— Dr. Daniel Sanchez
Director of the Scarborough Institute of Church Growth
Southwestern Baptist Theological Seminary

Church Planting Movements

Church Planting Movements

How God is Redeeming a Lost World

by David Garrison

WIGTake Resources
www.churchplantingmovements.com
Printed in Bangalore, India

CHURCH PLANTING MOVEMENTS

by David Garrison

www.churchplantingmovements.com

ISBN-0-9747562-0-2

First printing, January 2004
Second Printing, March 2004
Third Printing, October 2004
Fourth Printing, May 2005
Fifth Printing, March 2006

Printed by Sri Sudhindra Offset Process, Bangalore, India
Cover design by Zia at www.grafixetc.com.
Maps created by Vance Worten.
Author photo by D.P. Smith

Garrison, V. David
  Church Planting Movements, how God is redeeming a lost
world/David Garrison.

Contents

Part Three: Lessons Learned

Part Four: Launch Pad

Additional Resources

Acknowledgements

So many faces peer over my shoulder as I finish this book. Thank you Sonia, Jeremiah, Seneca, Amanda and Marcus, my loving family who joined me in pursuing God's Church Planting Movements far beyond our comfort zone in America.

Over the past decade I have been a shameless plunderer of the best Church Planting Movement practices around the globe. Some individuals have been particularly helpful in providing me their riches. Bill and Susan Smith, Curtis Sergeant, Bruce Carlton, Brother Ying, Dr. Choudhrie, Brother Shahadat, David Watson, Jim Slack. Michael Barnett, Karen Simons, Vance Worten, Zia van der Veen, Scott Holste, Avery Willis, Larry Cox, and Jerry Rankin have also been invaluable contributors to and supporters of this work.

I'm also indebted to my fellow Regional Leaders at the Southern Baptist International Mission Board who have sharpened me with their insights into God's missionary activity around the world. Particular thanks go to Bill Fudge, Don Dent and John Brady from whom I have learned continuously.

Other gracious encouragement has come from Rick Warren and Bruce Wilkinson who simply said, *"Yes, my friend, you are a writer."* And my unending gratitude goes to my professor and friend, Martin Marty, whose demonstrated words, *"writers write"* still haunt and inspire me.

Without the enthusiastic embrace of the little booklet, *Church Planting Movements,* by the broader evangelical world, this larger tome might never have seen the light of day. So, I offer my thanks to every translator, publisher, and purveyor of the *Church Planting Movement* booklet and paradigm.

And to my dear colleagues in South Asia—there is no greater joy in life than to be on mission with God among such gifted and dedicated brothers and sisters. Thank you all.

Finally, to my father and mother, Vernon and Etheleen Garrison, who did not count the gift of their own son, daughter-in-law, and grandchildren to foreign mission fields too great a sacrifice to make for their Lord, and to Sonia's parents, Vernon and Patsy Hutchins, who joyfully did the same, thank you.

David Garrison
India, 2003

Preface

Some years ago while traveling in Southeast Asia, I met a talented young missionary who had invented a water purification system from a car battery and an ultraviolet lamp; then he designed a solar powered refrigerator fueled by the tropical sun. Amazed at his inventiveness, I asked what his occupation had been before coming to the mission field.

"I was a reverse engineer," he said. Seeing the puzzled look on my face, he went on to explain, "I worked for a large corporation that was involved in many different fields of production. My job was to monitor the competition, and whenever they came out with a new product, I was to reverse engineer it, taking the product apart and carefully analyzing how it had been constructed and how it worked. Then I reported my findings to my superiors who would determine whether or not to develop our own version of the same product."

In the years that followed, I don't suppose I gave much thought to *reverse engineering* until someone observed that my treatment of Church Planting Movements was a form of reverse engineering. Looking back, I suppose this is true.

This book tackles a complex subject, in this case a divinely produced phenomenon that we call Church Planting Movements. It seeks to understand these movements by beginning at the end, with an actual Church Planting Movement. Then it reverse engineers the movement, dismantling its component parts, analyzing how it was constructed and how it works. Done properly, reverse engineering can reveal volumes about the Creator's designs, desires, and method of operation.

In Church Planting Movements, it is easy to see God at work transforming hundreds of thousands of lives. But *how* is God at work, and how would he have us participate? These are the questions that demand further investigation and propel us on a course of reverse engineering.

Beginning at the end, with actual Church Planting Movements, we will proceed to carefully analyze each of their component parts. If we are successful, by God's grace, we just might come to understand the mind of their Creator and how *he* would have us participate in these miraculous works.

Part One

In the Beginning

1.

How It All Began

Look to the nations, watch and be utterly amazed for I am going to do something in your days that you would not believe even if you were told. (Habakkuk 1:5)

IN AUTUMN 1994 this verse came to life in ways I never dreamed possible. It was the time of year when missionaries send in their annual reports to agency headquarters. Missionaries are busy people and rarely enthusiastic about stopping long enough to tell how many new believers were baptized, how many new churches were started, or how many unreached people groups they had introduced to the gospel. Each year these reports typically show modest growth in each of these key areas.

But this year was different. The report from missionaries David and Jan Watson serving in India made an incredible claim. Their report listed nearly a hundred cities, towns, and villages with new churches and thousands of new believers.

Mission headquarters was skeptical. "This can't be," they said. "Either you've misunderstood the question or you're not telling us the truth."

The words stung, but David held his tongue. "Come and see," he said.

Later that year, a survey team headed by Watson's supervisor arrived in India to investigate. They visited Lucknow, Patna, Delhi, Varanasi, and numerous smaller Indian towns and villages that David had listed in his report. The supervisor later commented, "I personally went in very doubtful, but we were wrong. Everywhere we went it was exactly as Watson had reported. God was doing something amazing there."

Amazing...difficult to believe. It was around that time that the words of Habakkuk took on a new relevance. "Look to the nations, watch and be utterly amazed for I am going to do something in your days that you would not believe even if you were told."

A year later, a report from Southeast Asia described a similar eruption of new churches. The following year missionaries serving in Latin America witnessed the same sort of spontaneous multiplication of hundreds of new churches. That same year two more such reports came in from China. We began to refer to these amazing phenomena as *Church Planting Movements*.

The reports keep coming. As he promised, God is doing something extraordinary *in our day*. As he draws a lost world to himself, Church Planting Movements appear to be the *way* he is doing it. What began as a small trickle of reports a few years ago has now grown into a steady stream of previously unreached people groups pouring into God's Kingdom.

In East Asia, a missionary reported: "I launched my three-year plan in November, 2000. My vision was to see 200 new churches started among my people group over the next three years. But four months later, we had already reached that goal. After only six months, we had already seen 360 churches planted and more than 10,000 new believers baptized! Now I'm asking God to enlarge my vision."

During the decade of the 1990s, Christians in a Latin American country overcame relentless government persecution to grow from 235 churches to more than 4,000 churches with more than 30,000 converts awaiting baptism.

A pastor in Western Europe wrote: "Last year my wife and I started 15 new house churches. As we left for a six-month stateside assignment, we wondered what we'd find when we returned. It's wild! We can verify at least 30 churches now, but I believe that it could be two or even three times that many."

A missionary strategist in Africa reported: "It took us 30 years to plant four churches in this country. We've started 65 new churches in the last nine months."

In Southeast Asia, a missionary strategist began working with three small house churches of 85 members in 1993. Just seven years later, membership had swollen to more than 90,000 baptized believers worshiping in 920 new churches.

A missionary strategist assigned to a North Indian people group found just 28 churches among them in 1989. By the year 2000, a Church Planting Movement had erupted catapulting the number of churches to more than 4,500 with an estimated 300,000 baptized believers.

Over the past decade, literally millions of new believers have entered Christ's Kingdom through Church Planting Movements. This book aims to help you understand these movements. In the pages that follow, you'll see not only *what* God is doing, but also *how* he is doing it.

First, we will describe what is happening in these movements. Next, we will glean whatever lessons and principles we can learn from these movements. Then we will evaluate what we've seen in light of God's word. Finally, we will submit all that we've learned to the lordship of Christ, asking, "In light of what you've shown us, O Lord, what should we now do?"

YOU WILL SEE references in this book to a special type of missionary that figures prominently in many Church Planting Movements. They are called *Strategy Coordinators*. A Strategy Coordinator is a missionary who takes responsibility for developing and implementing a comprehensive strategy—one that would partner with the whole body of Christ—to bring an entire people group[1] to faith in Jesus Christ. This new paradigm

---

[1] You'll see frequent references to *people groups* in this book. A people group is a social grouping sharing a common language and sense of ethnic identity,

of 21st century missionaries is reshaping the world of missions and contributing immeasurably to the spread of Church Planting Movements.

In August 1998, nearly a dozen Strategy Coordinators and mission researchers who had experienced these Church Planting Movements gathered for discussions in Rockville, Virginia. Before the year was over, a second group of Church Planting Movement practitioners convened in Singapore. The purpose of both meetings was the same: *to understand Church Planting Movements.* Together, the participants crafted a working definition of a Church Planting Movement and then began listing the characteristics that were present in each of the movements they had seen.

Debate was lively and energy ran high as the strategists and researchers shuffled between three or four whiteboards with scribbled lists of qualities, characteristics, and obstacles.

Examining what God was doing was a heady experience. God surprised them in that many things they had long held to be essential were strangely absent from *his* Church Planting Movements, while other elements clearly present in each Church Planting Movement were so obvious they were nearly overlooked.

Out of these intense sessions with real Church Planting Movement practitioners, came a 57-page booklet published in January 2000 under the title *Church Planting Movements.* During the first year that the booklet was in print, it spread quickly around the world and was locally translated into more than 20 languages. New language translations continue to surface every few months.[2] Today, many evangelicals use the

---

sometimes referred to as an ethnolinguistic people group. An *unreached people group* is one that has yet to be presented with the gospel of Jesus Christ.

[2] Among the language translations are: *Japanese, Russian, Spanish, Shona, Portuguese, Arabic, Chinese, Serbian, Hausa, Turkish, Hindi, French, Thai, Korean, Norwegian, Kazakh, Gujarati, Bangla, Hebrew, Albanian, et al.*

booklet as a guide to understand how God is at work and how they might partner with him.

Now it is three years later. So much has happened since that little booklet was written. Unlike the early days when most Church Planting Movements seemed confined to Asia, today they are surfacing in all corners of the globe. Researchers are monitoring more than thirty locations around the world where variations of Church Planting Movements can be seen. It is out of this context that we are now offering this expanded understanding of Church Planting Movements around the world.

THIS BOOK IS written for any Christian who desires to understand how God is redeeming a lost world, but it is especially for those who want to be on mission with him, sharing in his great salvation story.

In the pages that follow, we will explore a number of Church Planting Movements and *near* Church Planting Movements worldwide. We'll carefully describe those unique elements and common characteristics that we see in these movements. Moreover, we will try to address some of the questions frequently raised concerning Church Planting Movements. Then, following our early church ancestors in Berea, we will "search the Scriptures to see if it is so."[3] Finally, we will ask God to show us how we can be involved. God always calls his people to action, and that's where the adventure really begins.

---

[3] Adapted from Acts 17:11

2

What are Church Planting Movements?

BEFORE WE CHASE after Church Planting Movements, we need to adopt a working definition to be sure we will recognize them when we see them. A Church Planting Movement is *a rapid multiplication of indigenous churches planting churches that sweeps through a people group or population segment.* There's a lot more we could add to this definition, but this one captures its essence.

You'll note that this definition describes what *is* happening in Church Planting Movements rather than *pre*scribing what *could* or *should* happen. Throughout this book we'll try to remain faithful to what God is actually doing in these movements and avoid the temptation to prescribe or predict how he ought to be working. By clinging to a descriptive approach, we are humbly admitting that the work is not ours; it belongs to God. So rather than trying to squeeze him into our flawed predictions or prescriptions, we'll let him be God and we will alter our understanding and behavior to be on mission with him.

It's not easy to stay descriptive. Each of us comes to the table with preconceived notions about the mighty acts of God. Church Planting Movements aren't immune to these tendencies to misunderstand. So let's begin by carefully unpacking our definition, and examining each of its five parts.

First, a Church Planting Movement **reproduces rapidly**. Within a very short time, newly planted churches are already starting new churches that follow the same pattern of rapid reproduction.

"How rapid is rapid?" you may ask. Perhaps the best answer is, "Faster than you think possible." Though the rate varies from place to place, Church Planting Movements always outstrip the population growth rate as they race toward reaching the entire people group. Once you've viewed a few of the case studies, you'll begin to get the idea.

The second key word in our definition of Church Planting Movements is **multiplication**. Church Planting Movements do not simply add new churches. Instead, they multiply. Surveys of Church Planting Movements indicate that virtually every church is engaged in starting multiple new churches. Church Planting Movements multiply churches and believers like Jesus multiplied the loaves and fishes.

Perhaps this is why Church Planting Movements are devoid of goals to start ten or twenty additional churches in a country or city. Instead, these churches are satisfied with nothing less than a vision to reach their entire people group or city—and eventually the whole world! As each church realizes that it has the capacity and responsibility to reproduce itself, the numbers start compounding exponentially.

The third word is **indigenous**. Indigenous literally means *generated from within*, as opposed to started by outsiders. In Church Planting Movements the first church or churches may be started by outsiders, but very quickly the momentum shifts from the outsiders to the insiders. Consequently, within a short time, the new believers coming to Christ in Church Planting Movements may not even know that a foreigner was ever involved in the work. In their eyes the movement looks, acts, and feels homegrown.

The fourth part of our definition is **churches planting churches**. Though church planters may start the first churches, at some point the churches themselves get into the act. When churches begin planting churches, a tipping point is reached and a movement is launched.

A tipping point occurs when new church starts reach a critical mass and, like falling dominoes, cascade into an out of control movement flowing from church to church to church. Many *near-*

Church Planting Movements fall short at this critical point, as church planters struggle to control the reproducing churches. But when the momentum of reproducing churches outstrips the ability of the planters to control it, a movement is underway.

Finally, Church Planting Movements occur within **people groups or interrelated population segments.** Because Church Planting Movements involve the communication of the gospel message, they naturally occur within shared language and ethnic boundaries. However, they rarely stop there. As the gospel works its changing power in the lives of these new believers, it compels them to take the message of hope to other people groups.

N OW THAT WE'VE clarified these five parts to our definition, let's use our understanding to eliminate some of the other acts of God that might be confused with Church Planting Movements.

Church Planting Movements are not just a revival or spiritual awakening. Unlike the great revivals or spiritual awakenings that periodically occur among Christians, Church Planting Movements are centered within unreached people groups or concentrations of lostness. The lost aren't merely dozing in Christ—needing a revival—they are *dead in their sins and trespasses* until Christ gives them life.

Church Planting Movements are not just mass evangelism. We've all known dynamic evangelists whose gospel proclamations have drawn hundreds of thousands to salvation. But what happens after the stadium is emptied and the evangelist has moved on to a new city? All too often, the commitment to Christ ends with a mass meeting.

Not so in Church Planting Movements. Church Planting Movements are church multiplying movements. While it's true that Church Planting Movements include massive evangelistic proclamation, they go the second mile—resulting in churches where discipleship, worship, and spiritual development continue.

In Church Planting Movements mass evangelism produces rapidly multiplying new church starts.

Church Planting Movements are not just people movements. Beyond mass evangelism is mass conversion where great numbers of lost people respond to the gospel. These are sometimes called "People Movements" which should not be confused with Church Planting Movements. In several locations around the world, these people movements are occurring today, but they do not always lead to multiplying churches.

Thousands of Muslims coming to Christ in Azerbaijan, Algeria, and other places show us that the Holy Spirit is doing his work of drawing the lost to faith in Jesus Christ. What distinguishes these mass conversions from Church Planting Movements is the troubling absence of new churches.

For a variety of reasons, many of these mass conversions aren't producing the pool of new churches needed to assimilate the converts. When this disparity occurs these mass conversions run the risk of being a miraculous *flash in the pan,* like a quick burst of light that dissipates into nothing. Mass conversion is part of Church Planting Movements, but in Church Planting Movements, the new believers gather into rapidly reproducing new churches.

Church Planting Movements are not the Church Growth Movement. The Church Growth Movement refers to a school of missions and church growth begun in the mid-1960s by Dr. Donald McGavran at Fuller Theological Seminary in Pasadena, California. At the risk of losing non-missionary readers, let's take a few minutes to draw some significant distinctions between the Church Growth Movement and Church Planting Movements.

There are at least three areas where the Church Growth Movement differs significantly from Church Planting Movements. First, the Church Growth Movement has come to associate bigger churches with better churches. Growing mega-churches has become an increasingly common part of the evangelical landscape. Church Planting Movements, on the other hand, adhere to the principle that *smaller is better*. Intimate house churches are at the heart of every Church Planting Movement.

Second, the Church Growth Movement has directed many missionaries to focus on perceived "harvest fields" or "responsive fields" at the expense of unreached and what may appear to be unresponsive fields. By contrast, our descriptive analysis reveals that God has chosen to launch most Church Planting Movements among the least likely candidates—unreached people groups, which have often been dismissed by those looking for responsive harvest fields.

Third, the Church Growth Movement advocates pouring resources (particularly missionaries) into responsive harvest fields. The rationale being that there are limited harvesters and so we should conserve them from difficult areas and invest them instead into people groups that have already proven to be responsive to the gospel.

Once again, as you'll see in the case studies that follow, the approach of pouring more and more resources into the harvest is actually *contrary* to what we see God doing in Church Planting Movements. In Church Planting Movements, the role of the missionary or outsider is heaviest at the beginning. Once the people group begins responding, it is vitally important for outsiders (i.e. missionaries) to become less and less dominant while the new believers themselves become the primary harvesters and leaders of the movement.

Keeping these distinctions in mind will help us avoid seeing Church Planting Movements through the lens of the Church Growth Movement and free us to see what God is doing and how he is at work.

Church Planting Movements are not just a divine miracle. Church Planting Movement practitioners have been quick to give the glory for the movement to God, so much so, in fact, that some have described the movements as purely an act of God. "We couldn't stop it if we wanted to," one fellow remarked. His humility was admirable, but misleading. Reducing a Church Planting Movement to a purely divine miracle has the effect of dismissing the role of human responsibility. If God alone is producing Church Planting Movements, then God alone is to blame when there are no Church Planting Movements.

The truth is God has given Christians vital roles to play in the success or failure of these movements. Over the past few years, we've learned that there are many ways that we can obstruct and even stop Church Planting Movements. In many instances, well-intentioned activities that are out of step with the ways of God have served to slow and even kill the movement. Church Planting Movements are miraculous in the way they transform lives, but they are also quite vulnerable to human tampering.

Church Planting Movements are not a Western invention. In January 2001, the author addressed a group of North African church leaders gathered to discuss the subject of Church Planting Movements. Just before the session began, someone warned me, "These brothers and sisters aren't looking for the latest church planting methods from the United States. If that's what you've brought from America, you're wasting your time and theirs."

With this admonition in mind, I began with an honest confession: "Church Planting Movements are not an American phenomenon. In fact, because I grew up in the United States I almost missed seeing this amazing thing that God was unfolding among the lost all over the world."

Church Planting Movements didn't originate in the West, though they have occurred in the Western world along with other parts of our globe. Church Planting Movements are a description of what God is doing in many countries, but they are not limited to one type of culture or another.

As for the North African church leaders, all they really wanted to know was that it was something God was doing. From that point on they enthusiastically embraced this powerful instrument of God's salvation.

Finally, a Church Planting Movement is not an end but rather a *means* to an end. Those who pursue Church Movements sometimes err on the side of exuberance. They get so excited about Church Planting Movements that they virtually sell their souls for the sake of the movement. When this happens they have allowed the movement to slip into the 'god role' and the results are disastrous for both the movement and for the individual.

Church Planting Movements are simply a way that God is drawing massive numbers of lost persons into saving community with himself. That saving relationship—rather than any movement or method—is what touches the end vision, the glory of God, that we so desire.

THIS BRINGS US to a final important question as we prepare to investigate Church Planting Movements further. Why are they so important? Why do you need to study and understand them? There are several reasons.

First, Church Planting Movements are important because God is mightily at work in them. Every Church Planting Movement practitioner comes to the same humble awareness that God is doing something awesome in their midst. Persons can scheme and dream, but only God can turn the hearts of unbelievers to himself.

If there were no other reason than this, it would be enough. If we want to be on mission with God and not simply pursuing our own agenda, then we *must* turn our attention to how he is using Church Planting Movements to bring entire people groups to himself.

Second, we need to learn all we can about Church Planting Movements because of the critical role God has reserved for us to play. The difference between Church Planting Movements and *near*-Church Planting Movements is often the difference between God's people properly aligning themselves with what he is doing or failing to align themselves with what he is doing.

Some aspects of Church Planting Movements are logical and intuitive, but many are not. Those who miss this point may well find themselves like the pre-converted apostle Paul *kicking against the goads*. A goad was a first-century cattle prod used by the herder to prod the livestock where he wanted them to go. When we act out of our own reasoning rather than aligning ourselves with God's ways, we are like an obstinate goat that puts itself at cross purposes with the Master's will. If we want to be on mission with God we simply *must* pause long enough to understand *how* God is on mission. Only then can we know with some degree of certainty that we are aligned as his instruments and not misaligned as his obstacles.

The third reason Church Planting Movements are so important is for what they accomplish. Without exaggeration we can say that Church Planting Movements are *the most effective means in the world today for drawing lost millions into saving, disciple-building relationships with Jesus Christ.* That may appear to be an ambitious claim, but it is an accurate one, and an honest description of how God is winning a lost world.

Finally, Church Planting Movements are important because they multiply the glory of God. The prophet Habakkuk set a benchmark for us with a vision of a time when "the knowledge of the glory of the Lord would cover the earth as the waters cover the sea."[4] The glory of the Lord is nothing less than the clear revelation of God himself. This is why Jesus came. To reveal to us God's glory. "We have seen his glory, the glory of the One and Only, who came from the Father, full of grace and truth."[5]

---

[4] Habakkuk 2:14

[5] John 1:14

The ultimate end for all Christians must be to glorify God. We glorify God when we reveal him in all of his fullness. Christians find the fullness of God in his Son and experience that fullness as his Son comes to dwell in our hearts and through our lives.

In his grace, Christ conveys this same glory to all who invite him into their lives as Savior and Lord. For those who submit to his reign in their lives, Christ fills them with his glory, the very glory of God. This is why Paul could say with confidence, "Christ in you (is) the hope of glory."[6] This is why Jesus told his disciples, "This is to my Father's glory, that you bear much fruit."[7]

Mankind without Jesus Christ may bear God's image, but not his glory. In Church Planting Movements, the glory of the Lord is spreading from person to person, people group to people group like a swelling river as it begins to spill out over its banks until it covers all *the earth as the waters cover the sea.*

No other avenue so quickly and effectively multiplies the glory of God in the hearts of so many people. No other means has drawn so many new believers into ongoing communities of faith where they can continue to grow in Christlikeness. This is why Church Planting Movements are so very important.

Now we've clarified our definition. We've addressed the usual suspects in a line-up of misconceptions and explained how Church Planting Movements are unique. The stage is now set. The rest of the book is dedicated to profiling actual Church Planting Movements learning all we can from them.

---

[6] Colossians 1:27

[7] John 15:8

Part Two

Church Planting Movements
Around the World

Part Two

Church Planting Movements Around the World

A S WE VISIT Church Planting Movements around the world, we'll find some that are models for study and learning, but we'll see others that were near misses, some that *used to be* Church Planting Movements, and a few that may yet turn into Church Planting Movements. Keep this in mind as you read these case studies. Use our descriptive definition to see which ones are true Church Planting Movements and which ones fall short. Afterwards, we'll see what lessons we can learn from these examples, and perhaps even diagnose reasons why some of them failed to fully develop.

Our journey will begin with Asia's two giants, India and China, and then sweep across the rest of Asia. Next, we'll visit the Muslim world where tens of thousands have come to Christ over the past decade. Then we'll cross the Atlantic to see what God is doing in Latin America. Finally, we'll turn our attention to the West and examine Church Planting Movements in Europe and the United States.

As we make this world tour, we'll resist the temptation to linger too long in any one place. We'll save the commentary and many of the insights until Part Three: Lessons Learned.

Some may ask why nearly half our examples come from Asia. In fact, God has reserved about half his miracles for half of the world's population. The two nations of India and China alone constitute almost forty percent of the world's people. So, it is only natural that we should begin our survey there.

3

India

In Madhya Pradesh State a Church Planting Movement produces 4,000 new churches in less than seven years.

In the 1990s, nearly 1,000 new churches are planted in Orissa with another 1,000 new outreach points. By 2001, a new church was being started every 24 hours.

A Church Planting Movement among Bhojpuri-speaking peoples results in more than 4,000 new churches and some 300,000 new believers.

WITH MORE THAN a billion citizens, India is a world within the world. India is a land of stark contrasts: urban and rural, rich and poor, educated and illiterate, mountain and delta, monsoon and desert. Add to these, the contrasts of lostness and Church Planting Movements.

India's enormity invites comparison with its Asian neighbor, China. Like China, India possesses about 17 percent of the world's population, but India differs in many important ways. Where China converges around a shared Han Chinese civilization, India is a prism of hundreds of diverse peoples and languages.

Beneath its myriad languages and dialects, India further divides itself with invisible boundaries of religion, caste, economic status, education, and racial origin. Over the millennia, waves of immigrants have washed over the subcontinent each one leaving a residue of language and ethnicity, from the earliest immigrants, Negritos, and Australoid peoples to the Dravidian, Tibeto-Burman, and finally Aryan conquerors.[8]

India features a smorgasbord of religions. A thin veneer of Hinduism, Islam, Buddhism, Christianity, Jainism, Sikhism or Animism glosses over a range of beliefs as individual as the people themselves. Perhaps the most accurate description of Indian religion comes from the common Hindu boast that "India is home to 330 million gods."

Within this great human cauldron, God is at work. In the next few pages, we'll see his hand among the multiple people groups of Madhya Pradesh, Orissa, Bihar, and Uttar Pradesh.

L ANDLOCKED IN CENTRAL India, the state of Madhya Pradesh has a population of more than 70 million people packed into an area a little larger than the state of California. Hinduism is the primary religion of the state, but it also contains a number of Muslims and Animists. There are 77 major people groups in Madhya Pradesh each with more than 100,000 population. Evangelical Christians make up less than one percent of the population, but this is rapidly changing.

In 1993, Dr. Victor Choudhrie, then a prominent cancer surgeon in India, surrendered to the Lord's calling to evangelize and plant churches among the peoples of Madhya Pradesh. Over the next eight years, God blessed his ministry. Today there are more than 4,000 churches in the state with more than 50,000 believers.

What is the nature of this Church Planting Movement? For Choudhrie it begins with a restoration of the New Testament understanding of church as opposed to the contemporary view of church as a building. He explains:

---

[8] Paul Hockings, volume editor *Encyclopedia of World Cultures, Volume III: South Asia* (Boston: G.K. Hall and Co., 1992), p. xxiii.

India lives in villages. There are six hundred thousand villages. Additionally most of our cities are a conglomeration of villages. As of today, we need at least one million churches. Many villages are big and have many castes living in them. Therefore, the accurate number is substantially higher. No one, not even Uncle Sam, has the capacity to build that number of church buildings. Nor do we have the capacity to maintain them even if someone gave them free to us. We don't really need them, as all the houses we need are already available to us in the villages and cities. Being the Bride of Christ, the house churches rapidly multiply so we do not need big houses.[9]

Choudhrie has shaped the Madhya Pradesh movement with a potent combination of biblical teaching, lay leadership and house church accommodations steering clear of energy-sapping dependency on foreign finances. He explains, "Finance is not a problem as most house churches run on 'low' or 'no' budget. There are simply no maintenance bills and salaries to be paid. So instead of frequently sermonizing on stewardship and tithing, the leaders can focus on completing the task of the Great Commission of making disciples of all nations."[10]

For those who question whether house churches can stand the test of time, Choudhrie points to their alternative. "The empty cathedrals in Europe are silent witnesses to the barrenness of the church. Why continue to imitate a failed model?"[11]

A lay church planter who joined Choudhrie shared a revealing testimony: "I came to Jesus in the late 1980's. Not long afterwards, I experienced a large evangelistic crusade in a city. Impressed, I returned to my village and organized similar crusades there and in the surrounding villages for years.

---

[9] In Victor Choudhrie, "House Church: A Bible Study," *House2House*, March 2001: 1. Available [Online]: www.house2house.tv [March 2001].

[10] Ibid.

[11] Ibid.

Thousands came, and everyone liked it. The crusades were so successful, that even the lame could walk again—and walked away, never to return; the blind could see—and they never looked back."[12]

Frustrated with the fleeting fruit of mass evangelism, the village church planter sought help. "In 1994, I attended a seminar about house church planting which completely changed my thinking. I gave up the costs and difficulties of organizing crusades and started to plant house churches with fiery evangelistic zeal, with the result that almost 500 house churches have been started in neighboring districts. We don't plant only one house church per village, because there are a number of people groups which require their own house churches. I hope that the number of house churches will double in the next 12 months."[13]

This church planter's story is not unusual. He lives in a remote corner of the state among the tribal peoples in the jungle villages of Madhya Pradesh. Like Choudhrie, he is people group focused and committed to multiplying house churches.

How does one raise up the thousands of church leaders needed to shepherd this explosive movement? Choudhrie sees the answer in the movement itself. "We need hundreds of thousands of pastors for the church who cannot be produced in seminaries but can easily be equipped in the house churches."

He continues, "Seminaries equip pastors for a single congregation while house churches follow the 222 formula (2 Timothy 2:2). They equip disciples to plant multiplying churches by multiplying leadership."[14]

---

[12] Victor Choudhrie, "India: 3,000 House Churches Planted in Madhya Pradesh Since 1994." Available [Online] www.youtharise.com/news/14feb2000 [May 2001].

[13] Ibid.

[14] Choudhrie adapted the principle from missionary trainer, Bruce Carlton (see chapter 5 below).

Choudhrie estimates that it will take 30,000 churches to reach the inhabitants of Madhya Pradesh, but some speculate that more than 100,000 churches will be needed. "Whatever must be done," says Choudhrie, "must be done."

SOUTHEAST OF MADHYA PRADESH lies the state of Orissa where 40 million inhabitants have a literacy rate of not more than 35 percent among men and far less among women. Orissa's dominant population are Oriya-speaking Hindus of Indo-European origins, but the state is also home to a number of Muslims and Animists of Dravidian stock. One of these tribal peoples, residing in the Khond Hills of southern Orissa, are known as the Kui.

The Kui are an agricultural people who retreated to the Khond Hills as a way of maintaining their ethnic identity in the face of encroaching Oriya-speaking settlers. The Kui are predominantly an oral culture with no literature of their own, though most of the men have become bilingual adding Oriya to their native tongue. For centuries, the Oriya-speaking Hindu majority have viewed the Kui tribes as social outcastes without status in society.

The first missionaries arrived in Orissa in 1822, but over-looked the Kui who remained hidden in the hill country. Over the next century, though, the gospel was introduced and a few churches were started among the Kui. After two World Wars and a Great Depression, the outside world lost touch with the remote tribes of Orissa's Khond Hills.

When itinerant missionaries returned to the region in the mid-1980s, they found about 100 Kui churches scattered throughout the Khond Hills. They immediately began to encourage these young churches to thrive and multiply. With renewed energy, the Kui churches began to spread. Over the next five years, the number of Kui churches nearly doubled. Then during the decade of the 1990s, they increased to more than 1,200 with another

1,000 emerging churches. By 2001, Orissa saw a new church start almost every 24 hours.

The modern resurgence of the Kui movement can be traced back to the appointment of agricultural missionary John Langston in the mid-1980s. Langston's agricultural work earned him the favor of the government because it addressed their hunger needs, but John's love for the Kui extended beyond their physical needs.

In the years that followed, Langston was joined by Calvin and Margaret Fox. Together they planned what it would take to reach all of the Kui with the gospel. Recognizing that the most important resource for winning the lost masses were the Kui Christians themselves, the missionaries concentrated on training Kui church members, rather than focusing on professional clergy, to become the frontline evangelists and church planters.

With no permission to establish a theological seminary, the missionaries opted for a non-institutional approach, offering short segments of training ranging from a few weeks to a few months at a time. Training often coupled agricultural and rural health education with biblical messages of evangelism and church planting. The Kui would sometimes travel to a central location for the training, but often the training came to them in their own village.

To accelerate the gospel spread into the interior, missionaries and Kui believers teamed together to produce a radio program that would communicate public health and agricultural information in the Oriya language followed by gospel stories in the Kui language. Rather than sowing the gospel to the wind, the missionaries devised systems for gathering those who responded into new church starts. They did this by training Kui Christians to gather groups of non-believers to listen to the radio broadcasts and then discussing the message they heard. These "listener groups" became the nurseries for developing new churches.

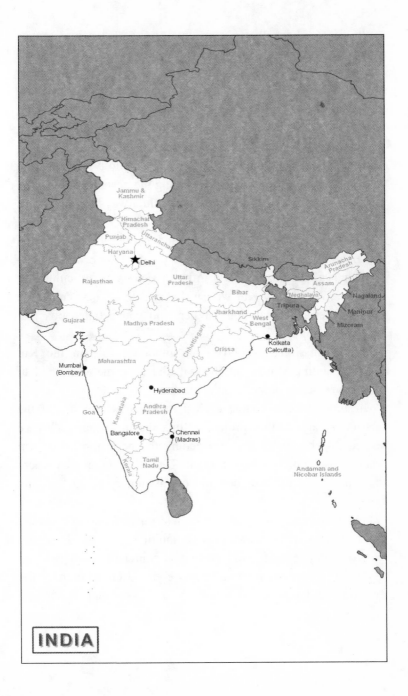

In 1997 alone there were at least 450 listener groups attentively following the two weekly broadcasts in their heart language. By the year 2000, there were more than 1,000 listener groups. Soon, the radio ministry was supplemented by audiocassettes. Traveling agricultural evangelists would spend a few days in a village teaching agricultural best practices during the day, but in the evening, they offered a deeper truth.

One evangelist explained, "All we had to do was sit in front of our hut with a cassette player playing the gospel stories in the Kui language. A crowd of listeners would always follow. These listeners soon became new church groups."

For a people whose language and culture had long been marginalized, the opportunity to hear the gospel—or anything—in their heart language was a gift as precious as agriculture or medicine. An elderly Kui woman listened in amazement to the program before exclaiming, "Where did you get that box that speaks my language?"

While missionaries played an important role in the Kui Church Planting Movement, the real advance came when the Kui themselves began propelling the advance.

In June 1997, a couple of Kui men visited the site of the missionary agricultural project, telling the missionary, "We've started 20 churches," and proceeding to show him on a map where those churches were located. They were in an area where there had been no churches and or missionary contact of any kind.

The missionary worried that he had misunderstood what the Kui were saying. "You mean twenty families?" he asked.

"No," they replied, "we have twenty churches."

"Well, how many families are in each church?" the missionary asked.

The Kui men replied, "Each church has about one hundred families in it."[15]

Today, both Langston and the Foxes have left Orissa, but indigenous momentum has long since carried the Kui Church Planting Movement. In addition to gaining the evangelism and church planting passion of the missionaries, the Kui believers have also begun exhibiting their zeal for cross-cultural missions. The Kui have identified several unevangelized people groups in the Khond Hills and have begun using the cross-cultural skills they learned from the missionaries to pass on their gospel treasure.

I N THE NORTH Indian states of Bihar and Uttar Pradesh you will find some 90 million people in a sprawling array of ethnic communities all speaking the Bhojpuri language. The author's 1999 booklet *Church Planting Movements* profiled this movement under the pseudonym "The Bholdari of India."[16] Even as the booklet was going to print the Bhojpuri movement was reaching a critical mass of such size and expanse that those involved in the work felt it could be openly described without jeopardizing the work. Here we will take a few paragraphs to review the Bhojpuri profile before bringing it up to date with the stunning growth that has occurred in the past few years.

Bhojpuri-speaking people are scattered through more than 170,000 villages in India and Nepal. The population includes each of the four major castes along with millions of casteless *Untouchables* or *Dalits*. The Bhojpuri heartland is a microcosm

---

[15] This story was printed in a report of the Southern Baptist International Mission Board: Mark Snowden, ed., *Toward Church Planting Movements*, p. 37. With an average family size of eight persons, this would indicate a membership of 16,000 in 20 churches.

[16] David Garrison, *Church Planting Movements* (Richmond: International Mission Board, 1999), pp. 21-26.

of the whole subcontinent. As such, the majority of the people group are extremely impoverished and illiterate while a small minority control much of the region's wealth and resources.

More than 85 percent of the Bhojpuri people are Hindu, the remainder being Muslim or Animist with a few scattered Buddhists. In years past, Jesuit missionaries drew sizable numbers of Untouchables into the Catholic Church, but their membership still accounts for less than one-tenth of one percent of the total Bhojpuri-speaking population.

In 1947, Baptists counted 28 small churches among the Bhojpuri, a number that would remain stagnant until the 1990s. By 1989, the dwindling Baptist congregations clung stubbornly to a few buildings and land, but their membership was aging and slowly losing vitality.

That same year, Southern Baptists appointed Strategy Coordinators David and Jan Watson to the Bhojpuri-speaking peoples. Following a year of language study and culture acquisition, the Watsons launched an aggressive plan of evangelism and church planting. The first efforts called for South Indian evangelists and church planters to preach the gospel in villages. This method had been highly successful in southern India though less widely used in the north.

To the Watsons' horror, the first six Indian evangelists were brutally murdered in separate events all within a year of each other. David was devastated and wanted to leave the Bhojpuri, but God would not release him.

What followed was a season of soul searching and re-evaluation. Abandoning his earlier strategy, Watson chose instead to adopt the approach Jesus had used when he sent out the 72 disciples two-by-two. The strategy is described in Luke chapter 10: "When you enter a house, first say 'Peace to this house, If a man of peace is there, your peace will rest on him; if not, it will return to you. Stay in that house... Do not move around from house to house." The instructions continue, "When you enter a town and are welcomed, eat what is set before you.

Heal the sick who are there and tell them, 'The kingdom of God is near you.'"[17]

Over the next couple of years, courageous Indian evangelists went out again, this time looking for a *person of peace*. When they found God's man of peace, they bonded with him, discipling him into the Christian faith. The man of peace then became the leader of the church in his household and his community.

The approach was surprisingly simple, yet sociologically profound. Outsiders who came into the village needed sponsorship and found it in the man of peace. The earlier evangelists who were martyred had been effective up to the point of baptizing new converts. Some reports indicated that it was the baptism of women and young men in the villages that had triggered the local hostility. This time, it was a Bhojpuri insider—the man of peace—who did the baptizing, beginning with his own family.

In 1993, the number of Bhojpuri churches grew from 28 to 36, the first increase in more than three decades. Watson quickly devised a training program to ensure a steady stream of evangelist-church planters would be available. The following years the number of churches climbed dramatically to 78 in 1994, then to 220 in 1995. Over the next two years, the numbers grew beyond Watson's ability to track them. his best estimates were that another 700 or so new churches were begun in 1997 and at least 800 the following year.

In a 1998 interview, Watson was cautious, "I don't want to exaggerate," he said, "but there must be at least 55,000 Bhojpuri who have come to faith in the past seven years." We later learned that he was far from exaggerating.

There were reasons for Watson's caution. It was difficult for any outsider to get a clear picture of what was happening among the Bhojpuri. Rife with crime, disease, and known as a missionary graveyard, Bihar is one of the poorest and most vola-

---

[17] Luke 10:8-9

tile states in India. Bihar and eastern Uttar Pradesh are also the heartland of Hindu nationalism and opposition to foreign missionary activity. These factors conspired to keep outsiders away from the leading edge of the movement, prompting many to question the very existence of the so-called Bhojpuri Church Planting Movement.

I N OCTOBER 2000, in an effort to clarify what was happening among the Bhojpuri, the Southern Baptist International Mission Board sent a team of researchers into Bihar to assess the movement. What they uncovered lay to rest any doubts about the Bhojpuri miracle.

Their investigations found that the movement had exploded across the sprawling Bhojpuri homeland. Taking multiple samples from various reference points, the researchers cautiously drew up three separate size projections for the movement: low, moderate, and high.

Their **lowest** projection estimated 3,277 churches among the Bhojpuri with nearly 250,000 members. The low estimate calculated annual baptisms for the year at nearly 50,000 with another 10,600 new outreach groups (embryonic church starts) currently under way.

The **moderate** estimate placed the total number of churches at more than 4,300 with just under 300,000 baptized members, more than 66,000 of whom had been baptized within the past twelve months. These were complemented by more than 14,000 new outreach groups currently underway.

The **high** estimate for October 2000, placed the number of believers at 374,500 worshiping regularly in more than 5,400 churches with a further 17,600 new outreach groups underway. In the high estimate, nearly 83,000 Bhojpuri would have been baptized in the past 12 months.

Low, medium, or high, the results revealed that God had been busy among the Bhojpuri speakers of North India and had great lessons to teach us.

The study revealed that most of the churches were led by a local lay pastor and a co-leader recruited and mentored by the pastor. The average church size was nearly 85 members. The Bhojpuri worshipped in their own heart language with an emphasis on prayer and the singing of hymns drawn from a Bhojpuri hymnbook published in October 2000.

The high rate of illiteracy among the Bhojpuri has made discipleship a challenge. Nonliterate Bhojpuri Christians listen to cassette tapes of the Scripture and are taught to govern their life decisions with the question: "How can I obey Christ in this situation?"

For the Bhojpuri, prayer is fervent, frequent, and faithfully answered. The climate of persecution, the routine bouts of illness and the common experiences of demonic assault have conspired to keep the Bhojpuri on their knees where they have found God waiting to lift them back up. An outside observer among the Bhojpuri commented, "These people come to know Jesus as healer first and then stay to know him as Savior." Among the believers, there is a sense that God has especially chosen to pour out his salvation upon them.

An air of divine power and assurance accompanies this conviction of God's favor, but it has not always been this way. A Bhojpuri pastor from one of the older Free Baptist churches in Bihar confessed, "I preached for over 20 years in this region with little result, but now if I witness to ten Hindus, seven will accept Christ. I do not know what has happened, but I hope it never stops."[18]

The Bhojpuri join a growing list of people groups experiencing Church Planting Movements across India. If the lost

---

[18] From an interview conducted by the IMB research team in October 2000.

millions of the subcontinent are to hear the gospel, many more Church Planting Movements will be needed.

Perhaps the only country currently reporting more Church Planting Movements than India is also the only country still larger than India. Let's turn our attention to China.

4

China

In China more than 30,000 believers are baptized every day.

A Church Planting Movement in a northern Chinese province sees 20,000 new believers and 500 new churches started in less than five years.

In Henan Province Christianity explodes from less than a million to more than five million in only eight years.

Chinese Christians in Qing'an County of Heilongjiang Province plant 236 new churches in a single month.

In southern China, a Church Planting Movement produces more than 90,000 baptized believers in 920 house churches in eight years time.

In 2001 a newly emerging Church Planting Movement yields 48,000 new believers and 1,700 new churches in one year.

T HE CULTURAL LANDSCAPE of Asia has always revolved around China. The Chinese have aptly named their country the "Middle Kingdom" or more to the point, *the center of the world*. Certainly this is true in terms of population, but also in terms of culture and influence.

China was the first foreign mission field for many Protestant mission agencies. It is encouraging to see that today China is home to the fastest growing church and to the most Church Planting Movements on earth. Only two decades ago few would have predicted this astonishing development.

After the turbulent years of World War II, missionaries returned to find China torn apart by civil war between Nationalist armies and Communist rebels. By 1949, the Communists had prevailed, driving the Nationalist forces into exile and foreign missionaries out of the country. Those who resisted were imprisoned or killed.[19]

At that critical juncture in the life of the church in China, there were less than a million Protestant Christians in a country whose population then exceeded 500 million. This seemed to be a low point for Christianity in China, but it paled in the face of what lay ahead.

In 1955, Chairman Mao Tse Tung initiated his *Great Leap Forward*, an aggressive campaign of agricultural development and export that lasted for five years and almost drove the country to ruin. Only recently have China watchers confirmed what many suspected and feared: the program was a charade of prosperity leaving an estimated 10 million Chinese dead from starvation and malnutrition-related diseases.

This calamity fell especially hard on the Christians. Viewed as foreign religionists, many Christians were sent to the countryside for re-education and to remove them from urban centers of influence. These same countryside settings were the most severely impacted by the *Great Leap Forward*. We will probably never know how many Christians died during this period.

Devastating as it was, the *Great Leap Forward* was not the lowest point in Christianity's history under Communist China. That distinction goes to the Cultural Revolution (1966-1976), an orgy of government-sponsored terror resulting in persecution and torment for millions. Anything deemed foreign or culturally inconsistent with Maoist ideology was subject to attack. Mobs of youth destroyed churches, confiscated and burned Bibles.

---

[19] See for example missionary doctor Bill Wallace in Jesse Fletcher, *Bill Wallace of China* (Nashville: Broadman Press, 1963), 155 pp.

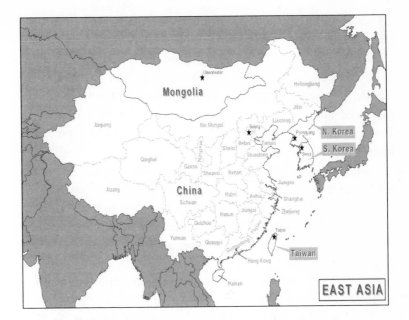

Pastors were beaten and paraded through the streets wearing dunce caps. Christian families were forcibly separated and relocated to re-education camps.

In 1989 I visited a remote Chinese province and was introduced to two Christian leaders. Only after we spent some time drinking tea together did they confide in me. One of them had spent 21 years in prison. The other had not seen his wife or two of his children since the Red Guard forced her to divorce him, and then exiled him to the countryside during the Cultural Revolution.

By the time of Mao's death in 1976, the church in China had been isolated from the outside world and under relentless attack for nearly three decades. When China re-opened to the West in 1982 foreign visitors saw that most of the old church buildings and Christian institutions had been converted to secular uses. There was little remaining of the Chinese church that had once been so vital. Yet beneath the surface, God was at work.

I N THE YEARS following Mao's death, there was little evidence of the looming revival of the church in China. In 1982, the *World Christian Encyclopedia* was accused of being overly optimistic when it claimed 1.3 million Christians in China. When the second edition was published 18 years later, the estimated number of Christians had risen to nearly 90 million. During the intervening decades, something remarkable had happened.

Students of China's Christian resurrection are divided over how large the Christian population in China is today, but there is a growing consensus that nowhere on earth are so many people coming to faith in Jesus Christ. Over the past two decades tens of millions of Chinese and ethnic minorities have become followers of Christ

An important window into China's religious life was opened in 1999 with the publication of *China's Christian Millions: the costly revival* by Tony Lambert.[20] Lambert, former British diplomat to Beijing and Tokyo and currently Director of China Research for the Overseas Missionary Fellowship (OMF), gleaned sources from across China to paint a picture of how God was at work.

For security reasons, Lambert was reluctant to speculate on the actual numbers of underground churches, but his calculations of the open, registered churches alone are stunning and are derived from published, official China sources or from OMF's extensive network of Christians across China.

If a picture is worth a thousand words, then consider the remarkable growth that these graphs reveal. What is striking is how much of the growth has occurred during the past two decades and continues today!

---

[20] Tony Lambert, *China's Christian Millions, the costly revival* (Singapore: OMF, 1999).

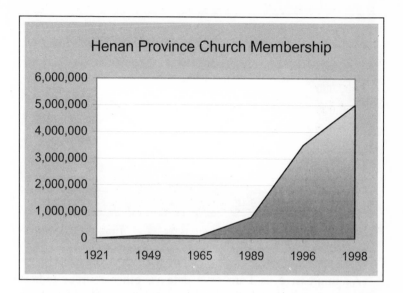

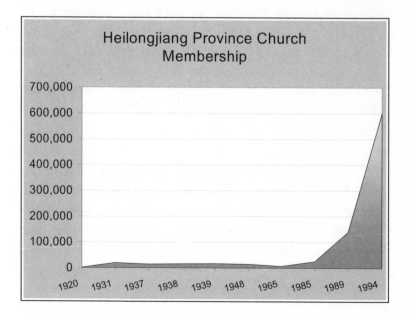

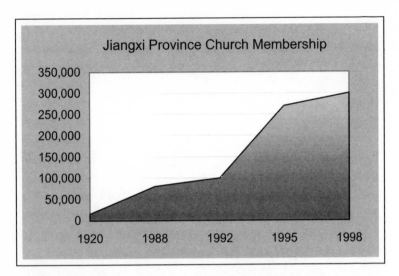

As impressive as Lambert's data is, other sources indicate that the conditions of the church in China, particularly in the underground house churches, are even more remarkable. One prominent underground church leader estimates that across China 30,000 persons are being baptized everyday.[21] Government officials admitted that the figures were probably even higher than that. Taking a closer look at two of these Chinese Church Planting Movements will shed light on how God is at work in this country.

A TYPICAL CHINESE Church Planting Movement can be seen in a city we'll call *Beishan*. In 1991, a veteran of missionary work in Taiwan took a new assignment to the city of Beishan[22] in northern China. He began his work with three prayers: 1) that God would do something so supernatural that it

---

[21] Anonymous source from an interview with Avery Willis, the International Mission Board's Vice President for Overseas Operations.

[22] Both names, *Siu Lam* and *Beishan* are contrived for security reasons, all other details are true and accurate.

could only be explained by the fact that God had done it; 2) that the work would last, and 3) that it would not be dependent upon him to keep it going. God granted all three requests.

In March 1993, God drew the missionary into a close friendship with a woman pastor named Siu Lam from one of the unregistered churches in Beishan. God used the relationship with Pastor Lam to launch a Church Planting Movement in the area around the city.

In 1986, Siu Lam had graduated from a registered seminary and returned to her home city of Beishan with plans to either begin or pastor a church.

Siu Lam was dissatisfied with the local registered church feeling that it was not aggressive enough in evangelism to the community. In 1987, she began a small church with 14 charter members. Six years later, the church had grown to more than 1,000 worshiping in several weekly services.

In December 1992, Siu Lam's church put together a Christmas drama as a means of outreach and gospel proclamation to the community. Each night 300 people filled the church to capacity while another 300 gathered in the courtyard. The first performance created such a stir that it caught the attention of Beishan's mayor and the local director of the Communist Religious Affairs Bureau (RAB).

Just before the opening of the second night's program, the mayor and RAB director confronted Siu Lam citing the issue of crowd control. They insisted that she go in and make a place for them to sit and monitor the drama. She refused. "The ground is level at the foot of the cross," she said. "First come first served. If you want seats, you will have to go in and tell the people to leave. I will not." And she walked away.

The next day the officials sent representatives early to hold seats for them on the front row. For the next several weeks, they attended the church services observing Rev. Lam's teaching.

At the end of February the mayor and Religious Affairs Bureau director contacted Siu Lam. "We've been watching you," they said. "You don't seem to have any political agenda and teach only what is in the Bible." She agreed that this was so. They then told her of the religious fanaticism (otherwise known as opposition to the State) that was prevalent in the countryside particularly among the rural peasants.

Because of her singular allegiance to the Bible with no political slant or activity, they asked her to go to the villages *to* "disciple them, so they will not become enemies of the State." She politely refused, citing lack of time and the heavy demands of her own large congregation.

Over the next few weeks, they pressured Siu Lam to help them, while she continued to decline. With the third invitation to help, they made it clear that she had no choice in the matter. "Just see that it gets done," they said.

Around this time Siu Lam met the missionary Strategy Coordinator. She told him her story and asked for counsel. The Strategy Coordinator encouraged her to take two weeks to fast and pray to see what God might want to show them. He told her that it just might be that God had caused the government leaders to give her this freedom to do what was normally prohibited— widely evangelize and train people throughout the region.

Two weeks later the two came together again, this time convinced that God was leading them to seize this opportunity. With time, travel, and financial constraints as mitigating factors, the Strategy Coordinator suggested that it would be easier to bring the trainees to a central location rather than try to take training to them in the towns and villages.

Siu Lam and her church colleagues agreed and began a Discipleship Training Center (DTC) ministry. The two parties covenanted together. Siu Lam and her church leaders would contact house church leaders in the region while the Strategy

Coordinator would prepare plans and materials for the training program.

In addition to gathering training materials, the Strategy Coordinator marshaled prayer support. He and his wife forged a prayer network spanning ten countries. The couple also began mobilizing Mandarin-speaking Chinese Christians from other countries to help teach in the DTC ministry.

Soon afterwards, Siu Lam arranged for the Strategy Coordinator to meet the mayor and Religious Affairs Bureau director to discuss the venture. In their meeting, the leading government official invited this American to assist Siu Lam's unregistered church to teach the entire province the word of God. The Baptist missionary concluded, "Only God could do such a thing."

The first Discipleship Training Center classes began in late June of

---

The First DTC Curriculum Included:

1) **Genesis 1-10** *Who is God? -the creation and God's relationship with man.*

2) **The Life of Christ** – *a study through the Gospels and the whole redemption story.*

3) **The Book of Romans** – *a study to teach the sinfulness of man and the provisions of God through Christ.*

4) **The Book of Jonah** – *a study of God's redemptive purposes for all mankind and the believer's role in that plan.*

5) **The Book of Ephesians** – *a study of the nature of church.*

6) **How to Study the Bible**

7) **How to Teach the Bible**

8) **Personal Evangelism Training**

1993 in less than ideal circumstances. At the first meeting 103 village-church leaders attended; 70 of them had no Bible. They were poor and bedraggled. They had no place to sleep and no money for food. So, they slept in the church building on benches and the floor. Local church members provided them one bowl of rice and vegetables per day.

The Strategy Coordinator was able to provide pens and paper while Siu Lam and the DTC teachers taught directly from the Bible. Sessions lasted 10-14 hours each day, six days a week for 20 days. Even under these conditions, the response was remarkable. The participants begged the leaders to continue for another 10 days. Exhausted, but elated, they agreed.

Siu Lam and the Strategy Coordinator took careful steps to ensure that they would be able to trace the participants and survey the effects of the training. After three months, the two met with the rest of the DTC leadership to assess the results.

During the three months from August through October the first class of participants were responsible for more than 1,300 conversions with over 1,200 of these already baptized. Most of these new believers were assimilated into existing churches, but some of the trainees had also started at least three new churches of 50 members each.

Over the next year, the Strategy Coordinator mobilized his network of prayer supporters to expand the training capacity of the Discipleship Training Center. They enlarged the little church building to be able to seat 1,200 persons. They added to the worship center a four-story training center. Its third and fourth floors serve as dormitories for women and men respectively. All of this was done with the support of the mayor and the local director of the Religious Affairs Bureau.

A year later the situation began to change. The ministry of the Discipleship Training Center had grown tremendously, but the window of favor with the local government officials was already beginning to close. The Religious Affairs Bureau director was promoted and moved on.

Results of the Beishan Movement

After **three months** there were
- More than 1300 professions of faith
- More than 1200 baptisms
- 3 new church starts

After **seven months** there were
- 15 new church starts

After **nine months** there were
- 25 new church starts

After **twenty-seven months** there were
- 57 new church starts

After **three years** there have been
- over 450 church starts scattered throughout three provinces that have roots in the DTC training
- over 18,000 professions of faith
- more than 500 house church leaders trained
- more than 1,000 other believers trained

His replacement was much more critical of the Center. Secrecy became standard operating procedure at the Center. Outsiders were curtailed from participating, leaving the responsibility for training on the shoulders of the pastor and her staff. This increased political pressure on the Discipleship Training Center prompted the leadership to take some of the training into the villages. The effects of this decentralized training have been promising, producing more than 450 new churches and 18,000 baptisms in three years.

T HE AUTHOR'S 1999 booklet *Church Planting Movements* described a Church Planting Movement that unfolded in another province of China that we called Yanyin.[23] Let's
revisit that movement today to see what has occurred since 1999.

The province where this Church Planting Movement occurred
has a population of about 8-10 million persons. The registered
Three-Self Patriotic Movement (TSPM) Church in the province
had 18 meeting places with about 4,000 members, roughly half
of whom attended services each week. These TSPM churches
had not grown in size or started new churches for many years.
They also closely followed government policies of opposing and
reporting underground church activity.

In 1991, an American Strategy Coordinator was assigned to
Yanyin. He began by surveying the existing church landscape.
The leaders of the registered TSPM churches indicated that they
were not interested in evangelism beyond their own walls, so the
Strategy Coordinator looked to the unregistered house churches.
He found three house churches with 85 members. The member-
ship was aging and had been in slow decline for years with little
vision for growth.

Aware of the enormous linguistic and cultural barriers
separating him from the people he hoped to reach, the Strategy
Coordinator began mobilizing ethnic Chinese from other
countries to assist with evangelism and church planting.

The first year these partners teamed up with Yanyin believers
to start six new house churches. The following year they started
17 more. The next year they began 50 churches. By 1997, the
total number of churches had climbed from three to 195. By this
time, the gospel had spread to every county in the province and
churches had been planted in each of the five ethnic people
groups.

---

[23] See the author's *Church Planting Movements*, pp. 16-21.

In 1998, the Strategy Coordinator left the assignment to begin new work elsewhere. In his absence, rather than decline, the movement accelerated in growth. By the end of 1998, there were 550 house churches in Yanyin province with more than 55,000 believers. Over the next two years, only sporadic reports surfaced from this province, but each report attested to great advances in the church.

In the summer of 2001, a careful survey was completed that revealed more than 900 churches with nearly 100,000 believers worshiping in them.

The Yanyin movement was characterized by widespread personal and mass evangelism. In pioneer areas, church planters would sometimes use the *Jesus Film* or a wide evangelistic campaign to identify inquirers who might then be followed up with further teaching. Church planters directed their message to the heads of households. As persons expressed an interest in the gospel, the church planters traced family lines to expand the base of people to involve in Bible studies, issuing invitations along relationship lines through relatives and friends. At the conclusion of a few weeks of witness and simple evangelistic Bible study, they invited participants to commit their lives to Christ.

Those who believed were immediately incorporated into basic discipleship Bible studies for a few more weeks. At the conclusion of the studies, the new believers were baptized. The church planters then identified those who were suitable for leadership and immediately turned over the leadership of the public meetings to them. One of the church planters stayed behind and mentored these leaders, teaching them doctrines and practices which those leaders would in turn teach to their new house churches.

At the core of the Yanyin movement was a house church model that combined multiple lay leadership development, mutual accountability, biblical authority and rapid reproducibility.

The Strategy Coordinator called this church model a POUCH church. POUCH is an acronym that stands for **P**articipative Bible study and worship, **O**bedience as the mark of success for every believer and church, **U**npaid and multiple leaders in each church, **C**ell groups of 10-20 believers meeting in **H**omes or storefronts. Rapidly reproducing POUCH churches served as the engine for the Yanyin Church Planting Movement.

> ### POUCH Churches
>
> **Participative** Bible Study and Worship
> **Obedience** to God's word as the mark of success for every believer and church
> **Unpaid** and multiple church leaders
> **Cell** groups of believers meeting in
> **Homes** or storefronts

In more established areas, churches reproduced whenever they reached a predetermined size that might jeopardize their security.

In cities or larger towns, house churches rarely exceeded thirty members. In rural areas, some churches grew much larger. When a house church divided, some leaders went with the new congregation and quickly named a local apprentice to begin training for the time when growth would demand a new division and fresh church start.

Most of the Yanyin churches met at least twice a week—though some met every day. In urban areas, a typical Sunday service aimed an evangelistic message at visiting seekers. A second weekday service was conducted that would concentrate on discipleship and training issues for believers.

In Yanyin, leadership development was built into the very structure of church life. By building the church around participative Bible study with multiple lay leaders there was a mutual accountability for what was taught and for how successfully the church developed and reproduced itself. The heavy emphasis on modeling also strengthened leadership development by compelling every believer to practice leading by doing.

Visiting Christians continued to provide the new church leaders with advanced training. These short-term trainers were typically ethnic Chinese who moved freely in and out of the region without attracting attention. After these trainers taught a group of Yanyin church leaders, the leaders would then cascade the training out through a network of meetings across the province.

Trying not to arouse suspicion from Communist officials, the Yanyin churches developed additional discrete means of leadership development. Each month the Yanyin believers conducted regular monthly meetings on the county level and two weeks later on the provincial level for a day of prayer, fasting, and training. They also created a system of cross-pollination for leaders. In this system, new potential leaders were encouraged to periodically attend house churches other than their own in order to learn other styles of worship, training, and leadership.

The Strategy Coordinator in the Yanyin Church Planting Movement was very helpful in providing insights from his experiences. He placed heavy emphasis on training of house church leaders and the preparation of ethnic Chinese evangelists, church planters, and trainers.

The Strategy Coordinator pointed to a dozen important lessons[24] he learned from the Yanyin Church Planting Movement:

1. Prayer was vital not only *for* unreached Yanyin people, but also *among* the new Yanyin believers.
2. Everything that we wanted the people to do, we had to *model* as well as teach.
3. We learned to emphasize application rather than knowledge, and found that the knowledge always followed.

---

[24] These and other lessons were first published in Snowden's *Toward Church Planting Movements*, pp. 17-22.

4. We always tried to include feedback loops with our mass evangelism efforts to ensure follow up of new believers.
5. We tried to make sure that everything we did in the areas of evangelism, church planting, and training could be reproduced by the Yanyin people.
6. We encouraged locally produced hymns and praise songs to spread the faith
7. We found that our expectations of the new converts were usually met, so we set the mark high for growth and new fruit!
8. We taught the new churches to quickly assimilate new believers into the life and work of the church.
9. We found that multiple leadership and unpaid leadership kept the movement growing while eliminating the gap between clergy and laity.
10. We learned to build accountability for both leaders and church members into the way they do church.
11. We learned that meeting in homes rather than dedicated buildings allowed the movement to stay below the radar of the government and spread rapidly without gaining notice.
12. We learned that the new Yanyin believers must take responsibility for fulfilling the Great Commission.

While the Yanyin Church Planting Movement may be unique in its well conceived church and leadership development structure, its rapid reproduction and multiplication are common-place across China. But China and India are not the only Asian countries where these movements are taking place. Let's now turn our attention to other Asian countries.

5

Other Asian Movements

During the decade of the nineties, Church Planting Movements in Outer Mongolia and Inner Mongolia produce more than 60,000 new believers.

A Church Planting Movement transforms Cambodia's killing fields into fields of new life with more than 60,000 new Christians and hundreds of new churches planted over the past ten years.

Despite government attempts to eliminate Christianity, a Church Planting Movement in one Southeast Asian country adds more than 50,000 new believers in five years.

IN DECEMBER 1990, the Republic of Mongolia had not yet shaken off its decades of subjugation to Soviet Communism. In the waning days of the Soviet Union, Mongolians were mired in poverty, illiteracy, crime, children born out of wedlock, unemployment, and an uncertain future.

Into this chaotic situation, God summoned adventurous missionaries such as a successful young pharmacist from Memphis, Tennessee named Stan Kirk. Stan and his wife Laura had been praying for the Mongolian people when God made it clear that he wanted them to serve as missionaries. In 1990 Stan and Laura took their one-year old daughter, Mary, and moved to Ulan Bator.

The Kirks' first winter in Mongolia was brutal. As the Communist economic system broke down, there was not yet a free market system to take its place. "We didn't have government-issued cards that all of the citizens had that would allow you to shop in the government-owned co-op," Stan explained. "Some days we were lucky if we could get anything at all to eat," said Laura. Stan's weight dropped 25 pounds that year, Laura who was nursing little Mary, lost more than twice that much.

During their second year, the free market system began to work. The Kirks were able to move into a small heated apartment and had regular access to the grocery store. As political conditions changed the Kirks began to see a growing harvest of Mongolian believers. A year earlier, they could find no more than six Mongolian Christians in the entire country. Most Mongols had never seen a Christian, unless it was a Russian, the foreign occupiers of their homeland.

By 1991 there were already two churches meeting in Ulan Bator and additional churches springing up in other towns. Stan spent his Saturdays meeting with a young Mongolian pastor. They discussed the questions that had come up on the previous Sunday and prepared the Bible lesson for the following day. When Sunday worship began, Stan sat quietly in the back of the meeting place.

As the nineties unfolded, missionaries began arriving from many different countries. Korean missionaries took advantage of their relative proximity to Mongolia and their shared Altaic language to adopt Mongolia as a major mission field. In 1996 an updated publication of the Mongolian New Testament further fueled the Mongolian movement. In the first month, the entire printing of 10,000 copies sold out.

By 1997 reports were radiating out of the country. "It's like the first century," one Christian worker said. "All the miracles, explosive growth and doctrinal challenges you find in the *Book of Acts* are happening today in Mongolia."

In July 1998, *Mission Frontiers* published a story on the phenomenal growth of the church in Mongolia. The article reported more than 10,000 Mongolian believers.[25] What had God done to bring this people to himself?

At the heart of the movement were some familiar qualities. In addition to the thousands of Christians who were praying for Mongolia, Mongolia missionary Rick Leatherwood identified the following key growth factors:

1. The missionaries' priority of loving the Mongolian people
2. Strong missiological principles of training indigenous leaders
3. Modeling the authority of the Bible for decision making
4. Establishing the church as a cell church movement
5. Encouraging Mongolian believers to write their own Christian songs

By the time the *Mission Frontiers* article was published, Stan and Laura Kirk were back in Memphis. Family health needs had forced them to return to the U.S. in 1997, but their hearts and prayers were still clearly in Mongolia.

A 1998 email from Stan confirmed the reports of the 10,000 new believers in Mongolia. "It has fulfilled my highest dream and aspiration," he said, "to be a part of what God has done in the rebirth of his church in Mongolia."

IN THE DAYS of Genghis Khan, Mongol hordes had so terrorized the peoples of Asia that when China and Russia finally recovered, they divided the Mongols into separate vassal states. The largest Mongolian population, some six million

---

[25] Rick Leatherwood, "Mongolia: As a People Movement to Christ Emerges, What Lessons Can We Learn?" in *Mission Frontiers* (July/August 1998).

Mongols, now live in China's province of Inner Mongolia that was seeing its own Church Planting Movement. This time it was the witness of Chinese house churches that prompted the movement.

In the summer of 2001, Chinese house church leaders reported baptizing 500,000 in the province of Inner Mongolia over a 12 month period. The provincial cities of Hailar, Yakeshi, Hohot, Zalantum, Ulanhot, and Huolin Gol have seen thousands added to the church. The majority of these new believers were ethnic Chinese, but the movement was also penetrating the Mongolian population. The *Voice of China* newsletter reported, "At least 50,000 converts are ethnic Mongols, both city-based Mongols and nomads who dwell in tents in the grasslands. Almost all the new Christians are people who had not previously heard the gospel."[26]

A T THE OTHER end of the continent, several Church Planting Movements were building momentum. Racked by decades of civil war and ideological strife, the peoples of Southeast Asia were broken and exhausted. Out of this broken soil, new life was springing up.

Security constraints prevent us from shining the light too brightly on many parts of Southeast Asia. However, Cambodia, offers insights that are comparable to those of other settings. Cambodia was one of the greatest victims of the decades-long Vietnam War. As the South Vietnamese government fell in 1975, Cambodia saw Pol Pot and his murderous Khmer Rouge rise to power.

---

[26] "Revival in Inner Mongolia- 500,000 Saved in Past 12 Months" in *Voice of China, the official voice of the house churches in China*, Vol. 1, Issue 1, Summer edition, 2001, pp. 13-14.

The horrors of Pol Pot's rule have scarcely been equaled in human history. Before the Khmer Rouge were forced from power in 1979, 3.3 million of Cambodia's less than 8 million citizens had been murdered, starved, or driven from the country.

The Khmer Rouge aimed its wrath at anyone with leadership potential: adults, urbanites, and the educated. Their paranoia also led them to attack anything perceived to be foreign, a judgment that fell heavily upon Christianity. By the 1980s, the fledgling evangelical population in Cambodia, which had never exceeded 5,000, was reduced to less than 600.

Today, Cambodia is changing. In the inner-city neighborhoods of Phnom Penh, one hears the sound of Christian hymns rising above the urban din. In a crowded meeting hall Cambodian Christians gather to sing praises, study their Bibles, and pour out their hearts to God in prayer.

Looking out of place in the service an elderly English woman accompanied the hymns with her violin. In years past she had been a concert violinist in England, before God redirected her to Southeast Asia where she had been serving as a missionary since 1959. After the service she took a few minutes to tell us what was happening.

"Pol Pot nearly destroyed the church," she said. "All the while he was ruining the country, though, Christians were ministering to Cambodian refugees in camps along the Thai border. I do believe that the Christian ministry during that time helped prepare their hearts for what is happening now."

What was happening now was extraordinary. She went on to explain, "Since 1990 the Christian population in Cambodia has risen from 600 to more than 60,000. The largest number of these are the Baptists with about 10,000 members followed by an indigenous denomination growing out of the Cambodian leadership of Campus Crusade for Christ." In the year 2001,

Baptist churches indeed reported 220 churches with more than 10,000 members.[27]

Before the movement began to wane, other denominations such as Christian and Missionary Alliance, Overseas Missionary Fellowship, Four-Square Gospel, and Presbyterians all reaped a harvest in Cambodia. By the year 2000, though, the Cambodia Church Planting Movement had passed. In the end it suffered, not from lack of missionary attention, but from too many well-intentioned intrusions from the outside. Foreign funds went to subsidize pastors and church planters who had previously done the work without remuneration. Salaries led to a sort of professsional minister class that created a gap between church leaders and common laypersons. Funds also accelerated the rate of institutionalization of training, ministry, and leadership. With funds and institutions came internal conflict within denominational hierarchies over who would control these resources.

We'll spend time examining these *movement poisons* in chapter 14. In the meantime, let's go back and examine how God was at work in the early stages of the movement, to see what we can learn.

One of the chief agents God used to spark the Cambodia movement was a young missionary couple named Bruce and Gloria Carlton.[28] The Carltons entered Cambodia as Strategy Coordinators in 1990. Although Bruce was already an experienced church planter, he determined that he would not plant any churches in Cambodia. Instead, he vowed to train Cambodians to launch a movement.

Bruce began by recruiting a promising Cambodian layman to assist him in translating a book he was writing on church

---

[27] Published by permission of the IMB's Regional Leader of the Southeast Asia & Oceania Region.

[28] Bruce Carlton, *Amazing Grace, lessons on Church Planting Movements from Cambodia* (Chennai: Mission Educational Books, 2000), 157 pp.

planting. As the project unfolded, Bruce transferred his own vision and skills into his Cambodian brother. Within a year, the Cambodian apprentice had recruited eight other Cambodian men and a woman, all of them anxious to learn how to plant churches.

The Carltons taught personal evangelism, how to study the Bible, church planting, and church leadership. The training was intensely practical, always aimed more at application than information.

By 1992, these church planters had multiplied the original church into six churches. In 1993, the number climbed to 10 and then 20 the following year. Over the next three years the number of Baptist churches climbed to 43, then 78, and then 123.

In his account of why this Church Planting Movement unfolded, Carlton cited the importance of prayer. "Over the past six years," he said, "there has been more mobilized prayer for the people of Cambodia than at any other time in their history." Prayers were aimed at protecting church planters and opening the hearts of lost Khmer people. God answered on both counts.

Prayer was also integrated into the lives of the new believers in Cambodia. They evidenced a strong sense of God's direct involvement in their lives. Signs and wonders, exorcisms, healing, and other manifestations of God's power were commonplace.

Training was another key to the success of Cambodia's Church Planting Movement. Carlton established the first Rural Leadership Training Program (known as RLTPs) in the country. The RLTPs became vital to the Church Planting Movement in Cambodia. Later, missionaries observed that, "where there were RLTPs in place, church planting always followed."

The Rural Leadership Training Programs consisted of eight modules of training, each one lasting two weeks, so that the entire program could be completed in about two years. Since most of the church leaders were bivocational, the pastors could not afford to be away from their homes for more than two weeks at a time. Furthermore, the meals for the trainees were provided by newly started churches in the area, and if the training went more than two weeks the poor church members would be hard-pressed to continue making this sacrifice.

Carlton also implemented a lifelong mentoring approach to leadership training. "I call it the 222 Principle," he said. "It's based on 2 Timothy 2:2 where Paul told Timothy: '...the things you have heard me say in the presence of many witnesses entrusts to reliable men who will also be qualified to teach others.'"

Carlton applied the 222 Principle as a means of multiplying the personal mentoring approach to leadership development. "Never do anything alone," he told the church planters, evangelists, and church leaders. "Always take someone with you so that you can model for them the vision, skills and values that shape your life."

At their departure in 1996, the Carltons left behind a small missionary band with a passionate commitment to serve the growing churches of Cambodia. One of these missionaries commented, "(we) earnestly seek to become the low-profile footman and avoid the temptation of being a high-profile front man."[29]

In a remote province near the Vietnam border, one could see where a Rural Leadership Training Center had been instrumental in spawning more than 40 new church starts. Dusty roads winding through acres of banana groves led to village after village each with scores of Cambodian believers meeting in thatched-roof homes.

Each village church told a similar story. They had been believers for less than six years. They met regularly with 30-50 members. Each house church had reproduced itself several times over the previous year.

---

[29] This and many other insights about the Cambodia Church Planting Movement are found in *Church Planting Movements*, pp. 26-31.

The churches organized around what they called "a seven-member central committee." They had adopted the notion of shared leadership from the selection of seven deacons in the *Book of Acts*, but the language of *central committee* had come from their Communist context. Bruce chuckled when he heard about it. "This didn't come from me," he said, "but it sounds like a great idea."

A Cambodian brother explained the seven lay leadership roles. "We have a worship leader, a Bible teacher, a men's minister, a women's minister, a youth minister, an outreach minister, and a literacy teacher," he explained. Each role met the needs of the Cambodian church, particularly the distinctly Cambodian need for a literacy teacher. Pol Pot's Red Guard had murdered so many of the educated Khmer people that every village now needed someone to teach the survivors how to read and write. These churches were literally rebuilding Cambodian society from the ground up.

In response to the question, "How do you start new churches?" One of the leaders smiled and pointed to a middle-aged woman standing nearby. She was a central committee member who was gifted in starting new work. She runs a small kiosk in the village market and when someone from out of town comes to her stall to buy things, she asks them, "Do you have a Baptist church in your village?" If they respond predictably with, "What is a Baptist church?" she replies, "Next week we will come and tell you about it."

In retrospect, it seems that the church planting vegetable seller always made it a point to ask her customers if they had a "Baptist" church in their village, not because she was an ardent denominationalist, but because she had correctly calculated that they were less likely to know what it was, which improved her chances of getting an invitation to come and explain.

The following week she and some members of the central committee would arrive in the village, and each one would share

how Jesus had changed his or her life and how they have now
dedicated their lives to serving the community. At the end of
their presentation they ask, "Would you like to have a Baptist
church in your village?" The villagers enthusiastically welcomed
the new faith as they began to form their own seven-member
central committee.

In Cambodia's rural villages houses are built on stilts with
wide spaces between the floor planks and heavy thatching on the
roof. A church member's one-room house typically served as the
sanctuary for forty to fifty church members who sit on the floor
for worship, filling the air with lively songs of praise.

At the close of the worship service, the church members
paraded slowly down the house church steps and then meandered
across the rice fields behind the village. In the distance, one
could see the hills that marked the border with Vietnam.

During the Vietnam War, this same borderland had formed
the infamous Ho Chi Minh Trail, a conduit for smuggling
Communist weapons into South Vietnam. The fields were all
peaceful now, but the landscape was still pockmarked with
muddy ponds, like scars from the war. "Those are bomb craters,"
the Cambodian brother explained, "made by your American
airplanes during the war." He paused to let the words sink in, and
then smiled. "Last Easter," he said, "we baptized 70 new
believers in that pond."

ACROSS SOUTHEAST ASIA, even greater reports are
surfacing. Since Christian ministry there is still under
government pressure, we can't tell all that is happening, but God
is clearly at work unfolding new Church Planting Movements in
remarkable ways.

One Strategy Coordinator has seen 65,000 come to Christ
over a ten-year period resulting in hundreds of new churches
despite severe government persecution.

Another has seen multiple Church Planting Movements spring up in both rural and urban settings. Rural Christians develop POUCH churches along the lines of those in China, while much of the urban growth has come as a result of training existing house church networks with more effective ways to survive and multiply.

In February 2000, a Strategy Coordinator working in one Communist country arranged a quiet meeting with the leader of a large home cell church network. The network was one of seven in the country, each containing more than 150 house churches. Together these networks were home to more than 180,000 believers.

The meeting took place on a floating restaurant where we could easily blend into the tourist traffic. The impressive night view of the city waterfront was overshadowed by the gravity of what the church leader and his two colleagues were saying.

In hushed tones, he told of how government agents had infiltrated churches and police had severely cracked down on unregistered church meetings. "Every few months," he said, "there is another report of a police raid on someone's home. Church leaders have been imprisoned and their parishioners scattered." Despite this opposition, Christianity continued to spread widely throughout the cities and countryside.

A crisis seemed to be reached every time a church grew to more than 30 members. "Perhaps our singing was too loud," he said. "Or maybe the neighbors became suspicious with so many visitors. Whatever the reason, the police were called. Our people were treated very severely. Some are still in prison." As he spoke his eyes seemed to see the faces of those who had been arrested.

Then he sat up and smiled, "That is when your missionary helped us. He invited several of us to go to Singapore for training. It has changed everything for us."

"How did it change things for you?"

He continued, "We learned about how to have small churches that multiply rather than growing large. That way we never attract too much attention. Before this training, we still were thinking like in the old days when we worshiped in open places. We were still trying to grow big. Now, we grow large by adding more cell churches. When we reach 15 or 20 members we start a new church."

"So how is it going?"

"Right now," he said, "we are training our people. This summer, in one week, we will start 70 new home cell churches."

By staying small, the church in Southeast Asia was growing large.

I N ADDITION TO its role as a center for home cell church and Church Planting Movement training, Singapore is also home to a surging evangelicalism that exhibits many characteristics of Church Planting Movements. Singapore is a virtual city-state with a population of 3.5 million. Across Asia, Singapore has earned a reputation as an economic powerhouse with its citizens boasting an annual per capita income of nearly $27,000. They are highly educated with 89 percent adult literacy, and increasingly, they are becoming evangelical Christians.

Over the past three decades, evangelical Christianity has more than doubled in Singapore. In 1900 there were only about 10,000 Christians of any kind in Singapore. Many of these were only nominally affiliated with the Catholic or Anglican Church. As recently as 1970, Singapore was only 1.86 percent Christian.[30] However, 14 years later, more than 12 percent of the country claimed allegiance to Jesus Christ. Today, the number of

---

[30] Keith Hinton, *Growing Churches Singapore Style* (Singapore: OMF, 1985), p. 110.

evangelical and Charismatic Christians has risen to more than 400,000.

What has contributed to this growth? While Singapore has not seen the same kind of house churches evident in Church Planting Movements, between 1970 and 1985, it has experienced an explosion of home-cell mega-churches. During those years, the total number of churches only increased from 189 to 320,[31] but the nature of those churches changed radically from traditional congregation-based worship to sprawling home-based cell groups.

One of these cell-based churches is Faith Community Baptist Church where Pastor Lawrence Khong leads a satellite network of more than 550 home cell groups with some 7,000 members.

---

[31] Hinton, p. 110.

Khong has been an ardent student and apostle of cell church methodology, instructing all who will listen.[32]

An even more dynamic Singapore cell church began in 1989 when Pastor Kong Hee and his wife Ho Yeow-Sun started the City Harvest Church. By the turn of the millennium, City Harvest counted nearly 13,000 members meeting in more than 400 home-based cell groups.[33]

Reverend Hee and his wife perfectly mirror the type of evangelicalism that is captivating Singapore. The young couple are still in their thirties and like the social group they seek to reach they come from the community of upwardly mobile Singapore professionals. To date, 57 percent of City Harvest Church's 13,000 members are salaried professionals.[34]

Singapore's urban evangelicals match this same demographic profile. In his 1985 study of the Singapore movement, Keith Hinton found that Singapore's evangelicals were 94.5 percent literate and comprised 28 percent of the nation's professional and technical class and 24 percent of its administrators and managers, while totaling less than 14 percent of the city's total population.[35] Likewise, evangelical affluence places more than 27 percent of Singapore's Christians in privately owned homes, a rarity in a city where space is a premium, and more than 90 percent of the population live in public housing.[36]

---

[32]See the Faith Community Baptist Church website at: http://www.fcbc.org.sg. In 2001, Khong shifted his church to a G-12 cell church model. The G-12 paradigm is discussed in chapter 8 below.

[33] Visit their website at www.chc.org.sg.

[34] Ibid.

[35] Hinton, p. 113.

[36] Hinton, p. 114.

If Singapore's rapid evangelical growth is structured around home cell groups, it is fueled by evangelism. Many trace this impulse to a December 1978 Billy Graham evangelistic meeting in the city's national stadium. Two and a half years later, in March 1981, Campus Crusade for Christ launched the *Jesus Film* across the city. With the permission of the Ministry of Education, *Jesus Film* promotional materials were sent to over 200 schools. By the end of the initiative, 215,408 persons had seen the film; 3,204 had returned decision cards indicating that they either wanted to receive Christ or rededicate themselves to Christ or receive further information.[37] The Billy Graham meetings were followed by even larger rallies by evangelists Reinhard Bonkke in 1985 and Luis Palau the following year.

In 1984 widespread evangelism received another boost when the Singapore government concluded that religious education was needed in the nation's school system.[38] Evangelicals took full advantage of the opportunity and quietly spread their faith wherever and whenever possible. The program was complemented by a host of evangelical student ministries (Inter-Varsity Fellowship, Youth With A Mission, Youth For Christ, Campus Crusade for Christ, and others). A 1985 survey revealed that 42 percent of Protestants in Singapore had attended some kind of Christian parachurch group while in tertiary school.[39]

Singapore's urban evangelicalism may not be a Church Planting Movement, but it is certainly a close relative. A local Singapore observer who has seen the evolution of Singapore's evangelical movement cited several similarities and differences

---

[37] Bobby E.K. Sng, *In His Good Time: the story of the church in Singapore, 1819-1992,* 2nd edition (Singapore: Singapore: Graduates' Christian Fellowship, 1993), p. 318.

[38] Sng, pp. 317 and 122. The government-sponsored religious education program was repealed in October 1989.

[39] Hinton, p. 120.

with Church Planting Movements. His insights are paraphrased below:

> As with Church Planting Movements, these mega-cell churches routinely see God's intervention in daily life; they spend lots of time and energy training lay people to lead small groups; they intentionally encourage the starting of new groups; they share their faith with a high number of their members witnessing; they empower their cell leaders; their cells are participative; they tend to emphasize the authority of the Bible...they are healthy, they are getting the gospel to thousands of non-believers.
>
> The difference is that none of these cell churches will reach their entire cities. They only grow to the size of the competence of the leadership. While mega-church pastors continue to look for cell church techniques to grow their own church larger, Church Planting Movement practitioners look to CPM principles to reach an entire people or city.[40]

Let's turn now to another urban movement that has flourished in northeast Asia.

IN SEOUL, KOREA, the world has witnessed another remarkable urban evangelical movement. Though also not a Church Planting Movement, Seoul, like Singapore, shares many qualities with Church Planting Movements. Seoul is a city of more than 12 million people and nearly 5.5 million of them profess allegiance to Jesus Christ.[41] Seoul's church multiplication has been unfolding for nearly four decades. Today there are more than 5,000 Protestant church buildings in the city of Seoul. Many of them have memberships numbering in the tens of thousands. Some even have more than 100,000 active members. However, as with Singapore, most of these mega-

---

[40] Paraphrased from an email from B. Smith, July 2003.

[41] *World Christian Encyclopedia, 2nd Edition, Vol. 2*, p. 601.

churches are actually mega-cell churches consisting of hundreds and even thousands of cell groups that meet in homes throughout the week.

The largest and best known of these is Pastor Cho Yonggi's Yoido Full Gospel Church with a membership of 780,000. Yoido Full Gospel Church is the largest single church in the world. At

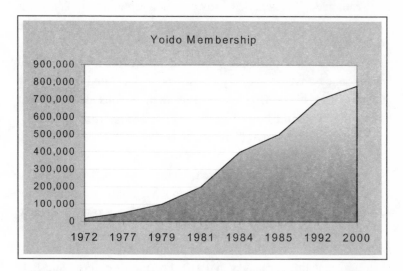

the heart of the Yoido church is a passionate commitment to prayer, evangelism, and Bible study in more than 20,000 home cell groups meeting each week all over the city.[42]

Some have asked, "How long can a Church Planting Movement last? Of course, if the movement lasts long enough it will eventually reach all the host people. As we have already seen, China's many Church Planting Movements have been building for about 20 years and show no sign of slowing. Korea's movement has an even longer history, but after more than 30 years of growth it is now in decline. Since its inception, though,

---

[42] The structure of the Yoido Full Gospel Church can be seen on the Internet at www.yfgc.org/n_english/fg.

more than ten million Koreans have been born again. To understand how this movement has continued for so long, we should examine its foundations.

Korea's church history took a decisive turn in the late 19th century when Protestant missionaries invited China missionary John L. Nevius to come to Korea to share his ideas on church self-reliance. Nevius had already gained a reputation in China for what has been termed the *three-self principle* or simply the *Nevius method*.

The three-self principle grew out of Nevius's alarm at the dependency that missionary subsidies had created among the Chinese Christians. To combat this evil, Nevius declared that "the church should be self-governing, self-supporting, and self-propagating." Dismissed by many of his colleagues in China, Nevius and his three-self principles were welcomed in Korea.

In 1900, Protestants in Korea counted only 6,500 adherents. Ten years later, the Presbyterian and Methodist churches that embraced Nevius's indigenous teachings had grown to nearly 30,000 members.[43]

Christian growth met fierce opposition when Japan invaded and annexed the peninsula in 1910. For the next three and half decades, Christians were persecuted and the faith was suppressed. The Japanese occupation was followed by a civil war, through which Communism virtually eradicated Christianity in the North. In the South, however, the gospel flourished. From 1940-2000, Protestant believers doubled in number every ten years.[44]

By the year 2000, there were more than 8.8 million Protestants in South Korea alone, and up to 40 percent of

---

[43] Stephen Neill, *A History of Christian Missions* (New York: Penguin, 1964), pp. 343-344.

[44] *World Christian Encyclopedia, 2nd Edition, Vol. 1*, p. 684.

Korea's population was affiliated with some denomination of the Christian faith.

For years evangelicals have watched Korea with reverent amusement. Many felt that it was a movement of God, but one that was uniquely Korean. Today, we can see that it has parallels in other Church Planting Movements that God is birthing across Asia and around the world.

We've covered Asia visiting Church Planting Movements from India to China to the Pacific Rim. Now let's go to Africa, where God is turning a lost continent to Christ.

6

Africa

Over the past century, the number of professing Christians in Africa grows from nine million to more than 360 million.

Each month an estimated 1,200 new churches are started in Africa.

In eight months, 28 Ethiopian evangelists led 681 persons to Christ and started 83 new churches.

Today, after years of resistance to the gospel, some 90,000 of Kenya's 600,000 Maasai are followers of Jesus Christ.

S TRANGERS TO AFRICA have described it as a vast, dark continent. But those who have ventured inside know of its beauty and rich diversity of peoples. From the nomads of the Sahara to the pygmies of the rainforests and the Bantu warriors of the southern plains, Africa is a colorful mosaic.

Ancient Cushitic tribes rule the eastern Sahara, while indigo-skinned Tuareg Berbers patrol its western reaches. Flowing southward through the Nile valley and around the river's legendary sources in the Mountains of the Moon are the tall and slender Nilotic peoples, such as the Dinka and the Tutsi. Farther south, the sprawling Bantu nations have staked out kingdoms in the savannah lands of the southern half of the continent.

While some outsiders have viewed Africans as one people, the continent is, in fact, a tangle of nations, tribes, and tongues. In many places these families of man are embroiled in genocidal conflict. Millions have died over the past decade as Rwanda,

Burundi, and the Congo with help from Uganda, Tanzania, and Zimbabwe have been locked in what one can only describe as a world war within the heart of Africa.

Under the feet of these great competing civilizations are the aborigines of Africa who once roamed the entire continent unchallenged, but today survive only in token groups such as the Pygmies, Bushmen, Hottentots, and Khoisan.

With all the ethnic diversity that is in Africa, it is no wonder that European colonizers reconfigured the continent into more recognizable patterns. However, as these European trading concessions evolved into colonies they completely disregarded Africa's ancient people group boundaries.

After World War II, Europe's African colonies began claiming their independence, but the road to nationhood has not been easy. Country after country has been torn by conflict stemming from ancient tribal enmities that were too easily papered over—and patched together—by the European colonizers.

Independence from Western control left ethnic people groups competing feverishly over which tribe would be dominant in the new state. Losers paid a bitter price. By the decade of the seventies, Africa's euphoria over independence had deteriorated into chronic ethnic conflict across most of the continent.

By the 1980s, missionaries grew increasingly aware of Africa's ethnic diversity and began shifting their attention to the people groups within those states. What did it matter, they reasoned, if millions of Kikuyu Kenyans were Christian if there were no churches among the Maasai or Turkana of the interior? The Yoruba of Nigeria had 7,000 Baptist churches, but what of the millions of Muslim Hausa, Fulani, and Bambara, among whom there was not a single church?

The refocus of missionary efforts beneath the veneer of political countries and into the reality of ethnolinguistic people groups has led to a virtual renaissance of gospel expansion and harvest in Africa. People groups that had long been neglected for reasons of hostility, linguistic complexity, or geographic isolation were now coming into focus.

Many of these unreached people groups of Africa have never heard the gospel before in their own language. It is in this context that God is now unfolding a number of Church Planting Movements in Africa.

While Africa has had many sweeping people group movements over the past century, many of these express themselves in Western-style church buildings and denominational hierarchies that linked them firmly to European or American control.[45] Today, African Christianity is expressing its own patterns and independence from the West.

By the end of the 20th century, the Kikuyu, Luo, Luhya tribes of Kenya had all exhibited long-term consistent church growth, but not the sort of rapid church growth one finds in a Church Planting Movement.[46] In Uganda, two decades of civil war created a different kind of church growth environment.

T HE 1.1 MILLION Teso people, living in Uganda's Teso Province comprise just over five percent of the nation's population. The gospel first reached Uganda in 1875 with Anglican explorers and missionaries. Since that time, there has been intermittent missionary activity among the Teso for nearly a century. During the early 1980s Southern Baptists assigned their first missionaries, Harry and Doris Garvin, to the Teso. The couple learned the Teso language well and soon began to find a

---

[45] See David B. Barrett's *Schism & Renewal in Africa, an analysis of six thousand contemporary religious movements* (Nairobi: Oxford University Press, 1968), 363 pp.

[46] Report by IMB's East Africa Strategy Associate Larry Pumpelly in January 2001.

response among the people. By 1986, about 90 Teso Baptist churches had been started.

In 1985 a military coup toppled the embattled government of Milton Obote. In the chaotic years that followed, missionaries were forced to withdraw from the country. When they returned in 1990, they found a country devastated by the war. Entire villages were destroyed. The missionaries didn't see how any of the Teso churches could have survived.

To their delight they found that rather than cowering in fear, the Teso believers had been boldly proclaiming the Good News and the people were responding enthusiastically to their message. During the five years of chaos, the 90 churches had multiplied into 320 churches. On a single Sunday 1,200 Teso converts were baptized.

The returning missionaries adopted a different role among the Teso. Rather than pursuing new church starts they concentrated on theological education and leadership development. Church growth among the Teso has slowed since the explosion of the late 1980s, but continues to be strong. Today there are 400-450 Baptist churches among the Teso. This represents more than 20,000 Teso who have come to faith in the past fifteen years.

T HE MAASAI OF East Africa are legendary for their courage and independence. They have resisted Western-style development and Western notions of modernization.

Scattered across the savannas of Kenya and Tanzania, the Maasai have long guarded Africa's interior from Arab slave traders and colonizers. The Maasai live in small clan units in homes constructed of mud and cow dung with thatched roofs. At first glance, their poverty is disturbing, but then you see that it is only a poverty of Western goods and services. Maasai men and women take great pride in their personal appearance and ancient customs. Their ornate necklaces, carefully braided hair, and sinewy muscles reveal an inner wealth that many Westerners have lost.

Missionaries have attempted to evangelize the Maasai over the past century. While some have met with scattered successes, the converts have generally been ostracized and driven out of their homes or have withdrawn themselves from the center of Maasai life and culture.

In the late 1980s, three missionary families gathered a few Maasai believers and began to develop a plan to reach all of the Maasai people. Following Jesus' pattern in Luke 10, they commissioned about 70 trained lay Maasai evangelists to go out two by two across the Maasai Plains. For training support, five Baptist missionary families moved into the Maasai Plains and related to the Maasai evangelists as they itinerated across the region.

Today, up to 15 percent of the 600,000 Maasai in Kenya will tell you they are followers of Jesus Christ. The majority of these can be traced back to those original Maasai lay evangelists.

To understand this unseen Church Planting Movement, requires a different set of eyes. For several years a photograph has hung on the wall of the waiting lounge near my office. It is a picture of an acacia tree set on a dry plain somewhere in Africa. You know that it's Africa because of the 30-40 dark figures gathered under its shade leaning against their spears. Only after visiting the Maasai Plains and seeing actual Maasai churches, did I realize that the photo outside my office was a Maasai church.

The worship style of the Maasai is a far cry from the Western forms that marked the colonial era of missions. Most Maasai churches gather under acacia trees, the traditional meeting places for Maasai councils. The Maasai will gather regularly for worship at the same tree again and again. Occasionally someone will pull a cluster of thorn bushes around to form a wall, a protection from wind, dust, and varmints.

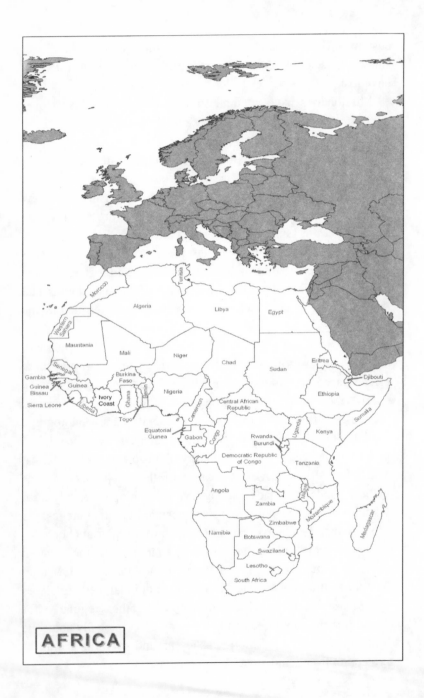

AFRICA

The heart of Maasai worship is found in their songs and prayers. The Maasai have an oral culture and have benefited from the telling of Bible stories in their native tongue. Not satisfied to hear the stories told, the Maasai often convert these great teaching stories into their native songs, and sing them with great enthusiasm.

In the cool dusk of the African savannah land, one can hear a seven-man Maasai chorus performing song after song adapted from Bible stories they have learned. Their Maasai rhythms are hypnotic as they accompany themselves with the throaty grunts, thumping on chests and thighs with spears tapping on the floor. Their faces flash vivid expressions as they act out the Bible stories with hand motions and choreographed steps.

It is difficult to know how many Maasai churches or believers there truly are. How do you count each "Acacia Tree Church?" Or why would you want to? The movement continues to spread in areas where Western missionaries have difficulty following. Maasai from Kenya share their faith with the 600,000 Maasai living in Tanzania who are also proving to be very responsive. Over the past year, Maasai evangelists have also begun learning the language of their neighboring tribe, the Samburu people, with a vision of taking the gospel to them.

WHEN THE MISSIONARIES of West Africa shifted their attention from countries to people groups, the Ife (EE-fay) of Togo soon felt the impact. The Ife are one of the tribes divided between two nations as they straddle both sides of the Togo and Benin borders. Numbering about 10 million, the Ife are the largest unevangelized non-Muslim people group south of the Sahara. In Togo they comprise about 36 percent of the nation's population; in Benin they make-up 55 percent of the country. Most Ife practice African traditional religion.[47]

The first Baptist missionaries to adopt the Ife assignment were Mike and Marsha Key. The Ife seemed to be waiting for the Keys to find them. Or perhaps they were simply waiting for someone to meet them on their own terms. Mike preached his first sermon to the Ife in 1981 and 24 Ife adults made commitments to Christ. After years of evangelicals avoiding the Ife, Mike could now see that the Ife were responsive to the gospel if only they could hear it. He also wondered if Togolese Christians might not multiply his efforts to reach the Ife.

Mike returned to Lome, the capital of Togo, where he recruited 24 Togolese evangelists to join him in the East Mono region where the Ife live. Mike and his Togolese Baptist team conducted a three-week preaching-teaching campaign in five separate villages. During the three-week period 5,700 persons viewed the *Jesus* film at night—446 persons made commitments to Christ. Among these converts were the chief and his sub-chiefs of an Ife village.

In 1983, the missionary initiated a partnership with North Carolina Baptists that was to last for three years. During the partnership, North Carolinians built a 210 foot-long bridge, dug 113 wells, 16 ponds, and constructed a conference center. By the end of the three-year period, there were 1,200 baptisms recorded and 1,000 additional converts awaiting baptism.

Over the next decade the Ife movement picked-up speed as 85 new churches were started among the Ife of Togo with more than 5,000 persons worshiping in them. Despite this progress in Togo, the missionaries were not allowed to extend their work across the border into the Ife tribes of Benin.

---

[47] Much of the profile of the early years of the Ife work is taken from "The Ife of Togo," by Bill Phillips in Mark Snowden, ed. *Toward Church Planting Movements* (Richmond, Virginia: International Mission Board, 1997), pp. 23-26.

After years of unsuccessful negotiations with Benin government officials, the Keys were denied permission to live among
the Ife of their country. Then, in the early 1990s, Mike Key was
diagnosed with cancer and had to leave West Africa. It would be
several years before any new missionaries were assigned to work
with the Ife.

In 1995, when Jess and Peggy Thompson were transferred
from Equatorial Guinea to live among the Ife of Benin, they
found that there were already five new churches underway. Soon
afterwards, the five churches were already reproducing themselves without missionary assistance. The movement that had
begun among the Ife of Togo was already spreading to the Ife of
Benin.

E THIOPIA HAS A special place in the Christian history of
sub-Saharan Africa. It is home to sub-Saharan Africa's only
indigenous Christian community with a history stretching back
to pre-Islamic times. If local traditions are true, Ethiopia's Orthodox Church began with a eunuch who was baptized by Philip on
the road to Gaza.[48]

Today more than 40 million Ethiopians profess allegiance to
the Ethiopian Orthodox Church. Christianity in Ethiopia has
been shaped by centuries of isolation from the outside world.
Religious festivals, icons, and traditions punctuate every aspect
of Ethiopian life. Over the course of centuries, religion has taken
on an ethnic identity that, for many, supercedes any sense of a
personal relationship with God through Jesus Christ.

Over the past few decades, evangelical missionaries have
entered the country. The bulk of their ministry has been among
the animistic Oromo tribes of southern Ethiopia. At the same
time, missionaries have encouraged their Ethiopian Orthodox

---

[48] Acts 8:26-39

brothers to let God's word reshape their understanding of Christ's ideal for a disciple and for a church.

In the early 1990s, an association of born-again Ethiopians began to take shape within the Orthodox Church. The movement was known as *Emmanuel Muhaber* (Emmanuel Fellowship). It centered around prayer, study and proclamation of the New Testament, and an emphasis on personal communion with God. The movement swelled in rapid fashion growing to several thousand adherents by the mid-1990s.

In 1990, the International Mission Board assigned David and Pam Emmert as missionaries to Ethiopia. In 1993, David became Strategy Coordinator for the city of Addis Ababa. With an eye toward what God was doing to reach the Amharic peoples, David soon noticed the vitality of the Emmanuel Muhaber.

By May of 1997, David had developed and implemented a comprehensive strategy to reach all quarters of Addis with a Church Planting Movement. Unlike many conservative evangelicals, David resisted the temptation to see the Orthodox Church as either the enemy or as competitors in the quest for Ethiopian faith. But he also refused to presume that Orthodox Church members had a personal relationship with Christ.

"The enemy," Emmert said, "is lostness. Our strategy is to work inside, outside, and alongside the church for purposes of sharing the gospel, planting churches, and seeing a Church Planting Movement."

Emmert's research of Addis revealed a huge unreached corridor in the heart of the old city. In a city flush with ancient basilicas, this inner city corridor was virtually devoid of Christian places of worship. Deeming this area *the red zone*, Emmert began devising and implementing a strategy to take the gospel into that zone.

About the time that David and Pam began their work, the growth and evangelical character of *Emmanuel Muhaber* reached a critical point within the Orthodox Church. By 1995, their numbers had risen to an estimated 70,000 born-again believers. Fearing their evangelical influence, the Orthodox Church hierarchy expelled Emmanuel Muhaber from their communion.

David engaged the leadership of the Muhaber with an offer of help and a request for help. The group wasn't difficult to find; they met every night for evangelistic prayer meetings in open-air tents in the city. David offered to provide them with theological training based on God's word in Theological Education by Extension (TEE) centers scattered around the city. In exchange, he asked them to help him reach the city's red zone for Jesus Christ.

Soon the TEE centers were filled with young Ethiopians passionately devouring the teachings on evangelism, biblical interpretation, personal discipleship, and cell-church planting. "Our emphasis is on practical training," David explained, "We try to give the guys very specific tools. The basic motto of our school is: 'No one cares what you know; they care what you do.'"[49]

In the first eight months of the program, twenty-eight Ethiopian evangelists led 681 persons to Christ and started 83 new house churches in the red zone.[50] During a 1997 visit, the author was able to see both the training centers and many of the house churches that had been planted in the red-zone. The ones we saw ranged in size from eight to 80 members. Their worship centered on prayer, singing of indigenous praise songs to God, and the teaching of God's word.

The Ethiopian believers lifted their hands and sang songs of praise in haunting melodies far removed from any Western influence. Their joy and passion were contagious. Emmert said,

---

[49] Tobin Perry, "Reaching a city, reaching the world," in *The Commission* (September 1999), p. 11.

[50] Ibid.

"Every week it seems that they are singing new songs they've written. Most of them are praises or prayers to God. It's hard for us to even keep up."

A SURVEY OF WHAT God is doing across Africa makes it clear that the people groups of that continent are very dear to his heart. You can see this in the Church Planting Movements that are just beginning to bloom in every corner of the continent. Yet for every Church Planting Movement we see, there are a dozen aborted movements and near misses that never made the transition from church planting to Church Planting Movements. Why is this?

A classic tale from Homer's *Odyssey* illustrates the challenge facing the African Church as it navigates Church Planting Movements. In Homer's epic, Odysseus and his crew had to sail through a dangerously narrow channel. There was no way to avoid it, and the shore was littered with shipwrecks. On one shore was the rocky precipice called Scylla and on the other the equally menacing whirlpool called Charybdis. Between them was a deep and safe channel, but Odysseus had to avoid the two perils.

As evidenced by the many shipwrecked Church Planting Movements in its history, Africa faces a similar challenge. On the one bank are the shipwrecks that have occurred as missionaries have overly protected the African Church. In Nigeria, for example, the 19th century Baptist missionaries waited 39 years before allowing a Nigerian to pastor the church they had started.[51] Missionaries are less paternalistic today, but some continue to feel that their role of safeguarding orthodoxy is indispensable and cannot be entrusted to an African.

---

[51] Travis Collins, *The Baptist Mission of Nigeria, 1850-1993* (Ibadan, Nigeria: Associated Book-Makers Nigeria Limited, 1993), pp. 12 & 25.

If paternalism is the Scylla, then Charybdis is the whirlpool of foreign dependency. How many Church Planting Movements have been lost to African dependency on outside funds, buildings, subsidies, and well-intentioned charity?[52]

Between the Scylla of paternalism and the Charybdis of dependency are the deep waters of indigenous African Church Planting Movements. Wherever African believers have found this deep channel, God has produced smooth sailing and a steady growth in reproducing churches.

---

[52] Glenn Schwartz has formed an organization called World Mission Associates aimed at exposing and combating dependency in missions. His website can be viewed at www.wmausa.org.

7

The Muslim World

More Muslims have come to Christ in the past two decades than at any other time in history.

In North Africa, more than 16,000 Berbers turn to Christ over a two-decade period.

A Central Asian Church Planting Movement sees 13,000 Kazakhs come to faith in Christ over a decade and a half.

Up to 12,000 Kashmiri Muslims turn from jihad to the Prince of Peace.

In an Asian Muslim country, more than 150,000 Muslims embrace Jesus and gather in more than 3,000 locally led Isa Jamaats (Jesus Groups).

I SLAM HAS CHALLENGED Christianity for more than 13 centuries. Its system of social laws, called *shariah*, have suffocated and virtually eliminated Christianity in much of the region that gave it birth.

Today, however, God is changing the Muslim world as never before. To understand how that change is occurring, it is important to have at least a small glimpse into how Islamic shariah has been so successful in its contest with Christianity Despite popular anecdotes of Arab conquerors sweeping through nations and forcing Christian conversion at sword point, the Muslim method of domination and control has been much more patient, insidious, and effective. Islamic shariah constitutes the only major religious system in the world designed to defeat Christianity. Let's briefly examine how it has worked.

As a beginning point, shariah prohibits Muslims from converting to Christianity or any other religion. Conversion from Islam is punishable by death. Likewise under shariah, Christians are prohibited from trying to convert Muslims to their faith. Not only are missionaries forbidden, but even local Christians are restricted to practicing their faith—including evangelism—only within the confines of their own church buildings. And while Christians are not allowed to speak ill of the Prophet or the Muslim religion under penalty of death, weekly sermons in the mosque openly ridicule and attack the most basic elements of the Christian faith.

Under Islamic law, a Muslim man is allowed to marry a Christian woman, and his bride can retain her Christian faith, but their children will be Muslim. Should a divorce occur, the children go to the custody of the Muslim father. Christian men are also welcomed to marry Muslim women, but only after they have converted to Islam. Should they later try to revert to their Christian faith, they will find it a capital offense.

In addition to closing the backdoor that would allow Muslims to leave their religion, shariah also created ingenious ways of incorporating and assimilating new converts into their faith.

One popular incentive was Islam's liberal divorce laws. Orthodox and Catholic Christianity prohibited divorce. Islam not only made it easy for a disgruntled husband to gain a quick divorce, it also allowed him up to four wives at a time.[53]

Non-Muslims also faced economic incentives to conversion. Shariah prohibited Christians from serving in the military, while requiring them to pay what was called a *dimmi tax* levied against

---

[53] By taking advantage of both the polygamy and liberal divorce laws in Islam, a man could have scores of wives in a lifetime.

non-Muslims, supposedly to pay for their 'protection' by the army. By converting to Islam, an oppressed Christian overcame two penalties. He gained access to a military career (forbidden to non-Muslims) while freeing himself from the hated dimmi tax. With so many incentives and ways to enter the Muslims religion, Islam grew rapidly. All roads led into the Muslim religion, but it offered no exit ramps, for Muslims the only way out of the religion was through death.

Not all of the reasons for Christianity's weak response to Islam could be blamed on shariah. In many cases the nature of the Christian societies that met Islam were their own worst enemy, offering many opportunities for Islamic advance.

Despite its humble beginnings, by the time of the prophet Mohammed, Christianity had grown wealthy and was expressing itself in ornate cathedrals festooned with icons of Christ and the saints. Prophetic voices within Christendom that denounced these *graven images* were branded heretics and imprisoned or exiled.[54]

Politics also undermined the health of the church. Byzantine rulers viewed local expressions of Christianity as a threat to their hold on Church and State. Consequently, local leadership or colloquial translations of the Bible were discouraged, keeping the word of God accessible only to those who could decipher Greek or Latin.

By the dawn of the Muslim era, many Catholic Church leaders were chosen primarily for their allegiance to Rome or Constantinople, rather than for their personal piety. This became evident when conquering Arab armies swept across North Africa prompting hundreds of European priests and bishops to flee their parishes and return to mother Europe.

---

[54] The *iconoclasm* (image shattering) *controversy* raged for centuries inside Christendom before it became a defining feature of Islam. see E. J. Martin, *A History of the Iconoclastic Controversy* (1930, repr. 1978); J. Pelikan, Imago Dei (1990).

Likewise when a small invading army of Arab Muslims assaulted the Byzantine stronghold of Alexandria, Egypt, it was an Egyptian Christian who secretly opened the gates for them. For him, it was an opportunity to rescue his persecuted church from Byzantine control. In response, one of the first acts of the new Muslim rulers was to release the Egyptian Coptic leadership from prison where the Byzantine hierarchy was holding them.

Christianity's failure to address the slavery problem also opened the door to Islamic advance. When small Arab armies swept across the Middle East and North Africa, they found millions of slaves owned by Roman and Byzantine Christians. Shariah simply prohibited the ownership of Muslim slaves by Christian masters. To gain his freedom, all a slave had to do was convert to Islam. This led to the conversion of countless slaves while garnering grassroots support for the new religion.[55]

TODAY, MANY OF the issues that once characterized the Muslim-Christian encounter are no longer at play. Barriers of slavery, church-state relations, and even marital incentives no longer exist. The free flow of information through satellite television and Internet undermine shariah's ability to suppress Muslim access to the gospel and the truth about their own declining civilization. After centuries of relative isolation, the growing interdependence between nations is once again thrusting Christians and Muslims into unavoidable contact.

In this forced encounter, many nominal and secular Christians are finding answers for life's uncertainties in the unchanging pages of Islam's holy book, the Qur'an. At the same time, though, it is clear that more Muslims have come to faith in Christ over the past two decades than at any other time in the history of the two great religions.

---

[55] Bernard Lewis, *Race and Slavery in the Middle East, an historical enquiry* (London: Oxford University Press, 1990), 184 pp.

Today, many of Christianity's internal obstacles to Muslim evangelization have been removed, but shariah remains a formidable challenge with Muslim converts facing persecution and even death. For this reason, we will sometimes have to veil the location and names of individuals involved in the growing communities of Muslim background believers.

The first glimpses of Church Planting Movements among Muslims are occurring in places where the smothering fabric of shariah has been frayed by war and rapid social change.

I N A NORTH African country that spent much of the 20th century embroiled in civil war, more than 16,000 Muslim Berbers have recently embraced Christianity. If asked why, they might well reply, "Because we can."

Between the extremes of a secular government and Islamic fundamentalism, these Berbers have chosen a third way, the gospel of peace. Working in partnership with a missionary Strategy Coordinator, local Berber leadership stimulated an emerging Church Planting Movement.

The North African movement rode the wave of rising Berber ethnic self-identity. Three vehicles carried the gospel most effectively: a Berber language version of the New Testament, Berber language gospel radio broadcasts, and a Berber language *Jesus Film* that some estimate up to four million Berbers have seen. In all three media, Berbers have been evangelized in their native tongue without dependence upon foreign missionaries.

F ROM THE MOUNTAINS of North Africa we turn to the war-ravaged Himalayan state of Kashmir. The only predominantly Muslim state in India, Kashmir's 9 million citizens have known little else but war since Pakistan and India gained their independence from Britain in 1947.

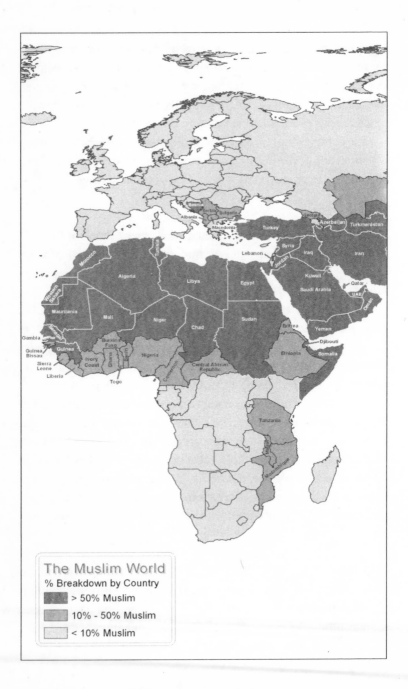

The Muslim World
% Breakdown by Country
> 50% Muslim
10% - 50% Muslim
< 10% Muslim

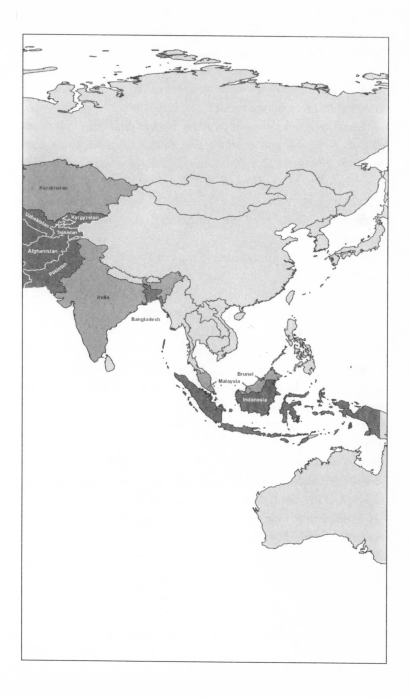

Since 1989, more than 35,000 Kashmiris have lost their lives to the conflict. In recent years, growing numbers of Kashmiri Muslims are turning from *jihad* to Jesus. Newspaper reports across India in 2003 spoke with alarm of the "cross in Kashmir" and "thousands who are turning to Christianity."[56]

Local evangelists from Muslim backgrounds now share the gospel of Christ and report rising numbers of baptisms from Muslim quarters. The price they have paid has been high. Yonathan Paljor, pastor of All Saints Church in Sri Nagar reports, "You will find thousands of people interested in Christianity, (but) they are threatened for life and socially boycotted."

Twice Muslim militants have burned Paljor's church building and pastoral house. While Paljor escaped with his life, a Gospel For Asia (GFA) worker named Neeraj was not so fortunate. In the summer of 2002, Neeraj was murdered.

A young woman named Masooda, 22, calls herself a "believer of Christ," although she is not yet baptized. "It's not a matter of religion," she says. "It's about finding God. I have found mine." Her face radiates with excitement as she describes how she saw two visions of Christ. In one, he sat on a huge rock. In the other, he was being nailed to the cross, with a pool of blood below him. Although Masooda told her mother and close friends about her new faith, she fears what Muslim radicals would do if she made a public declaration. "They would burn our house, and my family would be in danger."[57]

With so much opposition, why are people converting? Premi Gergan, a retired principal of a Catholic girl's school explains,

---

[56] Tariq Mir, "It's Conversion Time in the Valley," in *The Indian Express*, Srinagar, India, April 5, 2003, front page. also *The New Indian Express*, Bangalore Edition, April 8, 2003, p. 7.

[57] Manpreet Singh, "Harassed Kashmiri Christians Reach out to Discrete Muslims," in *Christianity Today*, September 9, 2002, Vol. 46, No. 10, Page 26.

"Militancy shook the inner being of many. And people, particularly the young, started inquiring. Every day one to two people come to me to know about [the] gospel. They say, 'In our religion, there is no forgiveness.'"

Paljor says, "Christians are not pressing for conversions. They are pressing for new conceptions, opening their mind by telling them stories from the Bible—the stories of love, harmony, and tolerance."

It remains difficult to assess all that is happening in this remote mountain valley, but it is beginning to sound a lot like other Muslim turnings around the world. Estimates of the number of converts range as high as 12,000.

In one of the more dramatic political changes of the 20th century, the collapse of the Soviet Union has provided another setting where Muslims are turning to Christ in significant numbers.

T HE FALL OF the Berlin wall in 1989 coincided with the first evangelical penetrations into Soviet Central Asia. At the time, there were no more than a handful of Turkic Christians among the millions living in the various Central Asian Republics. This scarcity of Turkic Christians was due largely to centuries of conflict between Central Asian Muslims and the Slavic Christians and atheists of Russia.

During the years 1928 - 1953, Stalin relocated thousands of ethnic German Protestants living in the Soviet Union to the Central Asian Republics of Kazakhstan, Uzbekistan, and Kyrgyzstan. These ethnic Germans, many of them passionate Baptists and Pentecostals, quickly established vibrant churches in the region. But after a half-century of coexistence, they had made little impact on the Turkic Muslims who lived around them.

Today, many of the ethnic German evangelicals have left the Central Asian republics for greener pastures in western Europe. Taking their place are scores of indigenous Turkic churches comprised of Kazakhs, Kyrgyz, and Uzbeks from Islamic backgrounds.

In one of the more open republics, Kazakhstan, more than 13,000 Kazakhs have come to faith in Christ over the past decade and a half. Today there are more than 300 indigenous Kazakh churches, led by Kazakh pastors shepherding these new believers.[58] Veteran Christian workers in the area speculate that there may be as many as 50,000 believers scattered across the republic.

The beginnings of evangelical outreach that eventually led to this movement can be traced back to the closing days of the Cold War. In 1989, missionaries approached Soviet Central Asia from two directions. Some came to the region through well-established Eastern European churches, such as the All-Union Evangelical Baptists (AUEB), a Baptist convention comprised mostly of Russian, Ukrainian, and ethnic Germans living in the Soviet Union. The AUEB had churches in all of the Central Asian republics, but had little rapport with the Turkic Muslim majority populations.

Other evangelicals took a people group approach. From their research into the history and culture of the Kazakh people, they came to understand the ancient hostilities between Turkic Muslims and Slavic Christians. This insight prompted them to establish direct relations with the Central Asian people groups rather than working through the neighboring Slavic churches. Leading this approach was a young Strategy Coordinator named Brian who went directly to the Kazakh Ministry of Education in 1989 offering to establish a Kazakh American joint venture.

---

[58] The 2000 Annual Statistical Report of the International Mission Board.

Brian's visit to the Ministry of Education laid the groundwork for a great movement.

The Kazakh Minister of Education warmly welcomed Brian, telling him, "Last year I was visited by representatives from two different Ivy League schools in the United States. They wanted to open an educational exchange with the universities of Kazakhstan. I told them 'No.' But to you I say 'Yes.'" When Brian asked why his offer was acceptable over that of the academically superior Ivy League schools, the Minister responded, "These Ivy League schools wanted to establish their headquarters in Moscow and open a branch in Alma-Aty (the Kazakh capital). You, on the other hand, have bypassed Moscow and come to work directly with us."

Brian's people group emphasis fit well with the Kazakhs' rising sense of national pride. Brian followed this first effort with more education and business-related proposals. Each of these ventures allowed scores of Christian workers to come into Kazakhstan, proclaim the gospel, translate the Bible and produce the *Jesus Film*.

The people group strategy also impacted the first church plants. Rather than try to assimilate the new Kazakh believers into existing European churches, the earliest church planters deliberately aimed at stimulating a Kazakh movement. The results have been impressive. Kazakhs today feel that they own the movement. Consequently, momentum is shifting from foreign workers to national leaders.

This people group focus has also yielded strong harvests in the other Turkic Republics of Central Asia. It is too early to tell if all of these harvest fields will produce Church Planting Movements, but there are encouraging signs. More Muslims have come to Christ in Central Asia over the past ten years than at any other time in history.

T HE EVENTS IN North Africa, northern India, and Central Asia were mere glimpses of what was to come. In an Asian Muslim country that we will call *Jedidistan* (jeh-DEED-ih-stan) the largest Church Planting Movement in the history of Christian missions to Muslims is presently unfolding.[59]

Jedidistan, like so many other predominantly Muslim countries, was also home to a dwindling minority of non-Muslims. A limited number of Christian missionaries were allowed to do relief and development in the impoverished country, but were required to restrict their evangelism to the non-Muslim minorities. The result was that more than 85 percent of the Jedidi people were unaddressed by the gospel.

By the early 1980s, several mission agencies and a handful of the traditional Jedidi churches were beginning to shift their attention to the Muslim majority. Around that same time, a Muslim sensitive version of the Jedidi New Testament was

---

[59] The case study is real, though the names such as Jedidistan, which means *the new place* and refers to the new life that is spreading among the people, is fictitious.

published and missionaries began experimenting with new forms of church that catered to the Muslim worldview.[60]

The Muslim sensitive New Testament was well received and reports filtered out of remote villages where entire mosques had come to worship Jesus as Messiah. However, these rumors of things to come were difficult to substantiate since foreigners were kept at a distance, and the converts in these areas still referred to themselves as Muslims.[61]

I NTO THIS CHURNING environment God reached out and touched a young Muslim teenager with his powerful gift of salvation. Sharif grew up in a crowded farming town in central Jedidistan. As was the custom with all young Muslim boys, five-year old Sharif was sent to the local madrasa to learn Arabic, the Qur'an, and the stories from the life of the Prophet.

Sharif absorbed his studies with a keen mind, perhaps too keen it seems for he soon found himself questioning his teachers.

"Why did Mohammed do this?" he would ask, or "Why does Allah say this or that?"

While curiosity may be prized in some educational systems it had no place in the madrasas of Jedidistan.

"The first time I asked these questions," Sharif recalls, "the teacher whacked me with a stick. 'You should not ask such questions,' he said, 'you are not to question these things.'"

But Sharif could not help himself. Soon he was questioning again. Repeated beatings did not stifle his curiosity. Before long,

---

[60] One of the more significant books to surface during this time was by Phil Parshall, *New Paths in Muslim Evangelism: evangelical approaches to contextualization* (Grand Rapids: Baker Books, 1981), 200 pp.

[61] This may seem stranger to an outsider than to an insider, since the name "Muslim" literally means 'one who submits to God,' a designation most Christians would accept.

he was branded *a sinner boy* who was going to hell for his insolence.

By the time Sharif had completed four years of schooling, the teacher decided it was enough. Sharif was expelled from the school, but the punishment didn't stop there. The teacher took Sharif to his father and said, "Your boy is very bad. He is a sinner boy and is going to hell. It is a disgrace for your family to keep him even in your home."

The curse of the religious teacher fell heavily on young Sharif. Sharif's father felt he had no choice but to expel the boy from his family. Sharif's mother interceded on his behalf and Sharif was allowed to live in a small hut perched on the back of the family property. Three times a day, Sharif's mother brought food and water to him, but no other family members would speak to him. This isolation continued for the remainder of Sharif's childhood, until one day when everything changed.

One hot summer day in 1983, a missionary named Tom was traveling home by rickshaw. Like most missionaries in the country, Tom had spent his years ministering and planting churches among the non-Muslim minorities of Jedidistan. Recently, though, Tom had been convicted of the need to reach out to Muslims. On this eventful day, he was listening to God when the Lord spoke and directed him to a Jedidi teenager.

The young man looked particularly alone and dejected as he made his way to the bus stop. Perhaps it was the sight of the white man in a rickshaw or maybe it was the rare sound of someone speaking directly to him that startled Sharif. The first words he heard were Tom asking him in fluent Jedidi, "Hey brother, do you want to get up in this rickshaw and ride with me?"

Sharif later recalled, "I was totally amazed because not many people were allowed, or even wanted, to talk with me because I was considered by family and community to be a rebel, thus shunned and seen as a Muslim sinner boy." As they rode together

Tom and Sharif talked and talked. Soon, Tom felt God encouraging him to invite Sharif to his home to meet his wife.

"Tom's wife, Gloria, was so kind to me," Sharif said, "She gave me fresh cookies from the oven and my first cup of coffee. Before I left their house that day, she and Tom also gave me a copy of the New Testament in the Jedidi language."

That night, alone in his room, Sharif read his New Testament. The pages seemed to turn themselves and they held him in rapt attention until the sun began to rise the next morning. It wasn't until the second night, that the Holy Spirit grabbed Sharif's heart.

"I was reading the Gospel of John, chapter three. When I got to verse seventeen it hit me. John says, 'Jesus did not come into the world to condemn the world, but that the world through him might be saved.'"

Years later, as Sharif recounted the story, the tears still stream down his cheeks. "You see, I wasn't condemned, I wasn't just a sinner boy. Jesus had come into the world to save me."

Soon, Sharif was attending church with Tom and Gloria, but all of this changed the day a neighbor saw what the young rebel was doing. That Sunday as he returned from church, his father was waiting for him.

"My father had my brothers beat me. They said I had a demon and that they would beat the demon out of me. They asked me if I was a Christian. I told them, 'I don't know. I just want to know more about Christianity.' My father said, 'If you want to know anything about Christianity, I will tell you. But hear me now. You are never to go back to that church again.'"

Sharif responded, "I will try, father."

The next Sunday, Sharif did try, but found himself drawn to church once again. This time when he returned his father, brothers and cousins attacked and beat him. Naked, bruised, and bleeding, Sharif was tied to a pole in the backyard. He remained there alone throughout the day and into the night, wondering if he would ever be free again.

Just before dawn when Muslims rise to say their first prayers, Sharif's mother came to him. She brought him clothes and a few coins.

"Your father is coming to kill you," she said quietly. "You must run away to the city."

In the years that followed, Sharif went to the capital city, was secretly baptized in a traditional church, and earned a degree in Business Administration at the national university. After college, he began working for one of the mission agencies seeking to win Muslims to Christ without extracting them from their Islamic communities.

Though he learned many things from his experience with the new Muslim mission efforts, Sharif was troubled by two things: 1) the influence garnered by U.S. finances, and 2) the dubious identity of these Muslims who had supposedly turned to Christ and yet were still calling themselves Muslims. After less than a year with the mission agency, Sharif felt compelled to leave and return to his hometown.

No one welcomed Sharif at his homecoming. His mother had died after many years of mistreatment by his father. No one in Sharif's family would acknowledge his presence. Only his childhood friend, Bilal, would receive him.

"You can stay in my home," Bilal said cheerfully, "My bed is large and we can put a rolled-up blanket in between us. One half will be for you and the other for me."

And so Sharif made his home with Bilal.

In the days that followed, Bilal could see the changes that had taken place in Sharif's life. Sharif read his Bible and prayed, not ritualistically as the Muslims did, but personally and fervently. Bilal and Sharif often talked of Christ and the New Testament until one day when events triggered a change.

Bilal had to leave town on business that day, and Sharif thought nothing of it. But some of the goons from the madrasa had been waiting for just such an opportunity. They recruited a local soccer team to ambush Sharif.

"They beat me until I collapsed and then they kicked me until blood was coming out of my mouth," Sharif recalls. "I suppose they would have killed me, but one of the town elders stopped them. 'What are you doing?' he said, 'Don't you know that if soldiers come they will put you in jail?'"

As the soccer team stepped away from Sharif, each one of them spit on him until his body was covered with bruises, blood, and spittle.

Bilal found Sharif in that mangled condition the next morning. Bilal wept as he tended to his friend's wounds.

"Why have they done this?" he asked.

"It is because I am a Christian," Sharif replied.

"Then I will become a Christian too," said Bilal.

Sharif was alarmed, "No, you cannot. Don't you see what they have done to me?"

"Yes, I will," said Bilal, "After all, Jesus suffered even more for both of us."

The baptism of Bilal and his partnership with Sharif mark a beginning point. The year was 1991. The following year, the two men led their first Muslim family to Christ and started the first church of Muslim background believers. Over the next decade, they would see nearly four thousand churches planted and more than 150,000 Muslims come to faith in Christ.

In this whole Jedidi Church Planting Movement, Sharif only baptized two persons. The first was Bilal. The second was his own father, but that is another story. Today, all of Sharif's family has accepted Jesus Christ and a church meets in the same home that had once expelled the young boy.

The Jedidi Church Planting Movement has been costly. Twice Sharif was beaten so severely that his tormentors thought him dead. Once he was nailed to a makeshift cross. On two separate occasions parcel couriers delivered death shrouds to his home as a warning of what was to come. The greatest blow to Sharif came in January 2003 when his dear friend, Bilal, was dragged from his home at night and beaten to death.

T HE WORK OF Sharif and Bilal moved at a slow and steady rate for the first three or four years. They received a major boost in 1997, when a Western agency appointed its first missionary Strategy Coordinator to engage the sprawling Jedidi Muslim population. It didn't take the missionary long to find Sharif and develop a deep friendship built around a shared commitment to the Jedidi people.

The Strategy Coordinator gave Sharif encouragement and safety when local police were pursuing him. He provided Sharif with the kind of research that prompted him to spread the movement beyond the confines of southern Jedidistan and into every state in the country. Finally, in 2001, the Western Strategy Coordinator arranged for Sharif to receive training as a Strategy Coordinator himself.

For his part, Sharif taught the Strategy Coordinator how to use the Qur'an as a bridge to open conversations with Muslims about Jesus and the New Testament. The Western missionary also found courage in Sharif's sufferings.

"Sharif taught me to be bold," he said, "How could I be afraid to walk into a mosque or witness to an Imam? The worst thing that could happen would be expulsion from the country. I was paying a far lower price than my brother Sharif."

By the year 2000, there were still many questions surrounding the rise and growth of the Jedidi Church Planting Movement. How extensive was the movement? Could it really be as vital as the rumors indicated?

I N MAY 2002, a research team from the International Mission Board descended on Jedidistan and conducted an investigation. The research team used the best research methods they could muster with random samplings and widespread input. What they found was unprecedented.

The researchers wanted to understand the extent and nature of the Church Planting Movement, but they also wanted to study the effectiveness of the Western Strategy Coordinator and his team.

Of the 21 districts where the Western Strategy Coordinator had work, there were an estimated 1,951 baptisms in 2001. This brought the total number of believers in this missionary sector of the work to 4,140 since its inception in 1998. And the work was clearly gaining momentum. In the first five months of 2002 there were an additional 2,277 baptisms.

Sharif's work was older and consequently much larger. Estimates for the year 2001 indicated 89,315 believers scattered across each of the 64 districts in Jedidistan. In 2001, there were an estimated 23,323 baptism, more than 2,000 per month.

For the year 2001, the combined number of Muslim background believers in the two works was well over 93,000. And with baptism figures of 23,323 for 2001 in one work and a 280 percent increase in the other work, the movement was clearly accelerating at remarkable rate!

The 2001 study identified 3,973 churches in the movement associated with Sharif and another 165 churches in the sister work. Given the rapid multiplication of new churches, it is probably not surprising that there were only 2,293 local pastors for the 3,973 churches. Likewise in the sister work there were only 149 local pastors for the 165 churches. This means new church starts are outstripping leadership development, a problem that will have to be addressed if the movement is to continue.

The churches in the Jedidi Church Planting Movement naturally carry with them the DNA of the first churches founded by Sharif and Bilal. Sharif brought with him an influence from both the traditional Christian churches he had attended and his own Islamic upbringing.

The resulting church was a blending of both worlds. Church meets on Friday mornings, a holiday in Jedidistan. The believers call their churches, *Isa Jamaats*, or literally, *Jesus Groups* and their pastors, *Imams*, the same term given to the one who 'stands in front' to lead prayers in a mosque.[62] New believers refer to themselves as *Isahi*, literally "belonging to Jesus." The typical church in Jedidistan will have about 30 members or three families, which is about as much as one house can contain.

Church members typically sit on the floor in a circle, but unlike many Muslim settings the women are included, albeit sitting opposite from the men. As with traditional churches, the worship service begins with prayer, loud boisterous prayer with all members praying aloud until the leader finally pronounces '*Amen*' at the end. Then, they pass a tithe box, collecting tithes and offerings which are used for ministry to the poor and to support new church planting. Like a traditional church, they sing songs, but these are songs they have written themselves with words that reflect their own prayers, praises, and favorite Scriptures.

A distinctly indigenous component in many of the Isa Jamaats was the recitation of a poem that someone had written. These poems are typically meditations on some Bible story, Bible character or the implications of some Bible teaching on the life of the individual.

"I remember one time hearing a poem about Joseph, the husband of Mary" recalls the Strategy Coordinator. "I had never thought about it, but this brother wrote an entire poem around the perspective of Joseph and what he must have felt to know that his betrothed was expecting a child and it wasn't his."

---

[62] *Imam* literally means 'in front' and refers to the position of the leader of the prayers.

Finally, someone shares a message from the Bible. In the Jedidi Jamaats this person may change every week; the *Imams*, as with the traditional church pastors in Jedidistan, love to share their pulpit.

When asked the question: "Have some Christians returned to Islam?" The apostasy rate was found to be far lower than what Christian workers in other Muslim ministry fields have experienced.

Yes	No	Do Not Know
8%	89%	3%

The researchers asked if these new *Isahi* were from fringe or active Muslim backgrounds.

Fringe	Active
33.6%	66.4%

In an effort to discover how far the new Isahi had come from their old Islamic practices, the research team simply asked those surveyed if the Isahi members of these new *Isa Jamaats* were still practicing old Islamic beliefs mingled with their new Christian ones.

Yes, Mixed	No, Not Mixed
22 %	77 %

Of course any mixture of non-Christian beliefs with new Christian beliefs is cause for concern, but the researchers pointed out that this level of self-awareness of mixed beliefs in a new movement was quite healthy, and pointed to an internal commitment to eliminate non-Christian beliefs and practices.

The researchers wanted to know where these *Isa Jamaats* were meeting. They found that 87% of the Jamaats met in homes, followed by 4% that met under a tree, and 3% in a school. Another 3% met in a mission-owned building, followed by 2% that met in a dedicated church building.

Meeting predominantly in homes helped insulate the movement from external persecution while forcing the believers to address the salvation needs of their own family members.

In a related question, the research team asked whether these Isahi perceived their church meetings to be secret, open, or somewhere in between. Here's what they found.

Secret	Open	Both-Mixed
22.3%	79.9%	4.7%

Despite the threat of persecution associated with leaving Islam and following Jesus, the great majority of these Jedidi Isahi saw themselves as openly professing and practicing their faith in Christ.

This boldness was evident in October 2001. There was a buzz in editorials of major newspapers across the country regarding an Imam in the south of the country who had apparently left his Muslim roots. The story went like this:

The local Imam had drawn a crowd of several thousand to air his grievances. At the end of his message, the Imam lifted a copy of the Qur'an over his head and shouted to the crowd, "This book has done nothing for us!"

With those words, he threw the Qur'an into the canal. Even more startling, scores of other disenchanted Muslims emerged from the crowd to throw their own Qur'ans into the canal.

HOW ARE THESE Muslim men and women coming to faith in Christ? Many factors are at play: Having a contextualized (i.e. Muslim-friendly) version of the New Testament; meeting in homes rather than buildings; adopting Muslim-friendly names for the church, pastors and new believers; using the Qur'an as a bridge to invite Muslims into discussions about Jesus and the New Testament. But the ultimate factor has been the bold witness of those converts like Sharif and Bilal who remained faithful in the face of death.

The first Isahi in Jedidistan to lay down his life for the gospel was a young man named Mejanur who went to be with the Lord in August 1997 about the same time the movement was beginning to unfold.

After learning that Mejanur and his family had converted from Islam, a mob of young Muslim militants turned up at his house. Over the protests of his young wife and father, the mob seized 22-year old Mejanur and dragged him into the local madrasa where he was pressured to renounce his faith in Jesus.. Mejanur refused.

The angry men took Mejanur's hand and cut off his fingers, one by one, but in his heart he clung to Jesus. Finally, the angry interrogators cut off Mejanur's hand at the wrist. Swooning from the pain, Mejanur was barely conscious as the frustrated men tied his arms behind his back and left him seated on the ground beneath a tree. In the cool night air the bleeding was slow, but sometime alone in the dark, Mejanur died.

Perhaps they didn't mean to kill him. Perhaps they only wanted to force him to renounce Jesus and return to Islam. Whatever their intentions, Mejanur was faithful to Christ even unto death.

But the story doesn't end there. Mejanur was an only son and the new husband of a young bride. Benevolent Christians who learned of Mejanur's story took pity on his family and gathered money to buy a small plot of land with some chickens to provide income for his widow and father. In the years that followed, life was hard with no Mejanur around to tend the farm. Then one day, two young men appeared at the home of Mejanur's father.

"We have come to ask your forgiveness," they said. "We were the ones who killed Mejanur. And now we give ourselves to you. We will be like sons and work for you. For you see, we too, have become followers of Isa."

T HE RESEARCHERS CONCLUDED their study of the Jedidi Church Planting Movement with the affirmation that this was indeed a bona fide Church Planting Movement and that it was still gaining momentum.

They also speculated that neither Sharif nor Bilal would survive the continued growth of the movement. At the same time, they predicted that martyring the leaders would not spell the end of the movement, it was simply too strong.

The same month their report was issued Bilal was murdered, and the number of Muslim background believers climbed to 150,000. Sharif has already surrendered his fate to the Lord's hands. Like Mejanur and Bilal before him, he knows that his blood may someday be required, as seed.

8

Latin America

Every Saturday night, 18,000 youth line up to enter a stadium for worship in Bogotá, Colombia. Each week another 500 youth commit their lives to Christ and the core values of prayer, fasting, and holiness. During the week they gather in 8,000 youth cell groups.

Among the Kekchi people in remote Guatemala, evangelical Christianity grows from 20,000 believers to more than 60,000 in three decades.

During the decade of the 1990s, Christians in a Latin American country overcame relentless government perse- cution to grow from 235 churches to more than 4,000 churches with a further 40,000 converts awaiting baptism.

L ATIN AMERICA PLAYS host to more Protestant mission- aries than any other region of the world. Brazil has nearly 4,000 Protestant foreign missionaries. Mexico has more than 2,000, while Ecuador and Peru each have more than 1,000.[63]

Despite these 15,000 Protestant cross cultural missionaries serving in Latin America, the region has a relatively small number of Church Planting Movements. Why is this? The answers to this question hold great lessons for understanding how God is at work and wants to use us in these movements.

---

[63] See Patrick Johnston, *Operation World* (Grand Rapids: Zondervan, 1993), p. 648.

A staple of Protestant missions in Latin America is the flow of tens of thousands of short-term North American mission volunteers. Each year countless North American evangelicals, brimming with goodwill, take advantage of the region's proximity to the United States to journey south of the border to share the love of Christ with their Latin neighbors.

Over the years these volunteers brought the gospel light to millions, and left behind immeasurable good will and acts of kindness, but their benevolence also had unintended consequences.

Surveys of several Latin American countries reveal that up to 90 percent of the church buildings were constructed by volunteers from the U.S., and this left many local believers with the sense that North American help is essential to starting a new church. Church Planting Movement practitioners often comment that when local Christians are encouraged to plant new churches, they respond, "How can we start churches without American help?"

For many Latin American Protestants, like their North American counterparts, church is synonymous with church buildings. Many of their church buildings, though modest by North American standards, are beyond the financial reach of the local Christians, reinforcing the opinion of volunteer and Latino alike that financial aid from America is indispensable.

So are there any Church Planting Movements in Latin America? The answer is *yes*, but each of the Church Planting Movements in Latin America has occurred in a place where the conventional norms of churches have been disrupted by drug wars, extreme isolation, or a military regime. Each of these *abnormal* disruptions in society have enabled new paradigms of church and church leadership to emerge—paradigms that are more conducive to Church Planting Movements.

Let's look at three examples of Latin American Church Planting Movements. The first comes from one of the most

violent countries on earth. The second is within the malaria-
infested jungles of Guatemala. The third exploded inside one of
Latin America's most restricted countries where dependence
upon God is the only option available.

F EW PEOPLE ON earth are more affected by pandemic
violence than the citizens of Colombia. Police report
roughly 70 persons die each day in killings that claim more than
25,000 lives each year. In addition to the killings, every day
another eight people are kidnapped, making Colombia one of the
world's most dangerous places to live.

The violence and resulting social upheaval have fractured all
of Colombia's traditional structures, including the religious
establishment. Citizens in much of the country live in daily fear
of kidnapping, murder, or conscription into one of the
paramilitary armies vying for control of the country. Perceived as
wealthy Americans, missionaries and volunteers have been
particularly vulnerable to this threat.

In the midst of this turmoil God is doing some remarkable
things. In the year 2001, Baptist press correspondent, Sue
Sprenkle, visited Colombia to see what God was doing. She
moved among the more than 2.2 million displaced Colombians
who fled the rebel insurgency in the countryside to find some
measure of safety in the city.

Sprenkle reported local efforts to build a church building met
with frustration. "As the new church building's walls reached
three-feet high, forces stormed the property and destroyed the
work. Members were told they could no longer meet. The threat
didn't stop the group. They still meet—but now they meet on
front porches of homes in groups of 10 to 12 people."[64]

---

[64] Unpublished story by Sue Sprenkle sent to the author by Bill Bangham in an
email titled "Colombia Story," March 14, 2001.

LATIN AMERICA

In this intimidating environment, God is opening the way to more flexible house-based worshiping communities. Evangelicals are now seeing unprecedented responsiveness to the gospel message with one town reporting more than 540 decisions for Christ in less than a month.

With declining numbers of missionaries and volunteers, local believers had to take stronger leadership roles. One example of this leadership can be seen in the capital city of Bogotá where Cesar Castellanos has founded the International Charismatic Mission.[65] Though not a Church Planting Movement (because it is one church rather than many), the International Charismatic Mission has many of the characteristics of a Church Planting Movement within a single church structure.

Using a creative cell-church model built around groups of twelve, "the church has grown from 70 small cell groups in 1983 to more than 20,000 cell groups in just eight years."[66]

The Groups of Twelve approach turned a hostile environment into a fertile field for sowing and reaping new believers. Pastor César—as he is known—began his ministry modeling what he had read about David Yonggi Cho's Full Gospel Church in Seoul, Korea. He later modified it to allow for even more rapid growth, multiplication, and assimilation of new members.

The results have been impressive. The church began in 1983 and by 1990 had already grown to 8,000 members. Then Castellanos shifted to his accelerated Groups of Twelve structure. From 1990 to 1999 the movement exploded from

---

[65] Castellanos explains the name of the group: "the International *Charismatic* Mission as an evangelistic strategy to reach Catholics. In the 1980s, the Colombian Catholic majority (97%) rejected the name 'evangelical' but was more open to the term 'Charismatic.'" Reported in Joel Comiskey, *Groups of 12* (Houston: Touch Publications, 1999), p. 21.

[66] Ibid., p. 13.

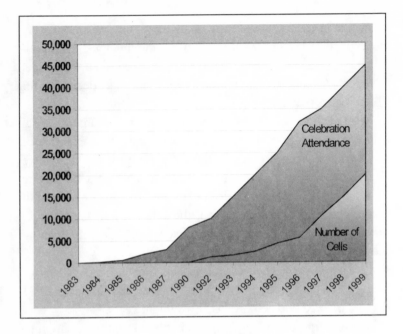

8,000 to more than 45,000 members meeting at an indoor stadium while others gathered in 10 satellite worship centers.

However, the International Charismatic Mission is more than a structural revolution. In fact, its leadership resists being identified with methods. Church leaders have infused its members with a passionate sense of God's presence and guidance. The church is characterized by indigenous Colombian leadership at every level, rapidly reproducing cell groups, and core values of prayer, fasting, and holiness.[67]

Persecution followed Pastor César's movement as virtually all of the church's membership has been impacted by the violence of Colombia. No one has felt the violence more personally than Pastor César himself. In May 1997, a motorcyclist pulled alongside the pastor's car and opened fire on him and his family. The children were unhurt, but César's wife,

---

[67] Ibid., pp. 32-33.

Claudia, was shot once and Pastor César was hit five times. Miraculously, God spared both their lives.

As for the future of the movement in Bogotá, you don't have to look much farther than the long lines of 18,000 youth who wait to enter the stadium for worship every Saturday night. Each week another 500 youth commit their lives to Christ and the core values of prayer, fasting, and holiness. During the week they gather in 8,000 youth cell groups.[68]

Over the past couple of decades, a number of other churches in Latin America have learned that they too, can redefine their concept of church and eliminate dependency on northern sources by developing their own cell-based churches. In 1998, Sergio Solórzano's Elim Christian Mission in El Salvador had 116,000 people regularly attending 5,300 cell groups. Each Sunday morning, the church rented 600 city buses to transport members to the weekly celebration services.[69] These mega-cell churches are not the sort of autonomous house church movements we have seen in other parts of the world, but cell churches are clearly related and can trace their growth to many of the same internal dynamics.[70]

I N THE REMOTE interior of Guatemala's northern Verapaz and Peten departments, descendents of the Mayan Indians, called the Kekchi (kek-CHEE) people, found sanctuary from centuries of domination by European settlers. Today there are between 500,000 and one million Kekchi living in the tropical land bordering coastal Belize. In recent years, tens of thousands

---

[68] *Groups of 12,* p. 38.

[69] Comiskey, *Home Cell Group Explosion*, Houston: Touch Publications, 1999, p. 25.

[70] We'll discuss the differences between cell churches and Church Planting Movements in chapter 15 below.

of these Kekchi have turned to evangelical Christianity as something akin to a Church Planting Movement appears to be unfolding among them.

For centuries, the Kekchi embraced a syncretistic mixture of Catholicism and ancient Mayan traditional religion. Their remoteness made it difficult for missionaries to reach them. Less than 50 percent of the Kekchi are literate in Spanish and even fewer in their native Kekchi language. Nonetheless, portions of the Bible were translated into the Kekchi language as early as 1937, with the New Testament being completed in 1984, and the entire Bible published in 1988.[71]

During the decades of the 1960s through the 1980s, Kekchi evangelicals saw their numbers triple from about 20,000 to more than 60,000. After spending many years living and working in Guatemala, missionary researcher Frank Johnson reflected on the Kekchi movement and cited six reasons for its rapid growth.[72]

1) A **people group focus** on the Kekchi, after years of missionary work in the national trade language of Spanish. "For centuries," wrote Johnson, "any Kekchi who came to faith in Christ had to do so in the Spanish, tantamount to embracing the dominant culture of European conquerors of the Mayan people. Baptist, Nazarene and Mennonite awareness of the need to reach beyond Spanish and into the local language grew with the translation of the Kekchi Bible."

2) The production of the **Kekchi Bible** and other Christian literature in the Kekchi language. "For the first time," Johnson explained, "the Kekchi could read the words: 'For

---

[71] Barbara Grimes, *Ethnologue, 14th Edition Vol. 1: Languages of the World* (Dallas: Summer Institute of Linguistics), p. 308.

[72] Johnson's profile of the Kek'chi is found in Snowden's, *Toward a Church Planting Movement*, pp. 31-34.

God so loved the world' in their own language. Nothing
more validates a people than to have their own literature."

3) Development of **indigenous Kekchi leadership**. "Rather
than importing seminary-trained clergy from other parts of
Guatemala," Johnson said, "we raised up Kekchi leaders,"
believing that "when God calls a group of people together to
form a church, from that same group (He) will call out the
leaders necessary to lead the church. A practical implication
of this concept is that the leaders will resemble the
background and preparation of those with whom they work.
For example, if the majority of people are illiterate farmers,
the pastor of the church may also be an illiterate farmer."[73]

4) The relative **physical isolation** of the Kekchi. "Remote
isolation prevented outside paternalism and promoted self-
reliance," Johnson noted. "The relative isolation of the
Kekchi Baptist leadership from the Spanish-speaking
leadership can be illustrated by the observation that the first
Kekchi leaders did not attend an annual national assembly
until 1969, five years after the Kekchi Baptist work had been
started. Kekchi leaders probably did not attend another
national assembly until 1974."[74]

5) **Financial self-support** of the Kekchi work. "The Kekchi
isolation shielded them from the generosity of well-
intentioned volunteers. Unlike most of Guatemala's
evangelical churches, Kekchi churches are built by the
Kekchi, and out of indigenous building materials. Likewise,
Kekchi pastors missed the stream of financial subsidies that

---

[73] Snowden, p. 33.

[74] Ibid.

have turned the heads of many Guatemalan pastors from their congregations and toward the donors living north of the border."

6) The Kekchi's own **evangelistic and missionary initiative.** Johnson writes, "the Kekchi have a great evangelistic spirit. Congregations are taught from the very beginning that they are responsible for starting new churches. The Kekchi believers say that a church without a mission congregation is a dead church."

The Kekchi growth has been exceptional in a country that has already had church structures and relationships established. As Johnson observed, it is the Kekchi's isolation that allowed it to develop its own patterns and directions of growth. However, it is not the only Latin American people group moving toward a Church Planting Movement.

T HE LARGEST CHURCH Planting Movements in Latin America are underway inside a country that has largely closed itself to the flow of outside influences. For security reasons, we will not name the country, but we will describe its significant features as accurately as possible.[75] Since the bulk of the movement has occurred within Baptist circles, we will limit our discussion here to two Baptist movements.

Like so many Latin American countries, this one has a population of mixed European, Hispanic, and African descent. The government has been a one-party socialist state for several decades. The people have limited freedoms, stifling poverty, but relatively high levels of literacy and education.

---

[75] Portions of this profile are taken from the author's 1999 booklet *Church Planting Movements*, pp. 11-16.

Historically the population has been more than 95 percent Roman Catholic, but for the past several decades, the government suppressed all religion. Today, religious freedom is still a distant hope, though conditions are slowly improving.

B APTISTS SENT THEIR first missionaries to the country more than a century ago. For the next 75 years, missionaries planted churches, trained leaders and formed two

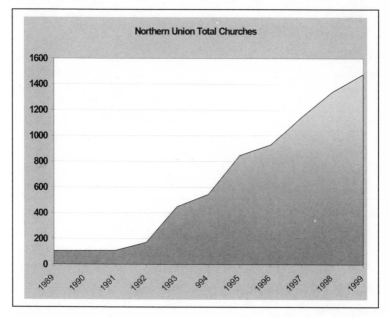

Northern Union Total Churches

Baptist unions with a combined membership of about 3,000. Following a military coup, all missionaries were imprisoned or expelled from the country. In the turbulent years following the coup, half the country's Baptist membership fled abroad.

Over the next few decades, the government tried to eliminate Christianity and its influence in the country. Persecution, imprisonment, and torture were widespread. After the initial plunge in church membership, Baptists in the country slowly began to rise again.

By 1989, the Northern Baptist Union had roughly 5,800 members worshiping in 100 churches. That same year they

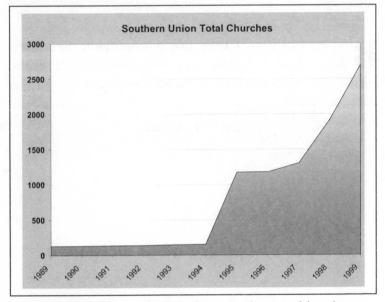

began to experience a spiritual awakening resulting in more prayer, evangelism and church planting. Membership rose five percent in 1989 and then nearly seven percent the following year.

By the end of the 1990s, the Northern Baptist Union's membership had climbed to more than 14,000 baptized members worshiping in 1,475 churches or houses of worship. Of these 1,475 meeting places, only 160 were constituted and registered with the convention as churches, but nearly 1,000 existed as *casas cultos,* or house churches. In addition to these 14,000 baptized church members, there are more than 38,000 regular church participants awaiting baptism.

A similar Church Planting Movement was unfolding in the Southern Baptist Union (SU). In 1989, the SU had 129 churches with a membership of almost 7,000. By the year 2000, they still had only 212 SU-constituted churches, but had more than 2,600 when factoring in the 1,620 house churches and 858 new church starts that were underway. Their membership had risen to nearly 19,000 with annual baptisms of more than 2,600. Another 12,000 non-members were enrolled in Bible teaching classes awaiting baptism. Over the decade, the total number of churches climbed from 129 to more than 2,600—a 1,900 percent increase.

A number of factors conspired to bring about the enormous growth in this Latin American country. Prayer for the people has been building since the military coup nearly forty years ago. Prayer also permeated the lives of the local Latino believers who describe themselves as a "people on their knees."

Persecution, which the government hoped would destroy the church, instead, purified and strengthened it. A Baptist union leader commented, "The prison was like a second seminary for us."

A missionary who recently visited the country reported, "All of the convention leaders have spent time in prison or work camps for their faith."

Foreign missionaries, though banned from living in the country, were instrumental in the development of this Church Planting Movement. First, by laying a firm foundation on God's word and on the concept of the priesthood of every believer, the missionaries ensured the church a means for surviving the coming storm of persecution. Then, during the years of government imposed isolation, missionaries continued to saturate the region with gospel radio broadcasts in the people's heart language.

In the early 1990s, when missionaries began to visit the country again, they found that the churches needed reassurance and training as they considered adopting unfamiliar house church structures. Had the missionaries criticized this move or tried to suppress it, the Church Planting Movement might well have been stifled. The missionaries also tried to protect the churches from dependency on outsiders. At the same time, they focused efforts on nurturing the vision of the emerging church leaders, offering training where appropriate and praying for continued advance.

Sometimes it is possible to look back on a movement and identify thresholds that, once successfully crossed, result in an almost inevitable movement. At the same time, we can sometimes identify these same crossroads as the point when a wrong choice may have derailed a Church Planting Movement.

This Latin American Church Planting Movement crossed a significant threshold in 1992. The Spirit of God was stirring the people of this region. Church meetings in the six modest buildings were regularly packed out. Unless new facilities could be found, the growth of the movement was in jeopardy. In addition to outgrowing their church buildings, the swelling number of believers faced fuel shortages that hampered their ability to commute to the church house.

Throughout this season of growing pains, the Baptist Union superintendent made repeated visits to the government ministry responsible for authorizing new building construction.

"Please, sir," he implored, "you must let us build more churches. We have no more space!"

Repeatedly, he was denied. Finally, one day, in exasperation, the government official shouted at him, "Buildings, buildings, buildings...that's all you Baptists can think about! Why don't you just meet in your homes!"[76]

The brusque response stimulated the thinking of the superintendent. Soon afterwards, he instructed the people to begin meeting in homes, and a threshold was crossed.

Moving the churches into homes as *casas cultos*, or house churches, stimulated several things simultaneously.

1. It freed the church from identification with buildings.

---

[76] As told to the author by leaders of the Baptist union.

2. It necessitated far more leaders than the seminaries could provide—provoking a major lay leadership movement.

3. It eliminated any time delay in starting a new church.

4. Many from Roman Catholic or atheist backgrounds felt uncomfortable entering a Baptist church building, but were less threatened by visiting a neighbor's home.

5. It allowed the movement to grow rapidly without attracting immediate public notice or government censure that would certainly have come if new church buildings had been constructed.

The laity responded vigorously to the move into their homes and neighborhoods. The Northern Baptist Union began a Lay Missionary School in the 1990s to provide training for the growing number of lay men and women starting and leading houses of worship. By 1998, there were 110 graduates and 40 more students enrolled. The Southern Baptist Union has not been far behind. Between them, the two unions have deployed nearly 800 home missionaries across the country. Today, Union leaders report that "hundreds are now expressing a call to missions."

This Church Planting Movement is now poised to spread the faith beyond national boundaries. Already some of these Baptists are finding employment opportunities in restricted countries where they can contribute to the Great Commission as tentmaker missionaries.

N O ONE CAN predict the future for Church Planting Movements in Latin America. But wherever missionaries, volunteers and Latin American evangelicals learn to trust indigenous leadership and depend on God rather than foreign funds, Church Planting Movements will likely follow.

9

Europe

Church Planting Movement practitioners report in 1999, among the refugees of the Netherlands, 45 new churches were started in a single year.

The Gypsy Evangelical Movement begins in France and Spain in the late 1950s. By 1964 there are 10,000 Gypsy believers. By 1979 there are 30-40,000 church members with 150,000 attending worship.

In 1996 two young Swiss evangelicals begin a cell church. In just five years the International Christian Fellowship grows to more than 3,000 members meeting in several hundred home cell groups.

N OWHERE IN THE world has Christianity received as much state support as it has in Europe. Even today, governments provide clergy with education and salaries, churches are tax exempt and church-based education is funded for children. Yet with all this support, Europe's Protestant churches are losing their grip on their post-modern parishioners.

In the place of vibrant Christianity are self-professed post-Christian societies that are searching for new avenues of spirituality. Secularism, complacency, and hedonism have all vied for the allegiance of Europe's masses. Something in the fabric of western Europe has staunchly resisted evangelical advances. Church Planting Movements have found a hard soil throughout western Europe.

Before one can ask, "Where are Europe's Church Planting Movements?" it might be more appropriate to search for those characteristic elements so commonly associated with Church Planting Movements.

Where are the house churches, the home-based cell groups, the lay leaders? Where is the fervent prayer, the abundant evangelism, and submission to the Bible? Only after we've addressed these questions are we likely to find Church Planting Movements.

Well intentioned churchmen of the past sought to ensure the Christianization of Europe's future generations by weaving into its legal structures and tax codes the support that would undergird that edifice. The beautiful cathedrals and basilicas of Europe are testament to that supporting structure. But today those cathedrals stand empty.

If conventional church structures and paradigms in Europe stand in contrast to Church Planting Movements, then it shouldn't be a surprise to see Church Planting Movements appear where the fabric of traditional society is torn and the key elements that shape Church Planting Movements are allowed to flourish. This is exactly what we find. God has chosen to reveal his power outside the centers of European Christendom. Instead, he has unleashed his work among the marginal and dispossessed of Europe: refugees and Gypsies.

EUROPE'S MARGINALIZED PEOPLES, such as the refugees of Holland, did not inherit the church-state legacy or the straightjacket of state support for the church. Each year thousands of refugees from troubled countries in Africa and Asia pour into Europe seeking safety and economic advancement. In Holland, these refugees are sent to processing camps where they

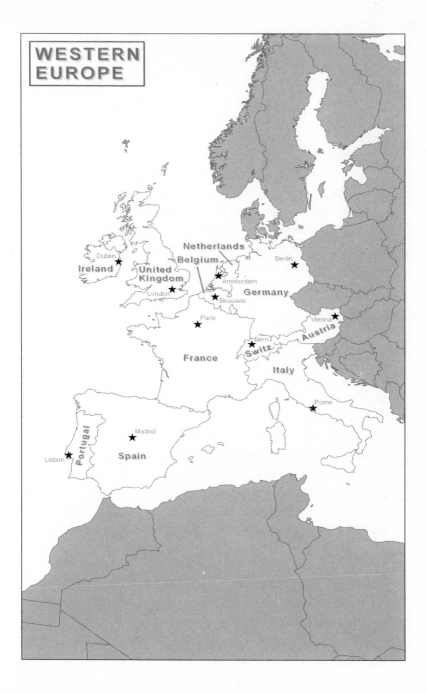

WESTERN EUROPE

remain for one month to several months while the government reviews their application for asylum.

The refugee processing camps provide a pleasant sanctuary for the traumatized refugee families before they enter Dutch society. In these settings, missionaries took the gospel and a concept of church planting that fit well with the transitional lifestyles of the refugees.

In 1995, missionaries Larry and Laura Hughes were appointed as missionaries to Eindhoven, Holland. After a year of Dutch language study, Larry began his ministry as pastor of the international community of Eindhoven. The Hughes soon discovered that many of their parishioners were newly arrived refugees from all over the world. The Netherlands has over 90,000 refugees in the northern region around Eindhoven alone.

Soon the Hughes began following their church members back to the refugee resettlement camps to minister to their friends and families. They enjoyed visiting with the newcomers from such places as Sierra Leone, Iran, Afghanistan, Rwanda, Nigeria, and Iraq. The refugees always seemed happy to receive the missionaries and welcomed their prayer and Bible teaching.

Larry and Laura longed for a way to do more than simply minister to the refugees. The analogy of teaching a person to fish in order to feed him for a lifetime seemed to fit the refugees' plight. If they could only teach the refugees how to minister to one another, perhaps the ministry would take on a life of its own.

In 1997, the Hughes began implementing their vision for a Church Planting Movement. They weren't sure it could happen. After all, this wasn't a single people group, but a mosaic of peoples. The one thread that linked all of the people groups was their transit through the Netherlands. Over the next few months, the Hughes intentionally set out to cast a vision and provide training for a Church Planting Movement.

The refugees proved remarkably receptive to the idea of starting their own churches. By the end of 1997, the Hughes were meeting with ten different cell groups each week.[77] The following year, the groups began to form into lay-led churches.

A 1999 email from Larry stated, "Last year (1998) my wife and I started 15 new church groups. As we left for a six month stateside assignment last July, we wondered what we'd find when we returned. It's wild! We can verify at least 30 churches now, but I believe that it could be two or even three times that many."[78]

When asked how these churches came to multiply so rapidly, Larry explained,

> All of our (house) churches have lay pastor/leaders because we turn over the work so fast that the missionary seldom leads as many as two or three Bible studies before God raises at least one leader. The new leader seems to be both saved and called to lead at the same time, so we baptize him and give him a Bible. After the new believer/leaders are baptized, they are so on fire that we simply cannot hold them back. They fan out all over the country starting Bible studies, and a few weeks later we begin to get word back how many have started. It's the craziest thing we ever saw! We did not start it, and we couldn't stop it if we tried.[79]

Over the years, evangelical missionaries to Holland had regarded it as one of the least gospel-responsive countries in the world. In the midst of this dry soil, however, God has produced a fertile garden among the refugees.

In July 2000, I visited the refugee ministry for myself. By this time, Larry and his wife had returned to the United States to care for gravely ill parents. The missionaries who followed them into the refugee ministry were wonderful, Spirit-filled saints who

---

[77] Mike Creswell, "The Netherlands: Providing An Anchor" in *The Commission* (November 1997), p. 22.

[78] Cited in the author's 1999 booklet *Church Planting Movements*, p. 4.

[79] Ibid., pp. 4-5.

loved the refugees and shared the gospel with them faithfully. One of them told us he had personally baptized more than 90 refugees in a single year. There was no doubt that these ministering missionaries had a vision for ministry, evangelism, and discipleship, but the understanding of a Church Planting Movement was absent.

One can thank God for the witness, love, and ministry of the missionaries who followed the Hughes, but one can only lament the twilight of the Church Planting Movement. The transient nature of the refugees meant that they only stayed for a short time in the refugee centers, then they were deployed into communities across Holland. With no one to transfer the vision of a Church Planting Movement to the new incoming refugees, the movement soon expired.

The team that succeeded the Hughes had a passion for evangelism and ministry, but little understanding of what is needed for a Church Planting Movement. Consequently, the movement regressed from a Church Planting Movement back into an evangelistic refugee ministry.

SOME YEARS AGO, a Baptist missionary working in Spain made an intriguing comment. "In Spain," he said, "we can't call ourselves evangelicals, or people will assume that we are Gypsies."

Imagine a people group so colored by the gospel that their very name has become synonymous with evangelical. Investigating the Gypsy evangelicals I was amazed to see how closely they matched the patterns of Church Planting Movements that have emerged all over the world.

Due to their marginalized status in European society, it's not always easy to find published reports in English of what God is doing among the Gypsies of Europe. Occasionally, however, the magnitude of the Gypsy movement catches the eye of the secular media. In a 1983 article in the *New York Times*, John Darnton described a movement of up to a quarter million strong, with a core of 60,000 who have been baptized.[80]

Ten years later, French Professor Jean-Pierre Liégois noted, "Over the last few years there has been very rapid growth in the Gypsy Pentecostalist movement, through the Gypsy evangelical Church; since its beginnings in France in the 1950s it has spread throughout Europe and beyond."[81]

In 1993, the movement was penetrating England's Gypsy population where it caught the attention of Andrew Hobbs, a correspondent for *The Observer*. Hobbs reported that in England, 5,000 out of Britain's estimated 60,000 Gypsies were committed Christians.[82] Another British journalist, Justin Webster, traced the movement back to Spain where the *Spanish Association of Gypsy Presence* claimed about 30 percent of Gypsies in Spain were associated with the movement.[83] By 1999, *Christianity Today* took note of the movement identifying 600 evangelical Gypsy churches in Spain alone.[84] At their annual assembly on a deserted NATO airbase in Chambley, France between 25,000 and 30,000 Gypsy Christians gathered in August 2000.[85]

---

[80] John Darnton, "Europe's Gypsies Hear the Call of the Evangelicals" in *The New York Times* (August 25, 1983), Late City Final Edition, Section A, p. 2.

[81] Jean-Pierre Liégeois, *Roma, Gypsies, Travellers*, transl. by Sinéad ní Shuinéar (Strasbourg: Council of Europe, 1994), pp. 91-92. Originally published in French as *Roma, Tsiganes, Voyageurs*, in 1992.

[82] Andrew Hobbs, "Gypsies take to highway to heaven" in *The Observer* (August 1, 1993), p. 20.

[83] Justin Webster, "Gypsies for Jesus," reported on p. 30 in the Features section of *The Independent* (London), February 11, 1995.

[84] Wendy Murray Zoba, "The Gypsy Reformation," in *Christianity Today* (February 8, 1999), pp. 50-54.

[85] Reported as "Around 25,000 Gypsies Gather in France" in *Agence France Presse*, August 24, 2000.

Clearly something was happening among the Gypsy peoples of western Europe, but was it a Church Planting Movement? The answers were hidden within Spanish sources and within the tightly knit Gypsy community, both of which are difficult for an outsider to penetrate.

Help came from an unexpected source when a librarian turned up a research paper on the Gypsy movement. In 1989, Stephanie Crider, a graduate student at Samford University and daughter of Baptist missionaries to Spain, wrote her senior honors thesis on "The Evangelical Movement among Spanish Gypsies." Fluent in Spanish, Crider had known many Gypsies personally and worshiped with them in her father's church in Grenada, Spain. In her thesis, Crider translated many of the sources that reveal the story of the Gypsy Church Planting Movement.

Crider writes,

The Gypsy revival can be dated back to 1950, in Normandy, France, in the little town of Liseuz. One day, in the market, a Gypsy lady named Duvil-Reinhart, was given a tract by a Christian from an Assembly of God church. She put it in her purse and forgot about it till several months later, when one of her sons became deathly ill. She then remembered the tract and the Christian who told her about healing miracles. Madame Duvil went to the Assembly of God Church and asked the pastor to pray for her son, because he was going to die. He went with her to the hospital and laid hands on the young man, who was completely healed. This miracle caused the whole family to surrender to Christ. They shared their conversion experience with the rest of their extended family members, and the great continuing revival that is still going on today, began here.[86]

---

[86] Stephanie P. Crider, "The Evangelical Movement Among Spanish Gypsies," a senior honors thesis submitted to the faculty of the Department of History and the Honors Council in partial fulfillment of Honors Program Requirements at Samford University, p. 34.

Le Cossec (the Assembly of God pastor who had prayed for Madame Duvil's son) picks up the story in his own words, "One day a family of Gypsies came to my church. They were searching. I invited them to a prayer meeting and they came. They received the Holy Spirit. The next Sunday I baptized 30 in the sea. The next year, 3,000."[87] Crider continues,

> The first conversions were among the Manouche tribe. The first Spanish or Gitano Gypsies were converted in 1960 while they were working in Bordeaux, France. In 1962 the movement spread to the Rom tribe that is widespread in Italy. In 1965, seven of the Spanish Gypsy converts returned as missionaries to Spain. The Gypsies always witnessed first to their families because of the great importance they give to family life.[88]

Crider writes, "The gospel spread among the Gypsies with great rapidity. By 1958, there were three thousand baptized and by 1964, there were ten thousand."[89]

By 1979, there were about 30-40,000 members with 150,000 attending worship groups. That same year, France counted 19,000 Gypsy believers and 230 pastors, and Spain had roughly 10,000 members with 400 pastors.[90]

By 1981 the Gypsy evangelical Church was working among Gypsies in France, Belgium, Switzerland, Canada, Spain, Italy, Germany, the U.S., Finland, Greece, India, England, Portugal, Argentina, and Romania.[91]

---

[87] Darnton, *The New York Times*, p. 2.

[88] Crider, p. 38. Crider draws, in part, from the Spanish language work of Lisardo Cano, *Un Pentecostes en el Siglo XX* (Sabadell: Imp. Serracanta, 1981) pp. 7-8.

[89] Ibid., p. 37.

[90] Ibid., p. 69 citing Lisardo Cano, p. 185.

[91] Ibid.

All sources confirm the role of Clement Le Cossec, the French Assemblies pastor. In 1983, Le Cossec estimated that 50,000 of the 100-150,000 Gypsies in France belonged to this movement. That same year, 12-15,000 Gypsy believers under the leadership of Le Cossec met for an international convention in southern France. Among the various Gypsy tribes were the Manouche of France and Germany, the Rom of Italy, the Gitano of Spain, and the Yediche of Germany. By the late 1980s, Rev. Le Cossec calculated that 250,000 had been drawn to the movement and that 60,000 had taken baptism. [92]

The first seven Gypsy missionaries who went to Spain in 1965 were later revered as the apostles to the Spanish Gypsies. They spread out across the country and endured great hardships in order to plant the church among their people. Persecution was nothing new for Gypsies, but for the new evangelical Gypsies, the persecution came from within the Gypsy population itself.

Opponents of the movement mocked the converts with the name "Alleluias," a reference to their frequent use of the term in worship and in everyday conversation. Gypsy lay-preachers were ridiculed and called "priests." Though intended as insults, these titles were appropriate designations for a people who are "a fragrance of praise to God" and "a nation of priests."

Signs and wonders accompanied the spread of the faith. Transformed lives including physical healing were commonplace among Gypsy believers. Gypsy Christians also brought with them the Pentecostal practice of speaking in tongues and receiving prophetic messages from God. Crider noted, "A Gypsy service is about 90% praise. It includes a lot of music interspersed with prayer. The music in the church has been adapted to their own Gypsy music. Usually accompanied by the

---

[92] John Darnton, "Europe's Gypsies Hear the Call of the Evangelicals" in *The New York Times* (August 25, 1983) Late City Final Edition, Section A p. 2.

guitar and clapping, the choruses have a distinct 'flamenco' sound to them."

Gypsies in Spain are famous for their flamenco dancing. After conversion, though, the lyrics of their songs were transformed such as in the following translated chorus:

> Before, Gypsies carried knives,
> Now we carry the Bible, the true Word.
> I don't want to sin anymore.
> Christ has taken away my bandages.
> Now I sing to him with joy;
> I want to follow his path.[93]

As for the role of the Bible in Gypsy worship, Crider reported that "biblical messages are interspersed amongst the praises, but these are usually short and simple because of the fact that many of the people in the congregation, sometimes even the speaker, cannot read. Therefore, the messages must be something easy to understand and assimilate. Parables are favorite forms used to teach God's word."[94]

Prayer was at the heart of the movement. In addition to prayers for healing and prayers for prophecy, believers often conduct all night prayer vigils on the weekend. Prayer was also the core of leadership training. Gypsy pastors described their preparation for the ministry as "coming from the mount," a reference perhaps to Moses who went to the mountain top where he talked with God.[95]

---

[93] Noted by former Operation Mobilization missionary, Hans van Bemmeten in an unpublished paper presented as a class requirement for Professor Gabino Fernandez at IBSTE, March 14, 1987, p. 1. Quoted in Crider, pp. 58-59.

[94] Crider, p. 59 quoting Juan Quero, a Baptist Spanish pastor.

[95] Ibid., p. 61 quoting Juan Quero.

Churches meet wherever they can, often beginning in homes before moving to rented facilities when they outgrow the house size. In addition to meetings in homes and random facilities, Gypsy churches "often move their place of worship." There are several reasons for this mobility, not all of them tied to the Gypsies' nomadic lifestyle. Renting facilities allowed them to grow without concern for limitations of building size, and to vacate a neighborhood when neighbors complained of their loud singing and shouts of praise.[96]

A few of the Gypsy pastors of large congregations received a salary from their flock, but most of the Gypsy preachers were bivocational. They continued to work their secular jobs often in common Gypsy trades such as market sales or construction work. The reason for this, according to an article in *The Ecumenical Review* was "mainly because of financial reasons; it is simply necessary to make ends meet, and to support a family."[97]

The *Review* went on to point out an interesting by-product of the bivocational pastorate that "the congregations devote their offerings to have conventions and to do missionary work, rather than to maintain a paid pastorate."

Crider identified a major reason for the growth in the Gypsy church being the emphasis on forming preachers. She writes, "Because many of the preachers were and still are illiterate, the Gypsy pastors do not receive the traditional training expected by other evangelical denominations. They are primarily lay preachers....There is no seminary. They train each other."[98]

---

[96] Ibid., p. 60.

[97] Ibid. pp. 61-62 quoting "The Gypsy Evangelical Church" in *The Ecumenical Review*, 31 (3), 1979, p. 292.

[98] Ibid., p. 60.

The training followed a pattern of mentorship. Those who wanted to enter the ministry presented themselves to the pastor who met with them two or three days a week. Once the pastor was satisfied that they were ready, he began giving them opportunities to lead music and preach in his church. After proving themselves to be faithful in their leadership for two years, the ministry candidates were presented to the national convention as new preachers or pastors.[99]

Why did this movement happen among Gypsies as opposed to some other people group in Europe? Gypsies have a long history of persecution in almost every country of Europe. Their status on the edge of respectable society may be one of the contributing factors to their openness to an evangelical faith.

In contrast with the more "respectable" sectors of European society, Gypsies were less conformed to the clergy-guided patterns of conventional European Christianity. Gypsy evangelicals allowed much greater congregational participation in worship. Spontaneous words of inspiration from lay members of the church were taken seriously. Though the Gypsies did meet in rented or modestly constructed church buildings, they were equally comfortable taking their faith on the road in caravans of vans and motor homes.

In the 1980s, many missionaries serving in Spain were still pastoring churches themselves rather than working with and through local Spanish pastors. These missionaries were also focused on Spaniards in general rather than identifying individual people groups such as the Gypsies. As Crider observed, "There are other churches and denominations working with the Gypsies in Spain besides the 'Iglesia Filadelfia (i.e. Gypsy Evangelical Movement).' They, however, are payo (i.e.

---

[99] Ibid., p. 61.

non-Gypsy) denominations that minister to Gypsies, rather than being a primarily Gypsy movement."[100]

As Crider noted, many of the Spanish evangelical churches had Gypsies as members, but none of them sought to form a Gypsy-based Church Planting Movement. Some even lamented that when payo (non-Gypsies) would visit the church and see the Gypsies, they would turn and leave.[101] Consequently, rather than seeing the Gypsies as a harvest field they were sometimes viewed as an obstacle to reaching the larger Spanish population.

I N THE HARDENED soil of western Europe one can still find occasional signs of hope for Church Planting Movements. After years of decline in Switzerland, evangelicals are beginning to sow the seeds of new approaches. In 1996 two young Swiss evangelicals began a cell church focused on 18-24 year olds. Over the next five years the *International Christian Fellowship of Zurich* grew to more than 3,000 members meeting in several hundred home cell groups.

In England we find another sign of hope in the *Alpha Program* of home-based evangelism. The Alpha Program is an introduction to the core truths of the Christian faith built around a setting of openness to inquiry. Lasting 15 weeks, the course focuses on non-Christians, often meeting in homes rather than in the church building, typically including a shared meal, welcoming skeptical questions, and resulting in an astonishing number of conversions. An Alpha practitioner shared his views on some of why Alpha Groups have been such effective evangelism tools.

---

[100] Ibid., p. 64.

[101] Ibid., p. 65.

First, it gets non-believers into small groups meeting in the homes of believers. Second, it actually encourages difficult questions that non-Christians have, without feeling a need to answer every question. This is very important. Christians think they have to have an answer for every question. Non-Christians want to know that they are free to ask—asking is more important to them than receiving a half-baked answer. Third, by the time the 15-weeks is over, it is often the small group itself that converts the non-Christian. A community of seekers is a winsome thing.[102]

Alpha Groups began in the 1980s when an Anglican clergyman, Charles Marnham, used the non-threatening program to introduce new believers to the Christian faith. In 1990, Nicky Gumbel took over the program and began looking for ways to share the methods with the larger Christian world. By 1999 more than 1.5 million persons were enrolled in Alpha Groups in more than 17,000 churches around the world.[103] By the year 2001, more than 65,000 church leaders had received Alpha training enabling them to use the Alpha program in their own churches. The program spread beyond church communities to universities, homes, and even prisons.

Alpha Groups are proving to be the most effective evangelism tool in western Europe in many years. Some of the components that are making it effective are reminiscent of Church Planting Movements, however, the primary users of the Alpha program continue to be conventional churches.

It remains to be seen whether this program will be able to break out of the conventional church and produce true Church

---

[102] From a conversation between author and a representative of the *Alpha Groups* at their display kiosk at the *Amsterdam 2000* meeting in Amsterdam, Holland July 2000.

[103] The official *Alpha Groups* home page for the U.K. is www.alpha.org.uk. In the United States related information can be found at www.alphana.org.

Planting Movements. What is clear is that much of Europe's efforts to undergird official Christianity have actually had the opposite effect, leaving Europe's fringes as the most fertile fields for Church Planting Movements.

Miracle-Gro

Blooming Houseplant food

10

North America

In 17 years, a Baptist church in North Carolina becomes the mother, grandmother, and great grandmother to 42 churches from which sprang 125 ministers.

In 20 years time, DOVE Christian Fellowship grows from three cell churches with 25 members to more than 80 cell church networks on five continents with more than 20,000 members.

Throughout 2001, Church Multiplication Associates saw a new church started every week.

Each week Saddleback Valley Community Church and Willow Creek Community Church shepherd some 40,000 members through a network of 4,000 home cell groups.

IN HIS SEVEN volume history of Christianity, Kenneth Scott Latourette identified the 19th century as an era of unprecedented advance for the body of Christ.[104] Of all the great advances that Christianity made during this period, none was more significant than the discipling and congregationalizing of North America.

The pioneer advance across the vast expanse of North America went hand-in-hand with its evangelization and the planting of new churches on the frontiers. By the end of the 19th

---

[104] Kenneth Scott Latourette, *A History of the Expansion of Christianity* (New York: Harper), 1937-1945.

century, virtually every town in North America had at least some small Protestant community striving to realize a vision of one nation under God.

How did this pioneering movement spread the gospel with such determination from the Atlantic to the Pacific shore? Twenty-first century denominations look back to their pioneer forefathers and struggle to understand the kind of zeal that subdued an untamed continent. Images of circuit riding preachers, brush arbor revivals, and Great Awakenings propelled the movement across the territory, but what kind of churches were able to keep pace with this rapid expansion?

One of the archetypal frontier churches that swept across North America in the 18th and 19th centuries was Sandy Creek Baptist Church founded in rural North Carolina in 1755. Historian Robert Baker described Sandy Creek church as

> the mother of all the Separate Baptists…(which) in 17 years, has spread branches westward as far as the great river Mississippi; southward as far as Georgia; eastward to the sea and Chesapeake Bay; and northward to the waters of the Potomac; it, in 17 years, is (sic) become the mother, grandmother, and great-grandmother to 42 churches, from which sprang 125 ministers.[105]

Baker continues,

> Within three years of the Separates' settlement at Sandy Creek there were three fully constituted churches with a combined membership of over nine hundred. Vigorous branches thrived in the region of Sandy Creek at Little River in Montgomery County and Grassy Creek in Granville County, and other branches were located well to the eastward at Southwest in Lenoir County, Black River in Duplin,

---

[105] Robert A. Baker, *The Southern Baptist Convention and Its People* (Nashville: Broadman Press, 1974), p. 50 quoting Morgan Edwards's *Materials Toward a History of American Baptists*. Of the twelve-volume work projected, only four have been published (Philadelphia 1770-1792).

New River in Onslow, and as far away as Lockwood's Folly in Brunswick. Preaching had been carried on from the Moravian settlements to the Cape Fear and northward into Virginia.[106]

Sandy Creek's expansion was no accident. Historian William Lumpkin "judged that a definite missionary strategy was planned by the leadership (as) Shubal Stearns worked primarily in eastern North Carolina and to the west of Sandy Creek; Daniel Marshall itinerated to the north; Philip Mulkey preached primarily in the east and southeast."[107]

By 1881, William Cathcart could write, "There are today probably thousands of churches that arose from the efforts of Shubal Stearns and the churches of Sandy Creek."[108] What was the DNA that produced this explosive frontier movement?

Morgan Edwards, another early chronicler of the Sandy Creek Church Planting Movement, noted the fierce belief in the autonomy of each local congregation and the conviction that God had been imparted authority to each independent church. "If power be fixed by Christ in a particular church," he wrote, "they can not transfer it; nay, should they formally give it away yet it is not gone away."[109]

Two centuries later, Baptists are still in awe of the dynamic impulse that flowed out of the Sandy Creek tradition. Historian Elliott Smith suggests several essential ingredients:

---

[106] Baker, p. 50 quoting William L. Lumpkin, *Baptist Foundations in the South* (Nashville: Broadman Press, 1961), p. 38.

[107] Baker, p. 51 quoting Lumpkin.

[108] Elliott Smith, *The Advance of Baptist Associations Across America* (Nashville: Broadman Press, 1979) p. 34 quoting William Cathcart, *The Baptist Encyclopedia* (Philadelphia: Louis H. Everts, 1881), vol. 2, p. 917.

[109] Baker, p. 51 quoting Morgan Edwards.

1) **Enthusiasm**: "The zeal and emotional preaching of the Separates, the use of uneducated ministers, the noisy meetings, and even the extensive ministry of women in the services alienated the more formal older Baptists."[110]

2) **Persistence in the face of persecution** - "But the more vigorously they were attacked the more vigorously the Separates preached and the faster they multiplied.... The Baptist response to oppression was rapid growth. Garnett Ryland wrote that Baptist churches were formed in every Virginia county where Baptists were imprisoned."[111]

3) **Evangelism** - Quoting Reuben E. Alley, "Those who committed themselves under this experience promptly received evidence of God's pleasure by seeking the salvation of men. True commitment required a person to be an evangelist for Christ."[112]

Under the heading of "ardor," Baptist historian Walter Shurden noted that the Sandy Creek Baptists "were a people possessed by ardor. And that ardor expressed itself in individualism, congregationalism, biblicism, and egalitarianism. They released a devotion to freedom which is without parallel in Baptist history."[113]

---

[110] Elliott Smith citing Baker in *The Southern Baptist Convention*, p. 32.

[111] Elliott Smith, pp. 36-37 quoting Garnett Ryland, *The Baptists of Virginia, 1699-1926* (Richmond: The Virginia Baptist Board of Missions and Education, 1955), pp. 85-86.

[112] Elliott Smith, p. 38 quoting Reuben E. Alley, *A History of Baptists in Virginia* (Richmond: Virginia Baptist General Board, 1974), p. 36.

[113] Walter Shurden, "The Southern Baptist Synthesis: Is it Cracking?" in *A Baptist History and Heritage*, Vol. XVI, no. 2, April 1981, p. 4.

Passion, evangelism, biblicism, local church autonomy, uneducated lay leaders, missionary zeal, rapid multiplication of converts, and new churches, fearless advance through persecution—all these were characteristics of the Sandy Creek tradition.

Viewed through the lens of modern day Church Planting Movements, it is easy to add the Sandy Creek tradition to the list. By today's standards, Sandy Creek seems exceptional, but it was only one of a number of frontier churches that won the North American continent in the 18th and 19th centuries. Those that lacked Sandy Creek's explosive DNA simply did not flourish or even survive.

If this was the legacy of 19th century American Protestantism, then where does that tradition stand today?

A T THE BEGINNING of the third millennium, North American Christianity is still vibrant. Up to 68 percent of America's 275 million citizens are members of some kind of church.[114] Even the National Council of Churches' annual study, which only includes those denominations that choose to report, identifies more than 151 million church members worshiping in nearly 321,000 congregations across the United States. These congregants report tithes and offerings of nearly $27 billion.[115]

In the 21st century, mega-churches are increasingly characterizing the North American evangelical landscape. First Baptist Churches in Atlanta, Houston, and Dallas all claim memberships larger than 20,000 as do Prestonwood Baptist Church, Second Baptist Houston, Bellevue Baptist in Cordova, Tennessee, and Jerry Falwell's Thomas Road Baptist Church in Lynchburg,

---

[114] Barrett, vol. 2, p. 607.

[115] Eileen W. Lindner, ed., *Yearbook of American and Canadian Churches, 2001* (Nashville: Abingdon Press, 2001), p. 366.

Virginia. But not all is healthy in these large mega-churches that can typically only account for one-third of their members on any given Sunday. For too many, church membership has become a spectator sport rather than a vital part of daily life.

A story is told in Kenya of a prominent pastor from the United States who visited Nairobi and was introduced to the Kenyan church leadership as "pastor of one of the largest churches in America, with more than 20,000 members. Each week more than 8,000 attend his preaching." Visibly moved, the Kenyan leader led his brothers to pray for the American pastor who could not find more than half of his church members on Sunday morning!

Besides the problem of absentee membership, North America faces the challenge of the unchurched. The United States, for example, can boast that 68 percent of its population are church members, but what about the 88 million other Americans who are unchurched? That number alone would be larger than most countries.

A study done of American Protestant Christianity in the 1980s revealed that American evangelicals have made little or no headway in reaching the unchurched. Church growth analyst Win Arn found that "not a single county in the United States grew in church attendance faster than general population growth in the whole decade of the 1980s."[116]

Many view North America's patterns as following the post-Christian trends of western Europe, but others recognize that North America demographics have been permanently altered by the millions of immigrants who have entered the U.S. and Canada from non-Christian countries around the world.

---

[116] David Mays, "Notes from Jim Montgomery's Great News About the Great Commission," Monthen.bk 1997. Available [Online] at www.davidmays.org/BookNotes/MONTHEN.pdf referencing Win Arn in *Leadership Journal*, Spring 1996, p.75.

Since World War II, though, the pace of non-Christian immigration to North America has outstripped the capacity of churches to assimilate them. Muslims, Hindus, and Buddhist populations have taken this opportunity to establish their own mosques, temples, ashrams and cultural centers across the continent. At the same time, Protestant churches in North America have watched their once prominent role in Western society and culture diminish.

In the face of this changing Church landscape is there hope for a Sandy Creek renaissance? Does North America still hold hope for a new wave of Church Planting Movements?

For a growing number of 21st century Christians, the answer is "Yes!" A surprising number of Christian leaders are adopting a radical new vision that looks surprisingly like other movements that we've witnessed around the world.

I N CITIES, TOWNS, and suburbs across North America, there is a quietly rising tide of ecclesiastical subversives. Dan Mahew, of the Portland, Oregon based, Summit House Church Network describes a typical church service in his home.

> It's Monday night. Familiar faces are coming through the door of our house. People are sitting or standing around the living room talking. A couple of the guests have casseroles and loaves of bread—it's their turn to provide food for this modest crowd of about fifteen. For the next three hours we will talk around the table, clean up after the meal, tell a story to the kids, pray over our burdens, sing, and discuss our discoveries in scripture. Before everyone drifts away, we will serve the cup of the Lord's Table, having already shared the bread at dinner.[117]

---

[117] Read more about Mahew's Summit Group at: www.worldaccessnet.com/~summit/welcome, July 20, 2003.

A far cry from traditional Protestant churches, but Mahew's experience is familiar to growing numbers of American evangelicals. How many house churches are there? No one knows for sure. A 1994 study by Robert Wuthnow estimated as many as 80 million Americans were part of a regularly meeting small group worship or Bible study.[118]

Some of these individuals such as the three million in Methodist Sunday School classes or the eight million enrolled in Southern Baptist Sunday Schools are easy to account for, but then, they are also present in traditional weekly worship services. Less obvious are the thousands of house and home-based cell churches that rarely appear in church census figures, but can sometimes be detected through Internet searches.[119]

Website home pages range from the simple businesslike Canadian house church's www.*HouseChurch.ca* to the restorationist www.TheEarlyChurch.com from the irreverent www.thechurchofnocrap.com to the sublime www.atHisfeet.com.

Across Canada, house churches have taken names such as *43rd House Group* in Calgary, *the Dwelling Place* in Ontario, *Face to Face* in Saskatchewan, *the Citywide* Church in Montreal or the convenient *J'snexdoor* in British Colombia.[120]

The growing ranks of individualistic house church practitioners find their voice in Wolfgang Simson's *Houses that Change the World,[121]* Drs. Tony and Felicity Dale's

---

[118] Robert Wuthnow, *I Come Away Stronger: How Small Groups are Shaping American Religion* (Grand Rapids, MI: William B. Eerdmans Publishing Company, 1994), p. 370 cited in Joel Comiskey's *Home Cell Group Explosion*.

[119] See for example the *Worldwide House Church Directory* at www.hccentral.com/directory/index.

[120]See www.HouseChurch.ca.

[121] Wolfgang Simson, *Houses that Change the World* (Carlisle, U.K.: Paternoster Publishing, 2001).

House2House on-line magazine,[122] and discussion groups that range across the spectrum of house life and polity.[123]

On-line web-log discussions reveals that these house churches are no utopia of consensus and conformity. Their members grapple with issues of organization, scheduling, authority, and freedom. The refreshing reality is that any member can enter the discussion and the only consistently persuasive authority appears to be the New Testament.[124]

In the Long Beach, California area, Neil and Dana Cole began worshiping in house churches over ten years ago. Today their *Church Multiplication Associates* (CMA) encompasses nine different house church networks spread across seven states and two countries. By 2001 the CMA network was cascading into a movement averaging one new church start a week.

Statements on CMA's website reveal the group's Church Planting Movement core values. Here are a few choice excerpts:

1. Bad people make good soil, there's lots of fertilizer in their lives.

2. Two kinds of lost people: moths and cockroaches. The way to tell the difference is to turn the light on - the moths will be drawn to the light and the cockroaches will flee.

---

[122] See www.House2House.tv.

[123] Such as the 17-page web-log found at: www.home-church.org/threads/ on July 20, 2003.

[124] Ibid.

3. We must lower the bar of how we do church, raise the bar of what it means to be a disciple of Christ and thus we will raise the standard of what church truly is.

4. Don't organize "it" until you have an "it" to organize.

5. Personal transformation precedes community transformation.

6. Worship has an audience of One.

7. To move others you must first be moved.

8. We must raise leaders for the harvest from the harvest, and all the resources for an abundant harvest are in the harvest.

9. Where you go the king goes!

10. When offering books and resources to growing Christians, give them the Bible! "We must plant the seed, not a seed substitute."

11. When mentoring: "Keep a bifocal leadership vision: start at the beginning, but begin with the end in mind."

12. We've got to get out of the barns and into the harvest![125]

In neighboring Riverside, California, Jonathan Campbell, Ph.D. and his wife Jennifer lead a flourishing network that now features house churches in the California cities of Riverside, Los

---

[125] See DAWN ministries U.S. website at: www.dawnministries.org/regions/nam.

Angeles, Pasadena, Santa Cruz, San Diego, San Jose, San Francisco, as well as in Orlando, Florida, Boise, Idaho, and in Seattle and Kitsap County, Washington State.[126]

Campbell's core values read like a Church Planting Movement start-up manual:

1. Love and obey Jesus Christ

2. Incarnate the gospel in the midst of the unreached and undiscipled - Focus on discipling "persons of peace."

3. Disciple social networks - We seek group conversions (oikos[127] evangelism) by sharing the gospel in and through relational networks and cultural systems.

4. Equip and empower every believer to actively participate in fulfilling Christ's mission in and through the church.

5. Give freely for the Kingdom – The New Testament provides two reasons for collecting money: benevolence and missions.

6. Empower indigenous teams - We identify, equip and empower indigenous leaders to partner together in relationship and mission.

7. Reproduce in every sphere - We intentionally reproduce in every sphere of church life: disciples, leaders, churches and teams.

8. Partner with the greater body of Christ - churches, teams and groups of like faith and mission for mutual edification.

Most North American house church networks seem to have formed as alternatives to traditional congregations that meet in

---

[126] Ibid.

[127] *oikos* is the Greek word for family or household.

buildings with professional clergy. However, a growing number are recognizing their own potential as seed for full-blown Church Planting Movements.

One example is DOVE Christian Fellowship International based in Lancaster, Pennsylvania.

I N 1978, A MENNONITE youth minister in Lancaster County, Pennsylvania received a challenge from the Lord, "Are you willing to be involved in the underground church?"

The question baffled Larry Kreider at first, but he and his wife LaVerne surrendered to the Lord's calling to form a new type of church that was in stark contrast to the hundreds of traditional Protestant churches that dotted the Pennsylvania countryside.

In 1980, the Kreiders gathered a handful of believers and formed DOVE Christian Fellowship. DOVE is an acronym for *Declaring Our Victory Emanuel*. The name is less important than the vision that propels it. Kreider sensed that the Lord wanted this new community to meet in homes, to rely on lay leadership and to focus its attention on reaching the lost unchurched society that would not participate in a traditional church structure.

By 1990, the original three cells had grown to include 2,300 members gathered in scores of home fellowships across southern Pennsylvania. In 1996, Kreider turned over the leadership and ministry of the church to eight pastors, twenty-one elders, and a whole host of cell leaders. Soon afterwards the church decentralized and become eight cell-based church networks and the movement began to roll.

By the year 2001 the DOVE family of churches had multiplied into 80 cell-based churches located in five continents of the world.[128] Though Kreider avoids touting total membership

---

[128] Read more about Kreider's pilgrimage and DOVE Christian Fellowship on their website at www.dcfi.org, October 2003.

figures, a simple extrapolation of his 1990 figures puts current adherents in the DOVE family of churches at more than 20,000.

Several of America's fastest growing mega-churches have created similar house-church dynamics within their larger community. Rick Warren's 20,000 member *Saddleback Valley Community Church* overcame the gap between clergy and laity through contemporary worship, seeker friendly atmosphere, and weekday meetings in the homes of 1,600 church members. The same is true at Bill Hybel's 17,000 member Willow Creek Community Church whose members gather each week in more than 2,600 home fellowships.[129]

Larry Stockstill's Bethany World Prayer Center in Baker, Louisiana shed its building-bound structure in 1993 and began reorganizing into home cell groups in the suburbs of Baton Rouge. Seven years later he had nearly 600 home cell groups with 3,000 adults in regular attendance.[130]

A S PROTESTANT DENOMINATIONS try to regain a foothold in the urban frontiers of North America, property costs alone are forcing church planting strategists to consider an alternative to planting 'cathedral style' churches.

In 1995, the Chicago Metro Baptist Association adopted a vision for nothing less than a Church Planting Movement across Chicagoland. In the greater Houston area, the Union Baptist Association embraced a similar vision.[131] Likewise, Dallas

---

[129] Verla Gillmor, "Community is Their Middle Name," in *Christianity Today*, November 23, 2000, p. 50.

[130] See their website at www.bethany.com.

[131] See their associational goals for Church Planting Movements on their website at: www.ubahouston.org.

Baptist Association appointed Joseph Cartwright to serve as a "house church planter catalyst to saturate the region with lay-led churches that do not meet in church buildings."[132]

Lending denomination-wide support to the trend, Southern Baptists' North American Mission Board has commissioned its *Church-Planting Group* to adopt a "New Testament church planting movement among all people groups in the United States, U.S. territories, and Canada."[133]

Can Church Planting Movements emerge in 21st century North America? Have North American evangelicals lost their Sandy Creek legacy to the comforts of the institutional church with its professional clergy, air-conditioned nurseries, and graded choir programs? Has America, like Esau, traded its Sandy Creek birthright for a bowl of pottage?

North America may yet have another Sandy Creek era ahead of it. These are yeasty times.

---

[132] See www.dawnministries.org/regions/nam/networks.

[133] See their website at www.namb.net.

Part Three

Lessons Learned

11

In *Every* Church Planting Movement

N OW THAT WE'VE completed our survey of Church Planting Movements, it's time to step back and see what we can learn. This is what we began in August 1998 as a handful of missionaries gathered around a conference room table in Virginia. The question we addressed was: "How is God at work in these Church Planting Movements, and how can we join him?"

Equipped with three whiteboards, a flipchart and an army of colored markers we scribbled on the boards while we discussed, analyzed, and debated the nature of what we saw God doing. Gradually, the patterns began to emerge.

After several hours we compiled our findings under three headings:

1. *Elements in Every Church Planting Movement* – ten universal elements at work in every Church Planting Movement.

2. *Elements in Most Church Planting Movements* – ten qualities and characteristics present in most, though not all, Church Planting Movements.

3. *Obstacles to Church Planting Movement* – barriers that, once removed, allowed Church Planting Movements to develop.

Since those initial studies in 1998, we've seen new Church Planting Movements spring-up around the world, but these original lists of ingredients and obstacles still stand as faithful guides to understanding and participating in Church Planting

Movements. Some of the findings seemed obvious at first, but there were also surprises.

Some characteristics we expected to find were strangely absent. While others, though present, were different in the ways they had contributed to their respective movements. These were often counter intuitive, and for that reason, their study and application are invaluable to anyone wishing to align themselves with the ways God is at work. Let's look now at the ten universal elements we found in every Church Planting Movement.

In *Every* Church Planting Movement

1. **Extraordinary Prayer**

2. **Abundant Evangelism**

3. **Intentional Planting of Reproducing Churches**

4. **The Authority of God's Word**

5. **Local Leadership**

6. **Lay Leadership**

7. **House Churches**

8. **Churches Planting Churches**

9. **Rapid Reproduction**

10. **Healthy Churches**

---

1. Extraordinary Prayer

Prayer permeates Church Planting Movements. Whether it's Koreans rising at four in the morning for a two-hour prayer time, or Spanish Gypsies *"going to the mountain,"* as they call their all night prayer vigils, Church Planting Movements are steeped in prayer.

Consequently, prayer has become the first priority of every Church Planting Movement strategist. As soon as a Strategy Coordinator senses the gravity of his calling he immediately falls to his knees and prays, "Oh God, only You can make this happen."

We've identified seven distinct roles that prayer plays in the life of a Church Planting Movement. In Church Planting Movements prayer occupies both intuitive and counter-intuitive roles.

Intuitive Roles of Prayer

#1 Prayer *for* the missionaries. Missionaries to the world's unreached people groups are invading hostile territory. Many of these unreached peoples have spent centuries, even millennia, under the dominion of "the god of this world"[134] and he does not surrender them lightly. Missionaries engaged in Church Planting Movements have come under severe attack on a spiritual level. Their health, their family members, their vocation are all subject to attack by Satan. Praying for them is the best defense they have.

#2 Prayer for the *lost people group*. One of our missionary leaders serving in Africa commented on a major goal he'd achieved that was yielding great results. "For years," he said, "our missionaries have had churches praying for them. Now, they are shifting the focus of prayer onto the lost people they are trying to reach."

This shift has been pronounced across the evangelical world. For years, it has been commonplace for Christians to tag

---

[134] 2 Corinthians 4:4

onto their prayers: "and God bless the missionaries." While Christians continue to pray for missionaries, they are increasingly pouring out their hearts for the *Kurds*, *Mongols*, *Uighurs, or Uzbeks*. People groups who have never been prayed for in all of history are now being lifted up before the throne of God.

I'm sometimes asked by faithful prayer warriors, "Do my prayers make a difference?" I love to tell them of people like Ibrahim. Ibrahim was a young convert from Islam that I met deep in Inner Asia in 1990. He was the first of his people group to come to faith in Christ. I remember how his face glowed with the radiance of the Holy Spirit in his life. I asked one of the church planters working in the area how they had led Ibrahim to Christ.

"We didn't," they said. "He came to faith through prayers."

"I don't understand," I said.

The church planter explained, "Ibrahim is a student at the university where I teach. He is the son of a mullah (Muslim religious leader). We normally stay away from people like him. But one day Ibrahim came to me and told me of a dream he'd had. In his dream an old man handed him a book and said, 'Read this.' Ibrahim asked me if I knew what the book in his dreams might be. Apparently he'd been asking his friends the same question because the dream had haunted him for weeks. His friends had always pointed him to the Qur'an, but Ibrahim said, 'No. It's not the Qur'an.'"

The church planter hesitated and then spoke softly, "In my drawer I had a tattered copy of the New Testament. It was written in the old script that most of Ibrahim's people could no longer understand so I had never used it in witnessing to them. I hesitated, but then sensed God wanted me to take a risk with this mullah's son. I showed it to Ibrahim. 'Could this be the book?'

Ibrahim opened the book and said, "Ah, I see it is in the old script. My father taught me how to read this. Do you mind if I borrow it?"

Over the next few weeks Ibrahim read all of it and led himself to faith in Christ."

We both knew that the true source of Ibrahim's conversion could only be found in the many saints who had prayed for so long for Ibrahim's people.

Counter-Intuitive Roles of Prayer

#3 Prayer modeled *by* the missionaries and church planters.
We often underestimate the way our actions overshadow our
words. Only when prayer comes to characterize the life of
the missionaries and church planters, does it spread to their
team members and to those they are trying to reach. If prayer
doesn't characterize the missionary's life then the new
believer will not grasp the true source of the missionary's
life-changing power. He will either view the missionary as
an extraordinary person whom he could never imitate, or
worse, a secular person whom he would not wish to imitate.

#4 Prayer *for* the new believers. In the course of Church
Planting Movements no one suffers as much as the first
converts into the movement. Missionary newsletters are
filled with pleas for churches to pray for Amal who has been
imprisoned or Mohammed whose family threatened to kill
him. New Church Planting Movements often pass through a
crucible of testing in which the first believers are harassed
and even killed. If the church survives this initial testing then
a Church Planting Movement is not far behind. If Satan can
crush the first fruits, then the Church Planting Movement
will die.

#5 Prayer *by* the new believers. In every Church Planting
Movement powerful prayer flows through the lives of the
believers and their churches, as God's mighty activity flows
through their lives. Vices are broken, diseases are healed,
opposition is crushed, and lives are changed. Often the
prayer was accompanied by a strong sense that God has his
hand on this people. It is *their* time—their appointed day of
salvation. This creates a powerful force within a people.
They witness with boldness, sensing that God is on their

side. They don't flinch under persecution, confident that God is with them.

Finally, we discovered that there were some collateral benefits that emerge from prayer in a Church Planting Movement, benefits we had not anticipated finding, but they have emerged as key factors in the success of many Strategy Coordinators' work.

#6 Prayer *between partners*. Strategy Coordinators in Church Planting Movements invariably have wide networks of partners who come from all over the world. How do they develop such close bonds so quickly that overcome enormous barriers of language, culture, and even theology? The secret is prayer. Strategy Coordinators pray for partners and pray with partners. The call to prayer for an unreached people group is the magnet that first draws these diverse partners together, and the glue that binds them over the years.

#7 Prayer *for more workers*. Jesus commanded us to "Pray to the Lord of the harvest to call out workers."[135] Prayer mobilizes harvesters to come to join the work. More importantly, though, prayer summons new workers to emerge *from within* the harvest. At the same time, it creates a sense of expectancy on the part of the missionaries and church planters to be watchful, always looking for the new harvesters, the co-laborers that God is raising up. These new co-laborers will take up the mantle of leadership within the movement and propel it to the next level.

We pray because our vision exceeds our abilities. Prayer is the soul's deepest cry of rebellion against the way things are,

---

[135] Matthew 9:38

seeing the lost of this world and crying out, "This does not glorify God, and so, by God's grace, it must change!" Prayer comes from God and ascends back to God on behalf of those who do not know God. Extraordinary prayer lays a firm foundation for a Church Planting Movement.

2. Abundant Evangelism

If prayer links a Church Planting Movement to God, then evangelism is its connection with the people. Essential to every movement is the principle of over-sowing. Just as nature requires a tree to drop thousands of seeds to produce a single sapling, or a human body to generate hundreds of eggs to yield a single baby, so it is with evangelism. In Church Planting Movements we find hundreds and thousands of people hearing the gospel every day and out of this abundant sowing, a growing harvest begins to take place.

Conventional wisdom in the West has often taught a reasonable yet much less effective pattern of gospel transmission. "You must first earn the right to share your faith," goes the traditional model. "Once you have developed a friendship and demonstrated that you are really different, your lost friend will ask you what is special about your life. Then, you can tell them about Jesus."

A passionate purveyor of Church Planting Movements denounced this Western model. "We teach that it's not about you or earning the right to share your faith. Jesus earned that right when He died on the cross for us. Then he commanded us to tell others!"

If nature's principle of sowing abundantly to reap abundantly is true, then so is its opposite: *if you sow sparingly, you will reap sparingly.* Wherever hostile governments or societal pressure has succeeded in stifling Christian witness, Church Planting Movements never get off the ground. This simple truth is so powerful, and yet many well-intentioned missionaries accomplish every lofty ideal *except* this one.

A colleague working in a Middle Eastern country expressed his frustration over the lack of seed sowing in his country. "In my country," he said, "everyone says, 'We're not reaping a harvest yet, but we're removing stones from the field.' The truth is they haven't even begun sowing the seeds yet. If you ask, they will tell you, 'We're still clearing the fields so we can plant the gospel. We're picking up stones, picking up stones, picking up stones.'

"I'M SICK TO DEATH OF PICKING UP STONES!" he exclaimed, "If God wants to, he can turn these stones into sons of Abraham! So let's stop picking up stones and start telling people about Jesus!"

To remind them of the importance of abundant gospel sowing, many Strategy Coordinators have prominently displayed a one-page sign at their workstation that reads: *How many of my people will hear the gospel today?* If there's going to be a movement, then the answer must be in the thousands.

In Church Planting Movements there is a buzz in the air about Jesus, about salvation, repentance, turning to God, and new life in Christ. A Strategy Coordinator working in an emerging Central Asian movement exclaimed, "This is the most responsive place I've ever been. The state-run newspaper last year reported that 5,000 adult Muslims in the capital city had become Christian. So the Legislature made it illegal to evangelize anyone, but they left a loophole that you can respond to questions about Christianity."

"And how has this affected the spread of the gospel?"

"It hasn't slowed it a bit," he laughed. "I'm telling you. A person will sneeze. Someone will say, 'God bless you' and a third person will say, 'How can I be saved?'"

The Strategy Coordinator may have been exaggerating, but not by much.

In Church Planting Movements personal evangelism and mass evangelism reinforce and contribute to one another. Mass evangelism always contains feedback loops to ensure that no one who comes to faith in Christ drifts away without discipleship, while personal evangelism ends by encouraging the new believer to share his faith with his family and friends.

Quantity *and* Quality

If quantity of gospel proclamation is of paramount importance, quality of communication can't be far behind. In its simplest form, evangelism means gospel proclamation, telling the Good News about the gift of new life in Jesus Christ. If it were this simple, though, we could simply translate John 3:16 into every language of the world and drop it from airplanes.

Too often missionaries get sidetracked from a gospel movement by questions of whether or not a people group is *responsive* to the Good News. Questions of responsiveness are often related, not to the news, but to the messenger.

True evangelism goes beyond proclamation to *communication*. Communication means someone has to hear and understand what is proclaimed. Often times, the subtle shift from proclamation to real communication triggers a response that was previously absent. Effective communication requires understanding the language and worldview of the people you are trying to reach.

Jesus said, "If I be lifted up, I will draw all men unto me."[136] The challenge is to lift Jesus up in a way that is not obscured by cultural barriers that would prevent all peoples coming to faith in him.

Uncovering the worldview of people groups can help to remove these barriers. Communicating the gospel requires us to get inside the mind of those we're trying to reach and that is

---

[136] John 12:32

impossible without learning the language and culture of the people.

One of many illustrations from the field that highlights the importance of a people group specific worldview study comes from Kenya. Two people groups in northern Kenya shared the same language and origins. They appeared identical to outside observers, except that one group inhabited the lowlands while the other resided in the adjacent mountains.

For years, missionaries had used the same approach to both groups with mixed results. The lowlanders had responded well to the gospel, resulting in many churches. The mountain tribe remained unresponsive. The missionaries had hoped that the lowlanders would take the gospel into the mountains to reach their resistant cousins.

Despite years of effort, the mountain tribe showed little interest in the gospel. Then the missionaries began researching the worldview of the tribes. They discovered the reason for the mountain tribe's lack of response. They found that in previous centuries the lowland tribes had been slave traders, often conducting slaving raids into the mountains to prey on their unwitting cousins. This history of victimization had left an indelible impression on the worldview of the mountain tribes. They could not receive Good News from their lowland neighbors.

Once the missionaries discovered this historical barrier, they were able to overcome it by using other messengers to take the gospel to the mountain tribes.

The quest for effective communication of the gospel has led to great advances in what has been called *contextualization*, i.e. presenting the timeless gospel message in the worldview and cultural forms of the people being reached.

Church Planting Movement practitioners, typically achieve this same end through *indigenization* – transferring responsibility for gospel communication to those who naturally present it through their own worldview perspective. Though missionaries often begin the evangelization of a people group, in Church Planting Movements, the primary evangelizers are always the new believers themselves, and they contextualized the gospel better than anyone.

3. Intentional Planting of Reproducing Churches

Intuitively, one might assume that the potent combination of extraordinary prayer and abundant evangelism would naturally result in spontaneously multiplying churches. Many missionaries and church planters have held this view, and so were surprised and disappointed when multiplying new churches did not follow. What we found instead was that Church Planting Movements did not emerge without a deliberate commitment to plant reproducing churches.

A wise person said "you will probably accomplish exactly what you set out to accomplish, nothing more, nothing less." If you aim to do a Bible translation, you will probably produce a Bible translation. If you aim to do ministry, you will likely succeed. But you cannot assume that a Bible translation or Christian ministry alone will result in a church plant. If you want to see churches planted, then you must set out to plant churches. The same axiom can be taken a step further to say, "If you want to see *reproducing* churches planted, then you must set out to plant *reproducing* churches."

In the Bhojpuri Church Planting Movement, for example, missionaries had been at work in the area for many years. They were evangelistic, pious models of Christian love and service, but they lacked a clear strategy for planting churches. A turning point occurred when the Strategy Coordinator developed an intensive church planter training school. Out of this practical training, Bhojpuri Christians began starting churches. Today, it seems that everyone working among the Bhojpuri is starting new churches.

Both missionaries and local believers are increasingly realizing the importance of intentional church planting. A number of mission agencies that were not previously known for church planting have begun actively pursuing training in this area. Among the Bhojpuri people, Youth With A Mission (YWAM) leads one of the largest denominations of churches. Not previously known for planting churches, today many YWAM missionaries have become ardent students of church planting and are producing new church starts around the world.

4. The Authority of God's Word

As Church Planting Movements produce multiple repro-ducing churches, what keeps the movement from fragmenting into a thousand heresies like a crack splintering across a car windshield? There can be only one answer: *the authority of God's word*. Like an invisible spinal cord aligning and supporting the movement, there runs through each Church Planting Movement a commitment to the authority of the Bible.

Even among the largely nonliterate peoples, for whom Scripture reading is rare, converts rely heavily on audiocassettes of the Bible clinging to every word. They have also learned to approach every faith and life situation with the question, "How can I best glorify Christ in this situation?" In following this principle they never venture far from biblical authority.

These two governing forces of biblical authority and Christ's lordship reinforce one another like parallel railroad tracks guiding the movement as it rolls far beyond the direct control of the missionary or initial church planters. Since this internal guide is independent of the missionary, it does not require the missionary's presence to advance. Even without the missionary the movement doesn't become disoriented, because its orienta-tion does not derive from an external source, but rather from the solid framework of God's authoritative word and the lordship of Jesus Christ.

This does not mean that the missionary has no role in the discipleship of new believers or training of the church leaders. He doesn't simply wind-up a Church Planting Movement like a toy and watch it go. Discipleship and leadership training are going on all the time. But even the missionary's teaching and training are evaluated by the same two criteria: is it consistent with God's word and the lordship of Jesus Christ? Any teaching that deviates from the twin tracks of Scripture and lordship are rejected whether they come from a heretical teacher or from the missionary Strategy Coordinator himself.

Consequently, missionaries and church planters engaged in Church Planting Movements learn very quickly to deflect questions of doctrine from themselves and onto these guiding tracks. When asked by a new believer or new church leader, "What should we do in this situation?" rather than answer from his own pool of wisdom or training, the CPM-savvy church planter replies, "Let's see what God's word says."

Those who have successfully navigated a Church Planting Movement are unanimous in their conviction that "it must be God's word that is authoritative for the new believers and the emerging church not the wisdom of the missionary nor some foreign creed nor even the local church authorities." By continually pointing back to the source of one's own authority, the church planter is modeling the proper pattern for the new believers who will soon become the new conveyers of the movement.

Nonliterate Peoples

So many of the world's remaining unreached peoples are non-literate that missionaries involved in Church Planting Movements have struggled to overcome the challenge of illiteracy. How do evangelicals, who are fundamentally a "people of the book," multiply among people who cannot read and write? Illi-

teracy doesn't diminish the importance of the Bible as a source
of authority; it simply poses new challenges for its transmission.
There are at least five patterns we've observed for transmitting biblical teaching to nonliterate peoples in the world today.

1) **Memorization** – though a lost art in the West, memorization
   of Scripture is still quite common in the non-Western world.
   This is particularly true among Muslims who have a long
   history of memorizing the entire Qur'an. In one South Asian
   Muslim country, where a shortage of Bibles coupled with
   widespread illiteracy threatened the advance of a Church
   Planting Movement, new converts found an ingenious
   solution—*they ripped their Bibles into pieces!* One believer
   was handed the Gospel of Matthew and told, "Here, you
   memorize this." Another was given the Gospel of Mark, and
   so on. Then, as the church convened, these "living Bibles"
   were called upon to faithfully recite the words of Scripture.

2) **Audio-visual** – Missionaries have been quick to adapt the
   Bible into nonliterate formats such as audio Bibles and the
   Jesus Film which have provided Scripture to many who are
   unable to read it.

3) **Bible Storying** – Recognizing that many people groups are
   essentially "oral cultures" who communicate great truths
   through story telling, missionaries and church planters have
   taken the key stories of the Bible and translated them into
   oral short stories that they then recite to their nonliterate
   hearers. These Bible stories have been used for evangelism,
   discipleship and leadership development. In Church Planting
   Movements, Bible storytellers are not satisfied until those
   hearing the stories are able to repeat them back accurately

and so multiply the great truths of Scripture throughout their community.[137]

4) **Songs** - A typical example comes from an African oral culture where the missionary had spent several weeks translating the gospel message into heart language stories for the people she was trying to reach. While she related the stories, a member of the group was listening intently and translating her message once again—he was putting it into song. "Our people don't just tell the story," he explained, "we sing our stories. It is too much for me to ask you to provide songs for us, but now that you have given us God's word, we will sing it to our children and grandchildren."

5) **Using Educated Youth** – The challenge of illiteracy in an increasingly literate world is not limited to those propagating the gospel. National governments face the same challenge when they want to communicate some important information regarding taxes or a new law or voting guidelines to a village that is illiterate. We asked a rural evangelist how this problem is surmounted locally. "They ask one of the children from the family to read the letter or message for them," he replied. The same is obviously true for reading God's word. Despite widespread illiteracy, there are usually some children who are attending school and learning to read and write. In the same way it is not uncommon for village elders to call on a schoolboy or girl to read from the *God Book*. Afterwards the elder is able to interpret and apply what he has heard to the benefit of the entire community.

In trying to reach nonliterate peoples, Church Planting Movement practitioners find encouragement in the New Testa-

---

[137] For more on *Chronological Bible Storying* visit the resourceful website: www.ChronologicalBibleStorying.com.

ment record of rapid church multiplication. The vast majority of the New Testament world was nonliterate, but still the Good News advanced.

Sometimes the question arises, "Why produce a Bible translation for this people group if the people are nonliterate?" A translation is important even if the people group cannot read or write. In the first place, more cultures today had their language reduced to writing for the first time by a Bible translator than by any other means. Out of these initial Bible translations have sprung entire literary traditions that have knitted a people together in a radically changing world.

More importantly, Bible translation into the heart language provides a resource pool for evangelism, discipleship, and leadership development. From a heart language translation of the New Testament a missionary can produce radio broadcasts of the gospel story, cassette testimonies with Scriptural promises, and even a videotape of the *Jesus Film* so that people can hear and respond to Jesus' story in their own heart language.

5. Local Leadership

Missionaries who successfully launch Church Planting Movements have learned to keep foreigners out of the spotlight. The principle has now been translated into an important watchword that accompanies Strategy Coordinators everywhere: "The resources are in the harvest." This axiom is a continual reminder to look for local leaders to get the job done. And it provides an important corrective for foreign missionaries whose strategies call for heavy reliance upon foreign teammates.

The most effective teams in Church Planting Movements have relatively few foreigners, but have large networks of local partners. Foreign missionaries understand that their role is to pass on their vision, passion, and skills to the local brothers and sisters with whom they serve.

So in Church Planting Movements, practitioners quickly develop local leaders and entrust to them the future of the movement. The earliest Strategy Coordinators who learned this lesson did so as much out of necessity as out of missiological reasoning. When faced with the overwhelming challenge of reaching millions of lost people, they had no choice but to raise up co-laborers from within the people they were seeking to reach.

The 222 Principle described in the Cambodia Church Planting Movement case study (chapter 5) has also become widespread. CPM practitioners have learned, *never do anything by yourself; always bring a brother along with you so you can model and mentor as you go.* In every instance the aim is to transfer the driving force of the vision into the hearts and lives of those being reached.

Passing the Torch
Relying on local leaders can be difficult for missionaries. Even today, some missionaries insist on pastoring the new churches they help to plant. Similarly, some missionaries still insist on mother churches sending an ordained pastor on an itinerant route to provide struggling new churches with rites of baptism and the Lord's Supper. This pattern of external dependency has never produced a Church Planting Movement.

Those who are reluctant to transfer this kind of authority quickly point to Paul's instructions in 1 Timothy 3:6 where Paul advises young Timothy that a bishop "must not be a recent convert..." However, Timothy's church was already well established enough to reference several generations of believers (see 2 Timothy 2:2). In such an environment it was natural for Paul to delegate church oversight to those who had been closest to the original message delivered by the apostles, but *nowhere* does Paul place church authority in the hands of outsiders.

When a new church is started, Paul does not hesitate to appoint local leaders right away. In Acts 14:23, immediately after winning converts in Lystra, Iconium, and Asia Minor's Antioch "Paul and Barnabas appointed elders for them in each church and, with prayer and fasting, committed them to the Lord, in whom they had put their trust." Likewise, he urges Titus to appoint elders, local men with families whom everyone knew, for every town of Crete.[138]

Meeting with the Church Planting Movement taskforce we posed the question, "When do you pass the torch to new leaders?"

Their unanimous response was, "In a Church Planting Movement you begin with the torch in their hand." The nods of approval around the room testified to the shared experience. Of course this is only possible when the churches are rooted in obedience to God's word and a lifelong commitment to discipleship.

Appointing local leaders rather than relying on the leadership of outsiders does several important things:

1) It makes a statement that we are all equally sinners; all equally saved by grace; all equally capable of being used by God.

2) It reinforces the truth that Christianity is not a Western religion, but an expression of Christ's body given to *all* believers.

3) It avoids setting standards of leadership that are unattainable. Most missionary church planters have far more experience and Bible training than the first generation of new believers will ever hope to achieve. But we shouldn't forget that it took many generations for Westerners to develop the kinds

---

[138] Titus 1:5-6

of training opportunities that we now enjoy. New believers need not think they have to reach the same level of education in order to lead God's people.

An African church leader said it well. "We think of you missionaries with great appreciation and affection. Like the person who first taught us to drive a car, we are grateful for what you have taught us. But we would not want our driving instructor sitting beside us every time we get behind the wheel!"

6. Lay Leadership

In Church Planting Movements the laity are clearly in the driver's seat. Unpaid, non-professional common men and women are leading the churches. Why is lay leadership important? There are several reasons:

1) **For Practical Reasons** - A movement that produces thousands of new churches needs thousands of new leaders and the largest source for finding these leaders is the local church membership itself. To produce these leaders, one must fish from the largest pool of candidates.

2) **For Theological Reasons** – Lay leadership is firmly grounded in the doctrine of the *priesthood of the believer*— the most egalitarian doctrine ever set forth. After centuries of reliance on a small tribe of Levitical priests, God turned to the church and said, "You are a chosen people, a royal priesthood..."[139]

It is not that Christianity has no special status for religious leaders; it is that now *every* Christian has this special status as a priest of the Lord God. Every believer is fully endowed with the right and responsibility to lead the lost to salvation and maturity in Christ.

---

[139] 1 Peter 2:9

3) **Following Jesus' Model** – Jesus' own pattern of calling laymen and women to come and follow him has not been wasted on Church Planting Movement practitioners. It is a great comfort to bolster a new believer's willingness to be a servant leader of the church by pointing him to the example of the Twelve and those who followed them.

4) **For the Purpose of Retention** - Around the world, the gospel's invitation to salvation has proven to be far more winsome than its call to a life of discipleship within the church. Within weeks of becoming a new Christian, far too many believers drift out the back door never to be seen again. Putting laymen and women to work within the church has proven to be the single most effective means of "closing the back door" to church membership and ensuring a lifetime of intimate involvement within the body of Christ.

5) **For Reasons of Relevance** - In traditional church structures, a clergyman is set apart from the congregation both in terms of education and livelihood. In the Catholic Church this is further compounded by vows of celibacy. In Church Planting Movements, the pastors remain one of the people sharing their lifestyles and struggles. This means, if the people are predominantly farmers the leaders will be farmers. If the people are urban, the leadership will be urban. If the people are nonliterate then the leaders will also be nonliterate. If the people are deaf, then the leadership will also be deaf.

6) **For Economic Reasons** - So many Church Planting Movements have occurred in developing countries where financial resources are minimal. By using multiple lay leaders and meeting in homes, these limited financial resources are

directed toward missions and ministry, rather than to church-staff salaries and facilities.

Lay leadership doesn't exclude professional ministers. There may be an ordained, seminary trained, professional clergyman or Strategy Coordinator involved at key points in the movement—as in the case with many of the sprawling home cell church networks—but on the cutting edge of its growth it is the laity who are leading the way.

For Church Planting Movements to be able to effectively rely upon lay leadership, two important factors must be present:

First, churches must remain *small enough* to be manageable by either one or several lay leaders. It is when churches exceed 20-30 members and begin using a separate church building that the task becomes too big for a layperson to lead without leaving their secular employment.

Second, church leaders must be *lifelong learners*. In Church Planting Movements, lay leaders typically have an insatiable hunger for training. Church Planting Movement practitioners have learned to continually feed and nurture leaders and potential leaders with on-the-job training and just-in-time training (which we'll discuss in greater depth later). Mentoring programs, rural leadership training programs, pastoral training schools, Internet and cassette training materials, pastor study Bibles and workshops all contribute to leadership development.

7. House Churches

The churches in Church Planting Movements begin as small fellowships of believers meeting in natural settings such as homes or their equivalent. Among the Maasai, the meetings take place under trees, among the Kui, in open courtyards. The key element in each of these Church Planting Movements was a beginning with an intimate community of believers who were not immediately saddled with the expense or upkeep of a church building.

Meeting in small groups[140] certainly has economic implications. Liberating the fledgling movement from the burden of financing a building and professional clergy is no small obstacle to overcome. But there is more. House churches create an atmosphere that fosters Church Planting Movement formation. Consider the following benefits.

1. Leadership responsibilities remain small and manageable.

2. If heresies do occur they are confined by the small size of the house church. Like a leak that appears in the hull of a great ship, the heresy can be sealed off in a single compartment without endangering the whole.

3. You can't hide in a small group, so accountability is amplified.

4. Member care is easier, because everyone knows everyone.

5. Because house church structure is simple, it is easier to reproduce.

6. Small groups tend to be much more efficient at evangelism and assimilation of new believers.

7. Meeting in homes positions the church closer to the lost.

8. House churches blend into the community rendering them less visible to persecutors.

---

[140] We'll explore the differences between house and cell churches in chapter 13 *Frequently Asked Questions.*

9. Basing in the home keeps the church's attention on daily life issues.

10. The very nature of rapidly multiplying house churches promotes the rapid development of new church leaders.

It is important to understand the role of small house and cell churches in the life of a Church Planting Movement. It's now easy to see why missionaries who want to start a Church Planting Movement without house or cell churches will find it so difficult.

8. Churches Planting Churches
Church Planting Movements are not in full flower until the churches begin spontaneously reproducing themselves. Traveling among the Khmer of Cambodia, each house church bore testimony to additional churches they had started in the previous year. Among the Bhojpuri, the average church had four new church starts underway. Many Chinese house church leaders taught their flock that the greatest joy was to train someone to start a church in their home.

In most of the Church Planting Movements we've studied there were already a few churches present among the people group before the first missionary arrived. For some reason, though, these churches had stagnated and ceased to reproduce. The missionary, often a Strategy Coordinator, brought a new vision, passion, and training for planting churches.

As the movement gained momentum, the missionary fades into the background and the churches themselves begin reproducing new churches. Only when the movement reaches this exponential stage of reproduction does it realize its full potential.

Church Planting Movement practitioners report looking for the fourth generation of church reproduction as a sign that the movement is proceeding under its own momentum. One of them explained, "When I see a church that I helped start reproduce a daughter church which itself reproduces a new church that produces yet another church, I know I've done my job. So long as this pattern of reproduction continues, I can move on to other less-reached population centers and know that this one will continue without me."

In Church Planting Movements, missionaries consciously progress along a four-stage process of *Modeling, Assisting, Watching, and Leaving.* First, they model the kind of patterns in evangelism, discipleship, and church planting that they want the new believers to imitate. Then, they assist the new believers in following this model. Next, they watch to see that their protégés are able to effectively reproduce what they have learned and experienced. When they see their students carrying out the same reproducing patterns, they know it is time to leave.

"Leaving can be difficult for missionaries, but it is absolutely essential," one missionary explained. "Otherwise the church will keep looking to the missionary rather than to the Lord and their own leaders for future direction. Departure guarantees the indigenous viability of the church."

Departure does not mean the missionary retires. Instead, he or she is now free to go to another, less reached sector of the people group to begin the process all over again.

9. Rapid Reproduction

Church Planting Movements reproduce churches rapidly. Of course, the word "rapid" is undefined. But missionary church planters often speak of church planting in birthing terms, asking, "How long does it take to birth a new church?" This gestation period varies around the world, just as it does within the animal kingdom. Elephants typically require 22 months to produce an offspring, while rabbits can yield a new litter every three months.

Church Planting Movements reproduce like rabbits! While a healthy gestation rate in a controlled environment might produce a new church every three to four years, a Church Planting

Movement might see a new church start every three to four months. Furthermore, because the new churches radiate out from each church rather than from the missionary church planter, the reproduction multiplies exponentially.

For this kind of multiplication, rapid reproduction must be built into the core values of each church being planted. Among the Kekchi people (in chapter 8) if a church didn't reproduce itself after six months it was considered an unhealthy church. Many of the sprawling cell church networks will not allow a home cell church to continue if it is unable to grow and multiply after a year of existence.

The rapid reproduction paradigm stands in sharp contrast to the more traditional view that a church must first grow large enough and mature enough to be able to afford to sacrifice some of its membership to begin a new work. In Church Planting Movements maturing in Christ is a never-ending process that is enhanced, rather than jeopardized, by starting new churches. In Church Planting Movements, both leadership development and every-member discipleship are built into the ongoing structures of church life—along with a passion for starting new churches.

When discipleship and leadership development are contained in the DNA of the first churches, they will naturally transfer that DNA to their offspring. The opposite is also true. When you teach your first churches to labor for many years under a missionary pastor while waiting to receive their own seminary trained leader; then require the church to purchase their own property and building; fill it with enough tithing members to support all of the above, you can't expect them to generate rapidly reproducing daughter churches. Rapid reproduction starts with the DNA of the first church.

In a Church Planting Movement the body of Christ reclaims the sense of urgency that characterized the Gospels and the New Testament churches. Rapid reproduction indicates that several healthy dynamics are present in the movement:

1)   The movement has gone beyond the control of the
      missionary or any other outsider.

2)   The movement has its own internal momentum.

3)   The new Christians passionately believe their message to
      be so important it must be spread rapidly.

4)   The fields are confirmed to be ripe unto harvest.

5)   All the elements that are foreign to the church—and not
      easily reproduced—have been eliminated.

Missionaries experienced in Church Planting Movements
would never admit to sacrificing orthodoxy for the sake of rapid
reproduction. Instead, they have learned to build the theological
controls into the DNA of each church rather than trying to
continually reinforce them from the outside.

10. Healthy Churches

What kind of churches do you find in Church Planting
Movements? This is the question many outsiders want to know.
In addressing this question, the panel of Church Planting Movement practitioners used several words to describe the nature of
the churches in the movements they had known. We can group
these qualities under the term *"healthy churches."*

One Strategy Coordinator put it this way, "I'll put these
churches up against any churches in the West and see how they
stack up. They are more vibrant; more committed to God's word;
more long-suffering...you name it."

One can forgive this missionary's pride in the churches'
character. It comes from an acute awareness not only of their
heroic courage in the face of tremendous persecution, but also
from a sad awareness of how anemic Western Christianity has
become.

What are the marks of a healthy church? Well, you don't measure it by the number of Sunday Schools, the size of its congregation or the credentials of its church staff.

In *The Purpose-Driven Church*, Rick Warren reminded the church of a more biblical standard for measuring church health. Drawing on Christ's Great Commandment and Great Commission, Warren points to five purposes in a healthy church:[141]

1) Fellowship
2) Discipleship
3) Ministry
4) Evangelism/Missions
5) Worship

Healthy churches exhibit all five purposes naturally, because these purposes flow from the church's identity with the living Christ. Jesus endowed the church with these purposes when he issued the Great Commandment to "Love the Lord your God with all your heart, soul strength and mind; and love your neighbor as yourself"[142] and the Great Commission to "Go and make disciples of all nations baptizing them…and teaching them to observe whatsoever things I have commanded you."[143]

When polled, the missionaries who had witnessed Church Planting Movements were unanimous in their opinion that the churches in these movements exhibited each of the five purposes. "They're all there," was their response, "but some of the purposes look different than they do in the West."

---

[141] Rick Warren, *The Purpose-Driven Church* (Grand Rapids: Zondervan, 1995).

[142] Matthew 22:37-40

[143] Matthew 28:20

This difference was particularly pronounced in the area of ministry. One Strategy Coordinator explained, "Their type of ministry is closer to what you find in the New Testament. They heal the sick, cast out demons, and share from their poverty with others in need." Sounds pretty healthy.

Of course the ultimate test of a healthy church is: "Does it glorify God?" Do these churches reveal and exhibit God's nature as revealed in Jesus Christ?

With this definition of health, each of the Church Planting Movements we've studied scored very well. This was the same sort of question that the imprisoned John the Baptist sent his disciples to ask of Jesus. "Are you the one who was to come, or should we expect someone else?"

The Lord's response to John's disciples still teaches us today. He said, "Go back and report to John what you hear and see."[144]

Jesus was saying, "If my words and deeds don't reveal to you the full glory of God, then you should look for someone else."

In the same manner, we should ask, "Is God's glory, his true nature as revealed in the person of Christ, evident in these movements?" The answer is seen in the millions of changed lives, healed bodies and souls, passion for holiness, intolerance of sin, submission to God's word, and vision to reach a lost world.

There is much more that we can learn about Church Planting Movements from our observations of case studies, but before we do, let's return to the Bible and see what it has to say about Church Planting Movements.

---

[144] Matthew 11:2-6

12

What Does the Bible Say?

I T'S GREAT TO know that so many people are coming to Christ and that new churches are springing up around the world. That reason alone may be enough for us to embrace Church Planting Movements. But as a people of the Book we are committed to filtering our understanding of the world through the lens of God's word.

As we do this, we follow the tradition of the first century Christians such as those in Berea who searched the Scriptures to see if these things were so.[145] So what does God's word say about Church Planting Movements? Let's the Berean dialogue begin!

You can search your exhaustive concordance *exhaustively* and you won't find a single entry for "Church Planting Movements." At the same time, the first century world was swirling with new converts and multiplying indigenous churches planting churches—in short, *Church Planting Movements.*

The origins of Church Planting Movements can be traced to the life and teachings of Jesus himself. The same Christ who mentored a small group of followers, moved from place to place across the Palestinian countryside, modeled prayer and fidelity to Scripture, worshiped in homes and hillsides, performed signs and wonders, and commissioned his disciples as the first missionaries, is the Christ of Church Planting Movements.

St. Luke, traveling companion of the apostle Paul and author of the largest portion of our New Testament, clearly linked Jesus'

---

[145] Acts 17:11

earthly ministry with the Church Planting Movements that followed.

In his second volume, the *Book of Acts*, Luke writes to Theophilus "In my former book, Theophilus, I wrote about all that Jesus began to do and to teach"[146] The implication is unavoidable, if volume one, the *Gospel of Luke*, covers all that Jesus *began* to do and teach then its sequel, the *Book of Acts*, will describe what Jesus *continues* to do and teach through his Body, the church. So it should not surprise us that the characteristics that mark Church Planting Movements today can be traced back through the New Testament church to the very life and teachings of Jesus.

Let's look at some of these characteristics.

Vision Driven

Church Planting Movement practitioners often speak of their vision or end vision. This describes where they hope to see when God's vision for their people or city is fulfilled. One brother put it this way, "If you can't see it before you see it, you're never going to see it."

Jesus filled his disciples with great expectations and a vision of the end fulfilled. He taught them to pray for the vision's realization, "Your kingdom come, your will be done on earth as it is in heaven."[147]

After the 72 missionaries returned from their mission, Jesus seemed to shout for joy: "I saw Satan fall like lightning from heaven," [148] he said.

---

[146] Acts 1:1

[147] Matthew 6:10

[148] Luke 10:18

In Revelation 12, the apostle John viewed the same image, "For the accuser of our brothers, who accuses them before our God day and night, has been hurled down."[149]

Jesus clearly initiated the overthrow of the *prince of this world*; it continued through the early church and through Church Planting Movements this divine subversion continues even to this day.[150]

Jesus prepared his disciples to expect even greater miracles than he himself performed. He also set a standard of harvest that far exceeded normal expectations. In his parable of the ten minas, Jesus taught his disciples that God expects an exponential return from his investment.[151] This expectation of great harvest enabled a motley crew of 120 followers to emerge from the upper room to tackle an entire world for Christ.

After walking with Jesus for three years and then seeing his death, burial, and resurrection, the disciples were ready to receive the Great Commission mandate to be his witnesses…to the ends of the earth.[152] Jesus filled his followers with a vision and an anticipation of the Church Planting Movements that followed. What other characteristics of Church Planting Movements can we find in the early church and teachings of Jesus?

Prayer

Prayer, the hallmark of Church Planting Movements, has deep roots in the New Testament Church that wend their way back to the lifestyle that Jesus modeled for his disciples. "Very

---

[149] Revelation 12:10

[150] John 12:31; 16:11; 14:30; 2 Corinthians 4:4; Ephesians 2:2

[151] Luke 19:11-27

[152] Acts 1:8

early in the morning, while it was still dark, Jesus got up, left the house and went off to a solitary place, where he prayed."[153] "This kind," he taught them, "can come out only by prayer."[154] His final meal with them was orchestrated around prayers that they were to rehearse until his return.[155] And then in the garden, "He said to them, 'Pray that you will not fall into temptation.' He withdrew about a stone's throw beyond them, knelt down and prayed."[156] And in keeping with his life's pattern, Jesus' final words on earth were a series of prayerful appeals to his Father.[157]

Following their Lord the early church was born in upper room prayer.[158] They frequented the temple for prayers,[159] dedicated their leaders to prayer and the ministry of the word,[160] and met daily in their homes for the breaking of bread and prayers.[161]

So it is no surprise that today's Church Planting Movements are steeped in prayer as they live out the legacy that Christ instilled in the foundations of the church some two thousand years ago.

---

[153] Mark 1:35

[154] Mark 9:29

[155] 1 Corinthians 11:23-26

[156] Luke 22:40-41

[157] Matthew 27:45-50

[158] Acts 1 & 2

[159] Acts 3:1

[160] Acts 6:4

[161] Acts 2:40

Abundant Evangelism

Jesus infused the early church with a passion for evangelism that flowed naturally from the One who began his ministry "proclaiming the good news of God."[162] At the midpoint of Christ's ministry he sent 72 of his followers "two by two ahead of him to every town and place where he was about to go," instructing them to "heal the sick who are there and tell them, 'The kingdom of God is near you.'"[163]

Before issuing his final Great Commission to preach the gospel to the whole world, Jesus even linked his return to the fulfillment of this evangelistic mandate. "This gospel of the kingdom," he said, "will be preached in the whole world as a testimony to all nations, and then the end will come."[164]

The early church obeyed these words with a passion. From Pentecost to Revelation, the church is taking the gospel from Jerusalem to the ends of the earth in anticipation of the return of Christ. Paul typified the ethos of the early church attitude toward abundant evangelism in his letter to the Corinthians when he reminded them, "Whoever sows sparingly will also reap sparingly, and whoever sows generously will also reap generously."[165]

The newly converted Paul ventured south into Arabia, north to Syrian Damascus,[166] and then on to the frontiers of Scythian Asia. What is surprising is how often he found that the gospel had already preceded him. Christianity was well established in Rome before Paul ever ventured there. The great Christian center

---

[162] Mark 1:14

[163] Luke 10:1,9

[164] Matthew 28:19-20 and Matthew 24:14

[165] 2 Corinthians 9:6

[166] Galatians 1:17

of Alexandria produced the likes of Apollos even though there is no record of how or when the gospel arrived. Paul commissioned Titus to appoint elders in every town of Crete—a relatively remote island off the coast of Libya. God only knows how the gospel came to permeate this distant outpost.[167]

During the half century in which the New Testament was written, the gospel swept from Golgotha to Gibraltar. The Pentecost miracle sprayed the message and its messengers eastward into the Persian Empire, west to Libyan North Africa, north across the Greco-Roman world, and south through Egypt to Ethiopia. Early church traditions from the Malabar Coast of south India attest to a first century missionary zeal that carried the gospel to the very ends of the known world.

This same zeal to abundantly sow the gospel flows through the life veins of modern Church Planting Movements. Today's missionaries develop creative ways to enter restricted countries, work through mass media, and through itinerant church planters. Like Paul, these 21st century apostles of the faith have "become all things to all men so that by all possible means (they) might save some"[168]

Scriptural Authority

Church Planting Movements are built on the authority of God's word. This is a vein that runs deep through the life of Jesus and the early Church. The Gospel writers all portray Jesus' life as a fulfillment of Scripture, and Jesus himself reminded his followers that "not the smallest letter, not the least stroke of a pen, will by any means disappear from the Law until everything is accomplished."[169] He then warned his disciples, "Anyone who

---

[167] Titus 1:5

[168] 1 Corinthians 9:22

[169] Matthew 5:18

breaks one of the least of these commandments and teaches others to do the same will be called least in the kingdom of heaven, but whoever practices and teaches these commands will be called great in the kingdom of heaven"[170]

Jesus modeled scriptural fidelity even at his moments of deepest trial. He answered Satan's temptations with verses from the Bible[171] and uttered a cry from Psalm 22 as he writhed in agony on the cross.[172] But even after his death, burial, and resurrection, Jesus returned his followers to Scripture to explain what had happened and what was to come: "This is what I told you while I was still with you: Everything must be fulfilled that is written about me in the Law of Moses, the Prophets and the Psalms." "Then," the Bible says, "he opened their minds so they could understand the Scriptures."[173]

Following this model of intimate commitment to Scripture, prompted Jesus' disciples to begin their own preaching with exposition of Scripture,[174] and face their eventual martyrdom—as in the case of Stephen—with echoes from the words of Jesus: "Lord, do not hold this sin against them."[175]

They reminded the church of the divine source of all scriptural authority insisting that "all Scripture is God-breathed and is useful for teaching, rebuking, correcting and training in righteousness, so that the man of God may be thoroughly equipped for every good work."[176] And to leave no doubt, they

---

[170] Matthew 5:19

[171] Matthew 4:6-10

[172] Matthew 27:46 (quoting Psalm 22:1)

[173] Luke 24:44-45

[174] Acts 2:17-21; 25-28: 34-35

[175] Acts 7:60

[176] 2 Timothy 3:16-17

explained that "no prophecy of Scripture came about by the prophet's own interpretation. For prophecy never had its origin in the will of man, but men spoke from God as they were carried along by the Holy Spirit."[177]

When modern day practitioners of Church Planting Movements refuse to counsel their converts with words of wisdom or time honored doctrines, but instead direct them to God's word, they are living out the New Testament model initiated by Jesus and transmitted through the apostles.

Models for Multiplication

Jesus and the early church practiced multiplication increase. In Luke chapter 5, Jesus chose 12 disciples. In Luke 9, he sent them out, and though it does not say it in this passage, we learn later that his pattern was to send them out 2-by-2. In the next chapter, Luke 10, Jesus sent out 72 disciples. Where did these 72 come from? If we understand the principle of multiplication, it is easy to imagine that the original 6 pairs of disciples did just what their Master had modeled: they discipled 12 others, resulting in 72 disciples (6 x 12 = 72).

If multiplication was truly at the core of Jesus' discipleship model, then we might expect these 72 disciples to have multiplied themselves as well. If they closely followed Jesus' example, then the 72 (comprising 36 pairs of disciples) would have produced 444 disciples (36 x 12 = 444). Adding these 444 to their 72 mentors would produce an early church of more than 500 disciples of Jesus.

Was this the pattern that the early church followed? In his first letter to the Corinthians, Paul described the community that

---

[177] 2 Peter 1:20-21

greeted Jesus after his resurrection, "he appeared to more than five hundred of the brothers at the same time."[178]

Did the multiplication pattern continue after Jesus' ascension? Let's see. If those same 500 brothers formed 2-by-2 teams and imitated Jesus' model of discipling 12 converts each, they would produce 3,000 disciples (250 pairs x 12 = 3,000). In Peter's Pentecost message of Acts 2:41, we read that 3,000 received the message and were baptized in a single day. Some may question whether Jesus had a precise formula for multiplying in groups of 12, but it is clear that Jesus intended for his followers to multiply, and multiply they did!

Preparation for Persecution

Missionaries engaged in Church Planting Movements understand that persecution will be the lot of those who renounce this world and follow Jesus Christ, so they prepare the new believers for this test. Modern day preparation for persecution extends a long shadow that stretches back to the cross of Christ.

Jesus warned his disciples, "A student is not above his teacher, nor a servant above his master."[179] Jesus could see that the prospect of "all men (hating) you because of Me"[180] would serve as a powerful deterrent to false or even timid faith.

Paul exhibited the same kind of fearlessness in persecution that marks those who have led and endured the cost of a Church Planting Movement. He tells the Corinthians, "I have...been in prison more frequently, been flogged more severely, and been exposed to death again and again."[181]

---

[178] 1 Corinthians 15:6

[179] Matthew 10:24

[180] Matthew 10:22

[181] 2 Corinthians 11:23-25

Suffering and persecution were so closely associated with the spread of the gospel that the Greek word for witness (martyria) became synonymous with death. Jesus knew this would happen so he boldly challenged, "If anyone would come after me, he must deny himself and take up his cross and follow me."[182]

For Paul, as for the early church, suffering was such an integral part of his life in Christ that he could say, "I rejoice in what was suffered for you, and I fill up in my flesh what is still lacking in regard to Christ's afflictions, for the sake of his body, which is the church."[183] Likewise James, the brother of our Lord, exclaimed, "Consider it pure joy, my brothers, whenever you face trials of many kinds."[184] And the author of Hebrews challenged the church to imitate "Jesus, the author and perfector of our faith, who for the joy set before him endured the cross."[185]

The early church response to persecution could be summed up in a single word, *boldness*. The word occurs eight times in the *Book of Acts*, each time associated with persecution or opposition to the gospel.

Peter set the tenor when he prayed, "Now, Lord, consider their threats and enable your servants to speak your word with great boldness. Stretch out your hand to heal and perform miraculous signs and wonders through the name of your holy servant Jesus."[186]

---

[182] Mark 8:34

[183] Colossians 1:24

[184] James 1:2

[185] Hebrews 12:2

[186] Acts 4:29-30

And Paul revealed the deep roots of the church's boldness when he wrote, "Therefore, since we have such a hope, we are very bold."[187]

By the end of Luke's early history of the Church, the pattern of bold witness in the face of certain death has become a recurrent theme for the entire book, so that he can conclude the *Book of Acts* with the declaration, "Boldly and without hindrance he preached the kingdom of God and taught about the Lord Jesus Christ."[188]

In today's Church Planting Movements, church members are refined by persecution and defined by their boldness. The tremendous price they pay to follow Christ ensures the purity of the movement against false motives and nominal conversions. And it links them personally to the life and path of Christ and the early church.

All in the Family

Unlike today's Western patterns of individual conversions, Church Planting Movements typically explode through a people group by moving through family relationships. How about the New Testament? What were its transmission patterns?

While it's true that the New Testament records plenty of dramatic individual conversions, the people of that era were much more communal in their decision making. This made it natural for the gospel to spread through family lines. You can see this in the interchange between Jesus' mother, Mary, and her relative Elizabeth who would soon give birth to John the Baptist.[189] Jesus later drew on this relationship as he built his

---

[187] 2 Corinthians 3:12

[188] Acts 28:31

[189] Luke 1:36

ministry on the advance work of his baptizing cousin.[190] Along
the way, Jesus' own brothers appear in his ministry even as his
mother, Mary, is found in the company of his followers.[191]

When Jesus called his disciples there were family
connections as Andrew drew his brother Peter[192] and the sons of
Zebedee, James and John followed Christ together.[193] In the
broader circle of followers, we see other family connections such
as the Bethany siblings, Mary, Martha and Lazarus.[194]

After Christ's resurrection and ascension, the gospel expansion continued to move through a natural web of family relationships. Peter preached to and baptized Cornelius and his household.[195] Paul did the same for the Philippian jailer,[196] and when
he met Lydia, the Thyatiran dealer in purple, she "and the
members of her household were (all) baptized."[197]

From Jesus to the early church to contemporary Church
Planting Movements, the gospel continues to flow through the
channels of family households and relationships.

Divine Power in Evangelism and Ministry

As with today's Church Planting Movements, New Testament gospel proclamation went hand-in-hand with divine

---

[190] Luke 7:20-29

[191] Matthew 13:55; Luke 8:20

[192] Matthew 4:18

[193] Matthew 4:21-22

[194] John 12:1-10

[195] Acts 10:24 & 48

[196] Acts 16:31

[197] Acts 16:15

demonstrations of God's power through healings, exorcisms, and miraculous signs. Jesus commanded the 72 to "preach this message: 'The kingdom of heaven is near.' Heal the sick, raise the dead, cleanse those who have leprosy, drive out demons."[198] And they returned with reports of the miraculous things God had done through them.[199]

As was his custom, Jesus first practiced all of these things before he commanded his disciples to do them. The Gospels use the word "healed" 39 times, and each occurrence is associated with the work of Jesus. The post-resurrection church carried on the same practice. They healed the sick, cast out demons, and even raised the dead as they proclaimed the Good News of God's salvation.

These practices which have become alien to so many of our contemporary Christian churches, were a central part of the ministry of Jesus and the expansion of the New Testament Church. And they are well represented in today's Church Planting Movements.

Person of Peace

Several of the Church Planting Movements we've examined attest to the missionary method of sending church planters into villages in search of God's "person of peace," that individual already chosen by God to receive the gospel message. Their motivation is to adhere to the model established by Jesus. When Jesus first dispatched his disciples as missionaries, he sent them out two-by-two and commanded them to enter every village in search of the "man of peace" who would welcome them and their message.[200]

---

[198] Matthew 10:7-8

[199] Luke 10:17

[200] Matthew 10:1-16; Luke 10:1-7

Jesus foreshadowed this approach in his redemptive dialogue with the Samaritan woman, a dialogue which prompted him to stay in the town for two days and gather a harvest of "many more believers."[201]

Later, Jesus seems to have taken the same path in relation to Mary, Martha and Lazarus: "As Jesus and his disciples were on their way, he came to a village where a woman named Martha opened her home to him."[202] The invitation led to a life changing relationship for Martha and her family.

Was this an isolated methodology that Jesus employed or did he intend for it to be a method for the early church to imitate? The two-by-two model of missionary deployment seems to have inspired Paul to always travel with a companion, whether it was Barnabas or Silas or Luke or Titus, whenever he ventured forth on a missionary journey. Though we cannot know about every missionary's practice, it does characterize Paul's pattern.

But did Paul also follow Christ's instructions to look for a "man of peace?" In Acts 16, Paul tells of a vision in which a Macedonian man calls for him to come and share the gospel. When Paul arrives in Macedonia, he discovers that God's man of peace is actually a woman named Lydia.[203]

Peter evidenced the same mindset when he followed God's leading to Cornelius, a Gentile man of peace, living in the coastal town of Caesarea. As with Lydia, Cornelius had already been chosen by God to welcome the Good News that the apostle was bringing.[204]

---

[201] John 4:1-42

[202] Luke 10:38

[203] Acts 16: 9-14

[204] Acts 10:1-31

Finding God's receptive person of peace was more than a pragmatic way of avoiding persecution; it was a demonstration of obedience to the teachings and patterns modeled by Jesus. This same motivation of obedience has reintroduced the quest for the man of peace in today's Church Planting Movements.

A House Church Movement

Today's Church Planting Movements grow large by focusing on small groups meeting in homes. The earliest model for this is the intimate circle of Jesus and his twelve disciples. Though Jesus did teach and perform miracles in large settings, he seemed to reserve his most precious teachings for the quiet time alone with his inner circle. Jesus appears to have had no home of his own, but he was comfortable teaching, evangelizing, healing, and discipling in the homes of others wherever he was invited. Whether it was the wedding feast of Cana,[205] the Capernaum home where he healed the paralytic,[206] the home of Zaccheus, or that of Mary, Martha, and Lazarus,[207] Jesus brought Christianity into the home.

The persecution of the early church prevented the believers from creating large sanctuaries or cathedrals. Meeting in homes instilled intimacy and reinforced small group accountability within the Church. The New Testament is filled with references to churches meeting in homes: Acts 5:42 (...from house to house....); Acts 8:3 (Saul began to destroy the Church. Going from house to house....); Acts 12:12 (...the house of Mary... where many people had gathered....); Romans 16:5 (Greet also the church that meets at their house); 1 Corinthians 16:19 (...the church that meets at their house); Colossians 4:15 (...the church

---

[205] John 2

[206] Mark 2

[207] Luke 10:38-42

in her house.); Philemon 2 (...the church that meets in your home.).

By the time the church grew strong enough to build its own cathedrals and basilicas, perhaps as late as the third or fourth century, it was also employing professional clergy. When the church left the home it left something vital behind: intimate contact with every facet of daily life. Today's Church Planting Movements are reintroducing this lost dimension by bringing the church back home.

Rapid Conversion

Rapid response and large-scale conversions have characterized each of the Church Planting Movements we've observed. Is this biblical? Once again the trail leads to Jesus who called forth disciples who "at once left their nets and followed him."[208]

Whether it was a blind man healed or a tax collector convicted, Jesus called for sinners to repent and expected an immediate response. This emboldened the apostles to take the same approach. They called for repentance and thousands responded.

Donald McGavran has highlighted the rapid response that characterized the people group movements of the New Testament Church:

It started with a large group—about a hundred and twenty adults not counting their children and dependents. Pentecost swept in about three thousand more. Within a short time the number of men Christians had risen to five thousand. After that, it is recorded that, 'More than ever believers were added to the Lord, multitudes of both men and women.' (Acts 5:14) A chapter later we read that 'the

---

[208] Matthew 4:20-21

number of the disciples multiplied greatly in Jerusalem and a great many of the priests (Levites) were obedient to the faith.'[209]

Today's Western Christians who have seen only individual commitments to Christ may have trouble understanding this spontaneous and sweeping response to the gospel, but it was common in the New Testament world. And it is common in today's Church Planting Movements.

Multiple Lay Leaders

Church Planting Movements are led by laypersons. Jesus pioneered this lay movement when he bypassed the Pharisees and Sadducees to call common men, fishermen, tax collectors, and political rebels. Out of this rabble he forged a community of disciples that changed the world.

This pattern of lay leadership continued in the years following Christ's resurrection. This effectiveness by laypersons astounded the Jewish Sanhedrin. "When they saw the courage of Peter and John and realized that they were *unschooled, ordinary men,* they were astonished and they took note that these men had been with Jesus."[210]

In the early Church, *being with Jesus* was always more important than academic credentials. In choosing a replacement for Judas Iscariot, the only requirement stated was that the candidate must have been with Jesus from his baptism to his ascension.[211] Paul, who might have had reason to boast in his training and credentials, treated them as worthless in contrast to

[209] Donald McGavran, *The Bridges of God* (New York: Friendship Press, 1955), pp. 18-19.

[210] Acts 4:13

[211] Acts 1:21-22

simply knowing Christ.[212] In his first letter to the Corinthians, he urged his readers to take this same attitude: "Brothers, think of what you were when you were called. Not many of you were wise by human standards; not many were influential; not many were of noble birth."[213]

Rather than seeing this "lack of nobility" as an impediment to serving the Lord, Paul saw it as an opportunity for God to reveal his power. "But God chose the foolish things of the world to shame the wise; God chose the weak things of the world to shame the strong.... so that no-one may boast before him."[214]

In Church Planting Movements, the laity not only lead the churches, they share responsibility widely with other lay members. In the New Testament, Paul describes this same phenomenon in his language of the "body of Christ." In his letter to the Ephesians Paul catalogued this broad lay leadership: "He... gave some to be apostles, some to be prophets, some to be evangelists, and some to be pastors and teachers, to prepare God's people for works of service, so that the body of Christ may be built up."[215]

Paul's first letter to the Corinthians describes a church bustling with a diverse and energized membership:

> To one there is given through the Spirit the message of wisdom, to another the message of knowledge by means of the same Spirit, to another faith by the same Spirit, to another gifts of healing by that one Spirit, to another miraculous powers, to another prophecy, to another distinguishing between spirits, to another speaking in

---

[212] Philippians 3:8-11

[213] 1 Corinthians 1:26

[214] 1 Corinthians 1:27, 29

[215] Ephesians 4:11-12

different kinds of tongues, and to still another the interpretation of tongues.[216]

The New Testament has a place for church office roles such as deacons, bishops, elders, and pastors, but also includes dynamic functions for apostles, evangelists, and prophets. In the New Testament church there was a place for all types of involvement. Paul had to exhort the churches to provide funds for the church leaders with the Old Testament admonition: "Do not muzzle an ox," and "the worker deserves his wages."[217] But he himself preferred to labor as a tentmaker to support his ministry and followed a Lord who was suspicious of "the hired hand"[218] and he himself had "nowhere to lay his head."[219]

All too soon the church abandoned its lay-powered engine and turned to a professional clergy to guide it. History has judged that these professionals guided the church into the Dark Ages. In modern Church Planting Movements the power of the unleashed laity is rediscovered, and with it New Testament church life is rekindled.

But Were They Church Planting Movements?

The world of the first century had much in common with the 21st. First century *Pax Romana* parallels 21st century *Pax Americana*, even as the famous Roman roads mirror our own Internet highways—both ideally suited for transmitting trade, ideas, and gospel.

The first century was keenly aware of people groups and a wide assortment of competing religions and cultures. It would be

---

[216] 1 Corinthians 12:8-10

[217] 1 Corinthians 9:9 and 1 Timothy 5:18

[218] John 10:12

[219] Matthew 8:20

difficult to find a modern heresy or philosophical persuasion that wasn't already being circulated in the first century. Each of these competing faiths persecuted converts from their ranks who joined the newly emerging body of Christ.

The cold war that has so shaped modern civilization had its parallel in the stalemate between the Roman and Persian empires of the first century. Just as Christianity has spread throughout both the Soviet and Western worlds, so too did it penetrate those first century giants.

So it is not surprising that contemporary Church Planting Movement practitioners find all that they need for their guidance in the New Testament. To those who are propagating the gospel and multiplying communities of faith in the midst of persecution, the New Testament reads like an indispensable road map.

But was the New Testament a running record of a first century Church Planting Movement? More likely, the pages of the New Testament reveal multiple Church Planting Movements sweeping across the known world. In an early letter to the Thessalonians Paul rejoices that "the Lord's message rang out from you not only in Macedonia and Achaia—your faith in God has become known everywhere."[220]

In the final years of his ministry Paul could say,

> From Jerusalem all the way round to Illyricum (modern day Albania), I have fully proclaimed the gospel of Christ. It has always been my ambition to preach the gospel where Christ was not known, so that I would not be building on someone else's foundation. Rather, as it is written: 'Those who were not told about him will see, and those who have not heard will understand.' This is why I have often been hindered from coming to you. But now that there is no more place for me to work in these regions, and since I

---

[220] 1 Thessalonians 1:8

have been longing for many years to see you, I plan to do so when I go to Spain.[221]

Why was Paul off to Spain? Because first century Church Planting Movements had already established the gospel throughout the eastern half of the Mediterranean world with hundreds of indigenous reproducing churches in their wake.

Yes, it is true that the term *Church Planting Movement* doesn't appear in the Bible. But having reviewed the biblical evidence, it is clear that rivers of Church Planting Movements flow through the New Testament and these rivers issue from the very life and ministry of Christ. Once you recognize this it is difficult to ever see your own church life in the same way again.

Today's Evangelicals want to believe that their church is patterned after a New Testament model. Certainly there is some truth to this aspiration. However, there are so many discrepancies between the world of modern Western Evangelicalism and that of the New Testament.

Today, the church of the New Testament world is only vaguely familiar to us. We look at it as we might stare at a photograph taken of us in our childhood. The resemblance is there, but so much has changed. When we visit Church Planting Movements, though, we are reminded of what the church was like in its youth—vulnerable, passionate, faithful, and explosive. For hundreds of thousands who are experiencing Church Planting Movements around the world today, it is the first century once again.

---

[221] Romans 15:19-24

13

In *Most* Church Planting Movements

NOW THAT WE'VE sifted through the biblical record regarding Church Planting Movements let's return to the characteristics that describe Church Planting Movements and their environment. We've already identified 10 elements that appear to be universal to every Church Planting Movement. What other factors contribute to these movements?

This question surfaced from our panel of practitioners as we found our whiteboards graffitied with several factors that were present in *most*, though not all, Church Planting Movements. We could not honestly call these universal elements, but to leave them out of our descriptive profile would greatly diminish our understanding of how God was at work in these movements.

The missionary church planter has influence over some of these factors, but others are beyond his control. Let's take a look at the 10 factors frequently involved in Church Planting Movements.

In *Most* Church Planting Movements

1. **A Climate of Uncertainty in Society**

2. **Insulation from Outsiders**

3. **A High Cost for Following Christ**

4. **Bold Fearless Faith**

5. **Family-Based Conversion Patterns**

---

6. **Rapid Incorporation of New Believers**

7. **Worship in the Heart Language**

8. **Divine Signs and Wonders**

9. **On-the-Job Leadership Training**

10. **Missionaries Suffered**

Let's examine each of these factors more closely.

1. Climate of Uncertainty in Society

Whether it's the waning days of Communism, the aftermath of a dictator's passing, or the unsettling chaos of an ancient tradition modernizing, Church Planting Movements seem to flourish in a state of societal transition, turmoil, or uncertainty. Cambodia's CPM followed the Khmer Rouge reign of terror. In Central Asia it was the collapse of Soviet Communism. In Latin America it was the realization that the old socialist ideology was no longer holding up against global market forces.

Sometimes the climate of social unrest is a longstanding condition. Such is the case with the grinding poverty of India's Bihar state where societal chaos has been the norm for decades. For centuries, Europe's Gypsies lived as social pariahs until God welcomed them into his own family through a Church Planting Movement.

For peoples like the Maasai of East Africa, the threat of modernity itself creates uneasiness and a quest for something permanent and true. Modernity has yet to encroach on many peoples in the interiors of Africa, Asia, and Latin America, but as it does it will topple old value systems and create openness to a more meaningful solution.

There are more than 14,000,000 refugees in the world today and an even larger number of internally displaced peoples fleeing oppression and economic hardship. As we've already seen in the refugee settlement camps of Holland, these displaced peoples are looking for a new reference point for their lives. In Christ they may find what they're seeking.

Unfortunately, the opposite is also true. Great social stability tends to lull people into a false sense of security. They forget that life is short and that one must prepare for eternity. This creates an obstacle for affluent Western Europe, Japan, and the United States where unparalleled economic health has fostered unparalleled spiritual malaise.

However, if social unrest is a precursor to a Church Planting Movement, the world of the 21st century offers many candidates—Africa, Asia, Eastern Europe, Latin America, and the Middle East—all quaking with uncertainty, reeling with change, and ripe for Church Planting Movements.

2. Insulation from Outsiders

Each of the panelists wanted to avoid this. After all, they too were outsiders. But we kept running into the factor again and again. Reviewing the list of Church Planting Movements unfolding around the world, the evidence mounted that most of them were insulated from contact with the outside world.

Finally someone asked, "Is it true that Church Planting Movements only occur in places that are difficult for Americans to reach?"

Cambodia, Mongolia, China, Maasai-land, Central Asia, Bihar, and Orissa States in India—these are all places that are insulated from outsiders.

Is this insulation coincidental or instrumental in the unfolding of Church Planting Movements? Perhaps it's a little of both. By definition Church Planting Movements are going to happen in places where lost people are coming to Christ. Since the world's greatest concentrations of lostness are, almost by definition, insulated from the world's greatest concentrations of Christians, we shouldn't be surprised that most of the world's Church Planting Movements are occurring in isolated locations.

An exception might appear to be the Gypsies of western Europe whose CPM has blossomed in several unfettered countries of Europe. However, even among the Gypsies, outsiders have not paid undue attention to the movement. On the contrary, most of the missionaries working in western Europe have avoided Gypsy ministry in favor of work among the majority population in their country.

Most Church Planting Movements do occur in insulated locations and there does appear to be a causal relationship. Easy access to evangelical resources can quickly lead to a dependency on the outsiders who offer them. When this happens the attention of the local church leaders turns from the lost in their own country and the resources within the harvest to the resource pool offered by foreigners.

This is not to deride the vital role that outsiders can and must play in the life of a Church Planting Movement. After all, the gospel has to come from somewhere. Every CPM can be traced back to some outsider who penetrated the difficult barriers surrounding unreached people group to introduce to them the gospel.

3. A High Cost for Following Christ

In most Church Planting Movements there is a tremendous price to pay to be a Christian. This trail of blood links today's martyrs with those of the early church who, like their suffering Savior, were obedient even to the death.

Persecution refines the church, guaranteeing the legitimacy of its life and witness. Persecution also filters out casual believers. In Church Planting Movements this happens every day.

In a coffee shop in North Africa, two Algerian men were lost in conversation. One of them, named Mohammed, has made his choice. He wears a cross and has a New Testament in his pocket. His friend, Ismail is still undecided. He's been reading the New

Testament, believes in Jesus, but is unwilling to break with his Muslim beliefs.

Suddenly three plain clothes policemen burst through the door, grab the two men and place them in the back of an unmarked police van. For the next three days, Ismail and Mohammed were detained by the Ministry of Internal Security.

Four days later, Ismail surfaced again and reported what happened. "Mohammed and I were separated. I was alone in a room with two men from the Ministry of the Interior.

'So you are a Christian?' they asked.

I told them that I was a Muslim like them.

'Then why do you carry a New Testament?'

I remained silent.

'Tell us. Who is right? Mohammed or Jesus?'

I hesitated and then said, *'They are both right...'*

Then one of them struck me on the face, knocking me to the floor. *'No,'* he said, *'Both cannot be right. One of them is right and one is wrong. Which do you believe?'*

Ismail said, *'I looked up at him and knew the answer,'*

'Jesus.' I said. *'Jesus is right.'"*

A few days later, Ismail was released, but his friend Mohammed was never seen again.

What happened to Ismail in 1996 happens in Church Planting Movements every day. Believers have lost jobs, families, been imprisoned, even murdered. But they stay true to their commitment even unto death. While persecution knocks some seekers from uncertainty to faith, for others like Ismail's friend Mohammed, the persecution claims their very lives.

4. Bold Fearless Faith

Most Western Christians will never know the terror that surrounds believers who live in persecution environments. Under Islamic law, a Muslim who converts from Islam merits the death penalty. The majority of Muslim countries today have signed the United Nation's *Declaration of Human Rights* guaranteeing freedom of conscience and freedom to convert, but this means little in a Muslim village.

An Egyptian friend who had converted from Islam explained it this way. "Under Islamic law," he said, "my blood is not forbidden."

He could see by my puzzled expression that I didn't understand so he continued, "Islam forbids the shedding of blood, but not the blood of an apostate."

For secret believers living in hostile environments, fear can take on an almost tangible quality. It grows beyond reason and stifles the Christian's ability to share his faith or even proclaim publicly his allegiance to Christ. If fear succeeds, a Church Planting Movement fails. However, when new believers choose bold witness in the face of persecution, they create an atmosphere that sustains a Church Planting Movement.

Visiting the emerging Maasai Church Planting Movement in 1999, I was asked to speak to a gathering of Maasai Christians who had come for a week of church planter training in the bush training school.

"The Maasai have never experienced persecution," the missionary said. "They've always been the persecutors rather than the ones being persecuted. But if they are going to follow Christ, they need to be ready to face persecution. Could you share with them some of what the Christians face in the Muslim world?"

I was glad to help, but a little intimidated by these silent, muscled warriors who had leaned their spears against the only door as they entered and now sat in rows between that same door and me. With feigned calmness, I stood before them and for the next hour told them of Muslim friends who had given their lives to Christ, and consequently lost their jobs, their families, even their personal security. I told them how each of these believers had emerged from their torment more committed to Christ than ever because he had given his life for them and was now living in their hearts.

After I finished, I sat down and waited for the next teacher to begin.

Before the next speaker could start, the Maasai began murmuring among themselves. Then one of them, visibly agitated, stood up, and then another. I nervously asked the missionary what was happening.

He told me, "They are calling for an invitation. Anyone who is willing to follow Jesus and be persecuted is invited to come forward." Within a few minutes, four Maasai men who had not yet decided about Jesus came forward to say, "If this is what it means to be a Christian, we will stand with Jesus."

With a reputation for being one of the most fearless people on earth, the Maasai are at the top of the food chain. But their boldness places them squarely in the company of new believers in Church Planting Movements everywhere.

5. Family-Based Conversion Patterns

The extent to which conversions follow family lines may vary from culture to culture, but in most Church Planting Movements the gospel flows through webs of family relationships. This pattern is as important as it is difficult for Western Christians to grasp. In the West, we have a strong tradition of individualism. Life changing decisions such as marriage, education choices and profession are all regarded as personal decisions. In fact, if a parent or other family member tries to influence the decision too strongly, the family member is seen as unreasonable and overbearing.

The rest of the world doesn't work that way. Those who are willing to make decisions without considering their community's counsel are generally individuals who are already on the edges of society and looking to escape. Too often individualistic Western missionaries have gravitated toward these marginal individuals and succeeded in leading them to Christ only to find that the gospel never moves beyond them to the broader community.

Historically, this tendency has led to the exodus of scores of marginalized Christian converts fleeing their society for a new life in the West. Missionaries today have become more deliberate about trying to avoid this sort of extraction of converts but continue to search for ways to penetrate the cultural center of the people group rather than plant a church of marginalized persons on the fringes.

In Church Planting Movements, new believers seize the initiative, taking the gospel to their family first, even in the face of severe persecution. One sees this among Muslim background believers in West Africa, among the evangelical Gypsies of Spain, and throughout Latin America, Asia, and Africa. Meeting in homes has greatly accelerated this family-based conversion pattern often leading to an entire clan's conversion to the faith.

In Pakistan, a missionary named Mark told the story of an extended family from Afghanistan who had come to faith in Christ all on the same day. Several Christians had befriended the clan, each one faithfully witnessing to each member of the family. The Christians made it a point to always share something God had taught them from the Bible that day. Over time, it was a natural occurrence to give a copy of the Bible to each member of the family.

One morning, Ali, the father of the Afghan family came to the missionary with great joy. "Mr. Mark, Mr. Mark, last night I had a dream."

Mark replied, "Tell me about your dream, Ali."

Ali said, "Last night before I went to sleep I put the Bible you gave me under my pillow. During the night a 'Being of Light' came into my room. He took the Bible from under my pillow and placed it on top of the pillow."

Ali could barely contain his excitement. "Don't you see what this means?" he asked.

Mark wisely responded, "Ali, why don't you tell me what it means."

Ali replied, "It is so clear. God is saying that I must not believe only a part of the Bible, I must believe all of it."

God had certainly spoken to Ali, but he was not yet ready to make a conversion to Christianity. Mark could have forced the issue and pressed Ali for a decision, but instead he affirmed Ali's vision and encouraged him to share the news with his father.

They both knew that Ali's father, the patriarch of the clan, was still living at home and was a force to reckon with in family decision making. Ali went home and told his father the story of his dream. That night Ali's father took his own Bible and placed it under his pillow. The next morning, the old patriarch reported the same revelation.

Within a week the entire clan, all 13 of them, had given their lives to Christ.

Missionaries in Church Planting Movements turn evangelistic encounters into family harvest times, resisting the temptation to extract converts one-by-one. They learn to let the natural love and respect that family members have for one another draw their entire clan to faith in Jesus Christ.

6. Immediate Enlistment of New Believers

In most Church Planting Movements, new converts are quickly incorporated into the life and work of the church. They are not only welcomed they are put to work!

In China, for example, church planters deliberately channel new believers into *new* churches rather than assimilate them into older fellowships. This integration forces them to take an active role in the church's life, and they are often up to the challenge.

In India, an elderly Bhojpuri man planted 42 churches in his first year as a believer; no one told him that he needed to mature in faith first!

In more traditional situations, churches are cautious about assimilating new believers until they have proven themselves.

Converts are put on a pew while they demonstrate their conversion through years of faithful church attendance. If the convert grows disinterested over time, the faithful conclude that his conversion was not genuine, when, in fact, he may have simply grown bored. This pattern has led to a staggering attrition rate for evangelical churches around the world. The passion and zeal of the new convert is slowly absorbed into the church pews until an anemic, nominal Christian finally drifts away. Lost people are finding the message of the gospel powerful both in its appeal and its ability to change their lives, but they find the life on the pews to be less satisfying.

In recent years, evangelical churches have improved discipleship training in an effort to conserve new converts. Some of these efforts have proven effective, but often they concentrate on indoctrination that results in better-educated Christians, but not necessarily better-assimilated Christians.

In Church Planting Movements prospective converts often begin serving Christ even before they become his follower. A Southeast Asia missionary began meeting regularly with a group of Vietnamese physicians. Though the physicians were not yet Christian, they met weekly for prayer, Bible study, and sharing a vision of what they perceived to be God's desire for them and their people.

After a few months, one of the doctors said, "I am not yet a Christian. But when I do become a Christian, I think I want to be the kind of Christian who brings a Church Planting Movement to my people both in this country and across the border."

The vision of this pre-Christian physician was surprising to everyone except the missionary.

"This is how it works with Church Planting Movements," he explained. "You begin practicing the end from the beginning."

In most Church Planting Movements, baptism is not delayed nor followed with lengthy probationary periods. Instead, new Christians immediately begin evangelizing others sharing the

discipleship teaching they themselves are receiving, and participating in new house church formation.

The movement focuses outward aimed at starting new works
and drawing in new believers rather looking than backward to the
past. This bias toward new church starts over against enlarging
older works is in sharp contrast with conventional practice where
it is often assumed that the church should not risk much on new
believers.

7. Worship in the Heart Language

Worship in the heart language allows the gospel to flow freely
through a people group. There are Church Planting Movements
that have erupted among people groups who do not yet have the
Bible translated into their heart language, but even then their
worship, songs and prayers are expressed in their heart language.

In a church service near the Caspian Sea, I listened to
haunting choruses of Azeri praises ascending to God. Stepping
into a dark and crowded room in Addis Ababa, I joined a wave of
Ethiopian believers as they closed their eyes and lifted holy
hands and Amharic songs of praise. In a crowded training center
in Uttar Pradesh, India, I was swept up with hundreds of Dalit
believers pouring out their hearts to God. I've joined Maasai
believers laughing joyfully as they sang and danced the great
stories of the Bible. In each place, the rhythm and flow of the
worship was local, natural, and powerful.

A missionary colleague returned from a visit to Myanmar
where he met a group of Buddhist monks who had just come to
faith in Christ. They had never heard Christian hymns, but they
couldn't help singing psalms and prayers to God.

"If you could call it singing," the missionary said. "They
sounded like Buddhist chants, but the words were all praises to
God."

Missionaries who take the time to adapt the gospel to the
heart language of the people are aligning themselves with the

way that God is at work. However, acquiring the heart language of unreached people groups is rarely easy.

Most of the world's least reached people groups are unreached today because their languages can't be learned at a local community college. Often the languages are unwritten and hidden behind other difficult trade languages. In some cases, the languages of the unreached people group have even been outlawed as subversive like that of the Turkish Kurds or the Kabyle Berbers of Algeria. For many years, the possession of literature in these languages could result in imprisonment or deportation.

Despite knowing the advantage of learning the heart language, some missionaries succumb to the temptation to provide the gospel in a trade language. Language learning is difficult and time consuming. So these missionaries stop after learning trade languages such as Hindi, Swahili, French, Russian, Chinese, or Arabic rather than penetrating to a deeper level to provide the gospel in one of hundreds of heart languages.

The difficulty of learning the languages of the world's least reached peoples makes receiving the gospel in their heart language all the more precious. A village woman in Southeast Asia watched the *Jesus Film* in her native tongue. "Who is this Jesus," she asked, "who knows and speaks my language?"

Among the Kabyle Berbers of North Africa, their own language has been suppressed for decades—first by the Arabs and then by the French. Today, they can hear the gospel radio broadcasts, read the Bible, and view the *Jesus Film* all in their Kabyli language. Small wonder that these historically Muslim people are now turning to Christ.

8. Divine Signs and Wonders

Church Planting Movements are born and nurtured in an atmosphere of God's mighty acts. For some, the power comes through healing. A friend recently returned from Bihar, India.

"I interviewed about 50 believers," he said, "Everyone of them knew Jesus as healer before they knew him as Savior."

For some, it is God's divine protection. A believer in a country torn by civil war observed, "In my country, Muslim fundamentalists and the government are killing each other in a war that has cost 100,000 lives. To this day, God has spared his Church; not one believer has died in the violence."

Missionaries who are unaccustomed to signs and wonders have become converts to the notion of God's direct intervention into the affairs of men. An American missionary who graduated top of his university class in America entered a new world when he immersed himself in China. After a few years there he confessed, "All of the Church Planting Movements I've seen in China are full of healings, miracles, and even resurrections."

Another Baptist missionary, who was serving in India, almost apologetically told of a resurrection from the dead that occurred among his people group.

In Bihar, India, the death of a young girl in the village coincided with the visit of an evangelist. As was the custom, the child was sown into a sarcophagus bag in preparation for a funeral pyre. RSS activists (an Indian nationalist vigilante group) used the opportunity to blame the itinerant preacher. Grief-stricken villagers were torn between the appeal of the gospel message and their bondage to the old ways. As a gang of thugs seized the evangelist and began to abuse him, the little girl in the sarcophagus bag suddenly sat up. Her family hastily freed her from the bag. And the evangelist was released.

Another church planter learned to expect the miraculous. "When we enter a village," he explained, "we look for God's man of peace who will be the leader of the new church. Then we do as Jesus commanded in Luke 10. We proclaim to him the Good News of the kingdom, and we pray for the healing of his family and anyone else who needs it. God doesn't always heal them but he does reveal himself to them. Our job is simply to obey his command to proclaim and pray."

9. On-the-Job Leadership Training

Leadership training is vital to Church Planting Movements. With new churches being produced so rapidly, there is a never-ending demand for the training of new leaders. For that reason alone, it is not surprising that Church Planting Movements have featured various types of practical, continual on-the-job training.

In Cambodia, training was conducted in two-week modules through the Rural Leadership Training Schools. The schools themselves were mobile, could be set-up close to the greatest area of need and then dismantled again until a new two-week session was organized. In the Latin American Church Planting Movement we saw that Lay Missionary Schools fueled the Church Planting Movement.

In the Gypsy Church Planting Movement, leaders developed within the church as experienced pastors mentored apprentices who sensed God's calling to be preachers. Across parts of China, leadership development followed several decentralized programs that complemented and sometimes took the place of training offered by the few seminaries in the country. In one Chinese Church Planting Movement, the house church pastors staggered the time of their worship services in order to attend other house churches to observe different methods of church leadership.

One of the more ingenious and effective leadership training methods is the **cascading model**. Widely used in India, this model allows training to multiply out without reliance on formal institutions by using cascading tiers of mentors who convey biblical training from level to level.

An Indian colleague explained it this way, "I relate directly to only 24 men, whom I call 'Master Trainers.' Each of these Master Trainers mentors 10-12 trainers. Each trainer mentors 10 pastors, while each pastor has at least 10 adult church members. What I teach the master trainers is cascaded out within two weeks to every church member."

I quickly did the math and saw that he was regularly training 36,000 people.

"How effective is it?" I asked.

"We'll know next week," he replied.

"And why is that?"

"Because next week I'm bringing in the second tier of trainers to see how effectively the message is reaching them."

For him, the quality inspection was as important as the cascading training model.

The cascading model has many benefits.

a. Allows for exponential multiplication of training that is able to keep pace with exponential church multiplication.

b. Can be transmitted with or without written materials, which makes it accessible to nonliterate as well as literate trainees.

c. Is interpersonal and relational. Because it can take place in restaurants, public parks, or sidewalk coffee shops, it stays below the radar of government opposition.

d. Finally, the requirement to immediately pass on the teaching is reinforced in the mind and life of all those involved in the process.

10. Missionaries Suffered

As the Church Planting Movement panel discussed the various Church Planting Movements we had witnessed, one unavoidable factor surfaced again and again. So many of the missionary colleagues we had known, who were instrumental in these Church Planting Movements, were no longer serving as missionaries. Others have continued on the mission field, but only after enduring staggering calamities.

Over the past decade, missionaries or their families, who have been involved in these movements, have been touched by lupus, multiple myloma, leukemia, lung cancer, lymphoma, fatal

attacks of asthma, scleroderma, heart disease, diabetes, chronic
back problems, fibromyalgia and chronic fatigue syndrome,
children's birth defects, and nervous breakdowns.

Sometimes the assaults are so insidious that they can only be
attributed to the Evil One. A missionary family who served on
some of the toughest fields in the world had their ministry come
to an end when the father accidentally struck and killed his own
toddler with his automobile. Another missionary's ministry
ended when he was charged with misappropriation of funds
following a famine and relief effort. There was never any
question of personal enrichment, but the misdirection of funds
from one cause to another tarnished the missionary's reputation
and temporarily sidelined him.

In other instances missionaries involved in Church Planting
Movements had to leave the work due to illness of parents or the
needs of their children. There have been departures over issues
of interpersonal conflict and inability to handle a changing
assignment.

The nature of the missionary suffering has been as diverse as
human suffering can be. The only common link in this catalog of
suffering is that each missionary was related to a Church
Planting Movement. For many, though not all of these missionaries, the suffering removed them from their vital role in the
movement.

Knowing that suffering is so frequently a part of the Church
Planting Movement environment can help prepare us and arm us
against this threat. Here are a few of the things missionaries are
learning to do to keep themselves in the Lord's service:

1) Find an accountability partner with whom to share openly
   and honestly. A good accountability partner will tell what
   you need to hear and not just what you'd like to hear. For the
   sake of objectivity, the accountability partner should be
   someone other than one's spouse.

2) Commit to the spiritual disciplines of daily quiet time and regular church involvement. It's easy for those in the 'religion business' to become stale in their personal walk with the Lord.

3) Commit to the disciplines of regular physical exercise and proper diet. Missionaries have a habit of de-prioritizing their own physical needs until it is too late.

4) Set limits to the number of nights each month or year to be away from home. Commit to regular date nights with one's spouse. Work at marriage with a goal of making it better this year than it was last year.

5) Schedule time with one's children. Put their school holidays and family vacation time on the calendar before everything else. Bring them into your inner prayer circle. As they see the ministry through your eyes, they will catch the vision and become your greatest team members.

6) Develop a strong prayer network of support. Watch, fight, and pray!

7) Stay humble and grateful that God has allowed you the privilege of serving him. Missionaries who maintain a posture of humility and gratitude serve longer and live longer!

8) Remember there is an Enemy. The adversary is not flesh and blood, but principalities and powers—spiritual darkness in high places. So avoid seeing individuals—Christian or non-Christian—as enemies.

These principles are helping to protect missionaries from the Evil One who would seek to destroy them. In the final analysis, we shouldn't be surprised at the measure of suffering that accompanies the missionary task around the world. Suffering was in the DNA of our Savior and so naturally passes on to us his offspring. Linking us closely to him it also binds us to those new believers whose suffering often exceeds our own.

Several Scripture passages have taken on renewed meaning in the light of God's great saving work through Church Planting Movements and the plight of so many great missionary brothers and sisters who have been involved in these movements. One of these is found in the book of Revelation, which clearly describes our own time.

> Now have come the salvation and the power
> and the kingdom of our God and the authority of his Christ.
> For the accuser of our brothers,
> who accuses them before our God day and night,
> has been hurled down.
> They overcame him by the blood of the Lamb
> and by the word of their testimony;
> they did not love their lives so much as to shrink from death.
> Therefore rejoice, you heavens and you who dwell in them!
> But woe to the earth and the sea,
> because the devil has gone down to you!
> He is filled with fury,
> because he knows that his time is short.[222]

---

[222] Revelation 12:10-12

14

Seven Deadly Sins

T HE QUESTION "HOW do you start a Church Planting Movement?" may be the wrong question. A better one might be "What is preventing a Church Planting Movement from happening here?"

Over the past few years we've discovered more ways to obstruct a Church Planting Movement than we care to recall. But, we've also found a number of ways to overcome these barriers. When Jesus encountered a demon, he exposed it, calling it by name before casting it out. The first step in overcoming obstacles to Church Planting Movements is to name them, and then drag them into the light before casting them out.

We'll call these obstacles *"Seven Deadly Sins for Church Planting Movements."*

Seven Deadly Sins for
Church Planting Movements

The First Deadly Sin: Blurred Vision (*You can't hit what you can't see.*)

The Second Deadly Sin: Improving the Bible (*Think it can't be done? Just watch.*)

The Third Deadly Sin: Sequentialism (*Inch by inch, step by step.*)

The Fourth Deadly Sin: Unsavory Salt (*When the salt loses its savor.*)

The Fifth Deadly Sin: The Devil's Candy (*Shortcuts to glory.*)

The Sixth Deadly Sin: Alien Abduction (*Who's in charge here?*)

The Seventh Deadly Sin: Blaming God (*Divine dismissal is still dismissal!*)

The First Deadly Sin: Blurred Vision

"Where there is no vision, the people perish," goes the often-quoted Proverb, but another version of the same passage reads, "Where there is no revelation, the people cast off restraint."[223]

Church Planting Movements depend on the cooperative efforts of scores of passionate believers with different talents and temperaments who set aside their differences to achieve God's perfect plan for an unreached people group. The only thing that binds these diverse teams together and compels them to restrain their differences is a shared vision. Without a common vision, they will cast off restraint and the people they are trying to reach will perish.

Missionary leaders are learning that they must clearly state and restate the vision for a Church Planting Movement. They must revisit the vision whenever team members gather to discuss the work and review past progress or plan for the future. The vision and its fulfillment become the touchstone for evaluating all that the team does.

Sharpening our vision is exercising our *faith*. "Now faith is being sure of what we hope for and certain of what we do not see."[224] Vision casting allows us to see what is coming.

If we don't really believe that a Church Planting Movement is possible, we won't take the actions needed to usher it into existence. Church Planting Movement practitioners come to

---

[223] Proverbs 29:18 in the King James Version first, followed by the New International Standard Version.

[224] Hebrews 11:1

believe, see, feel, and taste the movement well before it dawns into reality.

John Basham, a Strategy Coordinator trainer in England, devised a faith-building exercise that helps trainees to envision a Church Planting Movement among their own people group. Each morning trainees study the 28 chapters of the *Book of Acts* to see how Church Planting Movements unfolded in the first century. Then, at the close of their training, Basham directs the new Strategy Coordinators to write a 29th chapter of Acts that describes how a Church Planting Movement will reach their own people group.

This exercise connects Strategy Coordinators and their ministry to the New Testament roots from which every true Church Planting Movement emerges. The trainee is continuing God's redemptive work that has been unfolding for centuries. When a missionary can clearly envision a Church Planting Movement, he can align his team for its realization.

If you don't have a vision for a Church Planting Movement, you're not likely to achieve one. Vision is vitally important, because *you can't hit what you can't see.*

The Second Deadly Sin: Improving the Bible

Improve the Bible? Think it can't be done? Well, you're absolutely right. So why do we keep trying? Through the ages, God's people have tried to usurp his authority by expanding on his directions. Jesus condemned this in the Pharisees when he said, "You travel over land and sea to win a single convert and when he becomes one, you make him twice as much a son of hell as you are."[225]

Whenever we try to exceed the Bible's own requirements for Christian life, we mimic the Pharisees. There are many ways to yoke new believers with extrabiblical legalities, but two of them

---

[225] Matthew 23:16

are particularly deadly to Church Planting Movements. Satan knows that if he can distort God's teachings on the **church** and on **church leadership**, he can stop the flow of new believers into the Kingdom of God.

The Bible has clear guidelines for defining a church and its leadership. When we try to improve on these we don't create a better church we create a church that is less than what God intended. Church Planting Movements are often derailed by well intentioned, yet inflated, definitions for a church or overwhelming requirements for church leadership.

In the New Testament, Christ identified the church with himself. He foreshadowed this reality when he told his disciples, "Where two or three come together in my name, there am I with them."[226]   He confirmed it with Saul, the persecutor of the church when he said, "Saul, Saul, why do you persecute me?"[227] Paul took this lesson to heart, often referring to the church as the *body of Christ* while identifying church members as members of his body.[228]

In many older mission fields, church planters labor under the weight of years of tradition-built definitions of church and church leadership. This happens when well meaning Christians come to believe that they are not a church until they have been constituted by the national denomination, or have reached a certain congregation size, employed a seminary-trained pastor, secured church property, or constructed a building. All of these requirements exceed and encumber the biblical ideal.

When it came to church leadership, Jesus set the example by choosing disciples from all walks of life. He spent three years walking with them, and this became their license to lead. In

---

[226] Matthew 18:20

[227] Acts 9:4

[228] 1 Corinthians 12:13 and Ephesians 4

choosing a replacement for Judas Iscariot, the only requirement stated was that the candidate must have been with Jesus from his baptism to his ascension.[229] Paul helped us see that spending time with Christ results in godly character and that this same character is the greatest prerequisite for any church leader.[230]

To escape from the snare of this deadly sin, missionaries and church planters must get back to the Bible to define both church and church leadership. Ironically, some Christians claim that biblical literalism produces legalism, but nothing could be farther from the truth. A real return to the Bible liberates both the church and its leadership while overcoming the second deadly sin.

The Third Deadly Sin: Sequentialism

*Inch by inch, step by step...*this may be the way to make progress in normal human endeavors, but it is deadly to a Church Planting Movement. Sequentialism refers to thought and practice that adheres to linear, step-by-step processes.

Missionaries naturally think in sequential steps. First you learn the language, then you develop relationships with people, then you share a witness, then you win and disciple converts, then you draw them into a congregation, then you raise up leaders, then you start all over again. The sequence is perfectly logical but can take years to unfold. And like falling dominoes, the whole process comes to a halt if one plank doesn't fall.

In 1962, Christian science fiction writer Madeline L'Engle introduced millions of readers to the concept of wrinkling time. Her children's book by the same name poses the question: "What is the shortest distance between two points?"

---

[229] Acts 1:23-26

[230] 1 Timothy 3

Those mired in sequentialism will naturally respond, "A straight line."

L'Engle has a different perspective. "The shortest distance between two points is not a straight line. It's a wrinkle."[231]

Strategy Coordinators engaged in Church Planting Movements have learned to wrinkle time—combining multiple steps into a single model. They don't wait for the completion of step 1 before they are already tackling steps 2 through 20. They learn how to wrinkle these steps together and find them all unfolding in ways that mutually reinforce one another.

For example, they insist on witnessing from day one, even before the language is mastered (try it, it's a great way to improve your language skills). Learning the language from language helpers rather than in remote schools also gives the missionary a captive audience for sharing his deepest convictions about the *gospel* and new life in Christ.

By modeling house church with new believers, seekers, and others, missionaries wrinkle the time normally required for church planting. By the time house church participants have all become believers these new converts already understand how house churches function, and have even begun to catch a vision for reaching their entire community.

Some missionaries insist on taking the time to "lay a good foundation" with a small group, rather than sowing the gospel widely and expediting a Church Planting Movement. Time is not the precondition for a good foundation; sound doctrine and sound practice are. In fact, slow sowing and slow harvesting communicate to the hearer that the message isn't urgent so why bother responding to it?

When missionaries are yoked to sequentialism, they lose their sense of urgency. In the 16 chapters of Mark's Gospel the word "immediately" occurs 17 times, and is always used in relation to

[231] Madeline L'Engle, *A Wrinkle in Time* (New York: Bantam, 1976), 224 pp.

Jesus—either in his teachings or his actions. Mark's Gospel reveals something of the passion and urgency that Christ felt. When we draw deeply from his Spirit, we share this passion and urgency.

Paul knew this fervor as well. Just as Jesus had told his disciples, "As long as it is day, we must do the work of him who sent me. Night is coming, when no one can work,"[232] so Paul warned the Romans, "the hour has come for you to wake up from your slumber.... The night is nearly over; the day is almost here. So let us put aside the deeds of darkness and put on the armor of light."[233]

Though never lost in a frantic flurry of activity, both Jesus and Paul recognized that life on earth is defined by boundaries of birth and death and everything in between should be intensely purpose driven.

Missionaries are learning to incorporate this sense of urgency into their plans with ambitious three to five-year completion dates. They are asking, "What's it going to take to see a Church Planting Movement (this year or in the next three to five years)?" By building deadlines and target dates into their planning they keep a sense of urgency that is sensitive to the millions who will die each year without Christ. As they learn to wrinkle time, sequentialism disappears into the wrinkles.

The Fourth Deadly Sin: Unsavory Salt

Christianity that has compromised itself with sin is *unsavory salt*—a faith that has "lost its first love."[234] When missionaries try to launch a Church Planting Movement among a people group who already know Christians, and because of that know-

---

[232] John 9:4

[233] Romans 13:11-12

[234] Revelation 2:4

ledge, despise Christianity, the missionary faces a serious
challenge.

In William Dalrymple's travelogue of his journey on the Silk
Road from Jerusalem to Mongolia, he recorded a conversation
with a cultural Christian from Syria named Krikor. Krikor perceived Dalrymple to be a fellow Christian and so invited him to a
nightclub.

"My cousin has a nightclub. Nice place. Much drink, many
girls."

"I didn't realize there was a nightlife in Syria," said Dalrymple, "I thought Muslims disapproved of that sort of thing."

"They do. This nightclub is a Christian nightclub. No Muslims. Lots of fun."

Krikor took out a cassette from his bag, and told the driver to
put it on.

"Michael Jackson," he said. "Music for Christians."

He showed us the cross hanging around his neck and winked
conspiratorially.[235]

There are numerous sins of omission and commission that
can render Christianity impotent in the eyes of the lost. Whatever
the sin, when Christianity loses its savor, the missionary strategist faces an obstacle to a Church Planting Movement. Fortu-
nately, we've learned some effective strategies for overcoming
this obstacle.

Conventional wisdom holds that one should always work
through the local church to reach a neighboring people group.
Though logical and intuitively appropriate, this approach is often
not born out in reality. In too many instances the local church is
the major stumbling block that is preventing the unreached from
coming to Christ.

---

[235] William Dalrymple, *In Xanadu: A Quest* (London: Lonely Planet
Publications, 2000), pp. 54-55.

Despite this fact, some missionaries have spent their entire career trying to turn the local church in the direction of the lost. Others tied themselves so closely to the local church that they ended up sharing the church's unsavory characteristics.

Even in his own lifetime, the Apostle Paul saw the emergence of unsavory Christianity. He made it very clear how believers were to respond to those who had "a form of godliness (while) denying its power." He told Timothy to "have nothing to do with them."[236]

The best way to bring about change in a fallen expression of Christianity is by unleashing vibrant, living Christianity. Once authentic Christianity demonstrates Christlike virtues and begins drawing new converts into the fold, true Christians in the nominal churches will be attracted to the movement like moths to a flame. We have seen many instances of comatose Christianity awakened by the outbreak of a Church Planting Movement.

Different from comatose Christianity is another expression of unsavory Christianity—*contentious* Christianity. When there are several Christian denominations or mission agencies at work among a people group, they must not waste precious time and energy fighting against each other. Such distractions invariably war against a Church Planting Movement.

There will always be points of disagreement among the Lord's servants. Even the Apostles Peter and Paul were not immune to this problem.[237] If it persists, however, it becomes a distraction to a Church Planting Movement.

Jesus repeatedly confronted the barrier of contentious Christianity among his own followers, reminding them "By this will all

---

[236] 2 Timothy 3:5

[237] Galatians 2:11

men know that you are my disciples, if you have love for one another."[238]

In his parable of the wheat and the tares he addressed the problem directly. Recognizing that an enemy had sown tares among his wheat crop, the disciples asked if they could go and uproot the unwanted plants.

"No," the Master answered, "because while you are pulling the weeds, you may root up the wheat with them."[239]

Jesus recognized that we are not always capable of distinguishing all of those who are in his service, so he warned us to "let them both grow together until the harvest. At that time I will tell the harvesters: 'First collect the weeds and tie them in bundles to be burned; then gather the wheat and bring it into my barn.'"[240]

One of the best antidotes for contentious Christianity is a passionate and victorious ethos. Webster defines *ethos* as "the guiding beliefs, standards, or ideals that characterize or pervade a group, a community, a people...the spirit that motivates the ideas, customs, or practices of a people...."[241]

A team's ethos is like the air they breathe—healthy or unhealthy, a winning ethos or an ethos of failure. Sometimes a team of Christians cannot identify why they are unable to make progress toward their vision. Attitudes, methods of operation and ideals seem to be in perpetual conflict. There may be a need for an ethos transfusion.

Ethos is unavoidable. It can be a casual by-product of personality and circumstances, or it can be a chosen climate and work-

---

[238] John 13:35

[239] Matthew 13:29

[240] Matthew 13:30

[241] P.B. Gove, ed., *Webster's Third New International Dictionary, Unabridged* (Springfield, MA: Merriam-Webster, Inc., 1986), p. 781.

ing condition. Missionaries who know how to shape ethos have a great advantage in keeping the salt savory.

The Fifth Deadly Sin: The Devil's Candy

To a hungry child the sweet taste of candy is irresistible, but that sugary burst of energy is no substitute for the kind of good nutrition needed for long-term growth. In the same way there are *sweet* Christian virtues that Satan can use to seduce us away from a Church Planting Movement.

The Devil's Candy is deceptive, because it refers to good things that have real value, but if these good things keep us from our vision of churches planting churches, then they are a detour that we must avoid. Here are three examples of good Christian virtues that Satan has used to distract church planters from a Church Planting Movements:

1) Money – for pastors and church buildings
2) Ministry – as an end in itself
3) Unity – when it is a prerequisite to action

Money is not inherently evil, but neither is it foundational to a Church Planting Movement. When foreign church planters use funds to hire pastors and construct church buildings they may see quick results, but they will not see a sustainable movement. Building a movement on foreign funds is like running a machine with an extension cord that stretches across the ocean. When the movement reaches the end of the cords length, it will abruptly stop. A Church Planting Movement must have an internal engine and internal fuel if it is going to flourish.

Letting a movement grow with its own leadership and resources may seem slower and riskier,, but the risk is well worth the rewards. In his missiology classic, *The Spontaneous Expansion of the Church*, Roland Allen offered an instructive fable.

> It is said that when God announced to the angels his purpose to create man in his own image Lucifer, who was not yet fallen from heaven, cried: *'Surely he will not give them power to disobey him.'* And the Son answered him: *'Power to fall is power to rise.'* Lucifer knew neither power to rise, nor power to fall, but the word 'power to fall' sunk deep into his heart, and he began to desire to know that power....In the end, Satan achieved his greatest victories over man, not by pulling him down, but by *inducing the servants of Christ to deprive new converts of the power to fall...so that he might deprive them of the power to rise.*[242]

Whenever foreigners linger too long, refusing to turn over the reigns of church leadership, they are depriving the new church of the power to fall *and the power to rise.*

Another *good* thing that tempts church planters away from Church Planting Movement is the call of Christian ministry. Like Martha, who busied herself with many things, Christians can spend a lifetime pursuing ministries without ever making progress toward a Church Planting Movement.

The word "ministry" literally means "doing the little things." Ministry occurs naturally wherever Christians exists, but ministry is no substitute for planting multiplying churches. A missionary must never limit himself to his own personal ministry but must instead look beyond that ministry to see how it contributes to a Church Planting Movement.

In 1988, a bright young seminary graduate who had developed a passionate love for the peoples of Afghanistan emerged exhausted from years of leading summer mission teams to the refugee camps along Pakistan's border with Afghanistan.

Rather than continuing his annual refugee work, the young man decided to become a Strategy Coordinator. "I realized that the needs of these people are endless," he said. "When I go to

---

[242] Roland Allen, *The Spontaneous Expansion of the Church* (Grand Rapids, MI: Eerdmans, 1962), pp. 16-17.

work in the refugee camps, I pour myself into loving and caring for the people from early in the morning until late at night, but at the end of the summer I find that the needs just keep coming. I want to become a Strategy Coordinator," he explained, "so I can address the real reasons for the Afghans' suffering. These people need Jesus."

Part of the missionary vocation is working yourself out of a job. If missionaries satisfy themselves year in and year out with filling a ministry rather than mentoring, multiplying, and replacing themselves, they fall short of their vision and their missionary role.

To resist the temptation of ministry consumption, missionaries must continually ask the strategic question, "What's it going to take to see a Church Planting Movement among this people group?"

This question stands in sharp contrast to the personal question, "What can I do?" The personal question may lead to a vital ministry, but one that falls short of what is needed to stimulate a Church Planting Movement. Ultimately, the personal question is about *me*, but the strategic question is about *them*.

The strategic question, "What's it going to take?" invariably draws the missionary beyond himself to realize that a much larger resource pool is required to foster a Church Planting Movement.

Another good but distracting diversion from a Church Planting Movement is the yearning for Christian unity. The ecumenical impulse may appear in mission partnerships which demand evangelical unity before pursuing a Church Planting Movement. Or it may surface when mission partners insist on planting only one, unified national church that rises above the fractiousness of denominational expression.

Both of these ecumenical impulses have appealing aspects. After all, from Christ's prayer in John 17 to Paul's treatise in the

1 Corinthians 15, unity is lifted up as a virtue that cannot be ignored. Unity can also be a life-consuming pursuit.

With more than 25,000 Christian denominations in the world today and more being formed every year, we are unlikely to see the emergence of a unified Christian church in the near future, unless Christ returns. Instead, we might do well to see our diversity as a strength. By allowing tremendous freedom of perspective and diversity of emphasis within one Body, the church becomes unstoppable. Locking all of our diversity into a single spear point can actually make it easier for the opposition to stop it.

Missionaries pursuing Church Planting Movements have found a balance between diversity and unity in the image of a kaleidoscope. A kaleidoscope takes pieces of broken glass, colored paper, bits of metal and views them through a prism which reconfigures them into beautiful patterns that would otherwise be undetectable. Missionary efforts to reach a people group must be viewed through the kaleidoscope. From our limited vantage point the various ministries may appear to be conflicted and worthless, but from God's vantage point they coalesce into beautiful patterns of unity that can stimulate a Church Planting Movement.

The Sixth Deadly Sin: Alien Abduction

The origins of the gospel may be out of this world, but Church Planting Movements are at home in their environment. They don't have the smell of foreignness to them. Their leadership is local; they worship in the community's heart language; they meet in their own homes.

There are at least three ways that Church Planting Movements can succumb to alien abduction: 1) by forcing new believers to exchange their cultural forms for alien ones, 2) by creating a welfare state of foreign dependency, and 3) by injecting foreign elements into the life of the church that cannot be locally reproduced. Any one of these alien invaders can cripple a Church Planting Movement.

1) When the gospel is perceived to be alien to a culture or is viewed as belonging to another people group or culture, Church Planting Movements face an uphill battle.

For centuries Turkic Muslims in Central Asia have known Christianity as the religion of their enemies. Generations of conflict with neighboring Russians and Armenians both of whom have claimed some form of Orthodox Christianity have left them with little taste for the Christian faith.

In Central Asia, any Turks who wanted to accept the Christian religion had to embrace the culture and language of their historic enemies. Thus, becoming a believer in Christ was tantamount to high treason against their own people.

Today, tens of thousands of these Central Asian Turkic peoples have overcome this barrier and embraced Jesus Christ. How did it happen?

The missionary strategists who are seeing Church Planting Movements emerge across Central Asia have been very deliberate in their efforts to separate the gospel message from the Russian and Armenian cultures. They have consistently presented the gospel in the heart language of the people and helped plant Turkic churches led by Turkic leaders worshiping in their own language and cultural style.

2) When foreign funds tie the movement to outside sources, missionaries describe it as "help that hurts." When well meaning foreigners provide subsidies to pastors and construct local church buildings they sap local initiative. When disaster strikes, relief aid is quite appropriate, but if it continues for too long it creates dependency and eventually a state of puppets and welfare dependents. Church leaders learn to look to the donors rather than to the Lord and the lost for the direction of their ministry.

In Guatemala, Brazil, Honduras, Costa Rica, Romania, and the Ukraine Church Planting Movements were emerging, but instead stumbled over "help" from outsiders. A missionary in Latin America commented, "It's so hard to criticize these dear brothers, because their heart is in the right place, but their money and buildings are killing a Church Planting Movement."

3) When we inject foreign elements into the church that the local believers cannot reproduce for themselves we alienate a Church Planting Movement.

On a tour through Latin American with some Christian mission leaders, we came across a beautiful church building with tinted windows and large wooden doors. The grounds were swept clean, the cinderblock walls were recently whitewashed and the tiled roof was in fine form. We went inside to find a small electric organ, a piano, and wooden pews similar to those used in small town American churches.

The church had been built three decades earlier by American volunteers. The local church members admired the building and took great care in its upkeep. But they had never attempted to start any other churches, because they could not get any of these materials. Cinderblocks, ceramic tiles, tinted glass windows were all beyond their reach. They couldn't imagine how to reproduce a piano or electric organ. At the same time, they believed that a *real* church had to have these things, and so the movement died before it started.

Church Planting Movements take on the appearance of their context. If villages build homes out of bamboo, then church buildings are made of bamboo. If the people live in small apartments, the Church Planting Movement will occur in small apartments. Missionaries who are successful in seeing a Church Planting Movement have learned to begin each church plant with the question, "Can this church be reproduced by these believers?" If the answer is, "No," then the foreign elements are identified and discarded or replaced with reproducible elements.

The Seventh Deadly Sin: Blaming God

A number of Church Planting Movement practitioners have concluded that the single greatest barrier to Church Planting Movements is blaming God for their absence.

Certainly God is at the center of every Church Planting Movement, but there is also a place for human responsibility, a place that God reserves exclusively for us. When Christians complain, "I guess it's just not God's time for them," they are abrogating this human element and blaming God. This is a form of divine dismissal and is probably the most common excuse offered for not improving our own contributions to a Church Planting Movement. Divine dismissal is still dismissal. It just sounds holier.

The truth is Church Planting Movements are a lot like personal salvation. Of course God has done it all, paying the price through his Son's atonement, but he allows us the freedom to respond and requires us to take action in order to receive his saving gift. The same is true of Church Planting Movements; they are a divine-human cooperative. Yes, God is in charge, but he reserves many crucial roles for us. We have never seen a Church Planting Movements without human participation and cooperation.

There are two ways we see the sin of *blaming God* at work. The first occurs in the very human effort to do it all ourselves, as if following some prescribed formula must produce a Church Planting Movement. Then, when the movement doesn't follow, we become resentful, blaming God for the lack of results.

The other expression comes when we disregard the ways God has chosen to implement these movements. We go about our business and piously proclaim, "When God wants to create a movement, he will do so. It has nothing to do with me." Such a response conjures memories of a young Baptist layman in the 18th century who proposed missionary means to take the gospel to India. Staid church leaders rebuked him. "Sit down, young man!" they said, "If God wishes to save the heathen, he does not require your help."

These were the voices that opposed William Carey on the eve of his departure for India and the launching of the modern missionary movement. Whenever we ignore means and methods for stimulating Church Planting Movements, we are in the company of those who felt missionaries themselves were an unnecessary addition to God's sovereign intentions.

A wise friend said, "We should look to see where God is at work and join him."

In Hong Kong, venture capitalists who made a fortune investing in new business start-ups in China put it a little more crassly, "If it smokes," they say, "throw kerosene on it!"

The principle applies to Church Planting Movements as well. If God is drawing people to faith in Christ among a particular people group, find out what he is doing there and then discover how you can join him in this divine activity.

Perhaps you recognize some of these Seven Deadly Sins in your own ministry. Don't be dismayed. For every obstacle Satan puts in your path, God will provide a bridge to overcome it.

Ten Commandments for Church Planting Movements

As we look back over what we've learned so far from universals, characteristics, and obstacles, let's see if we can summarize. Consider these Ten Commandments for Church Planting Movements. While they don't include all of what we've learned thus far, they do encompass the most important points. You might want to reproduce them as a gift for your team or colleagues. Commit them to heart. Live by them, and let them live.

Ten Commandments
for Church Planting Movements

#1 Immerse Your Community in Prayer

#2 Saturate Your Community with the Gospel

#3 Cling to God's Word

#4 Fight Against Foreign Dependency

#5 Eliminate All Non-Reproducible Elements

#6 Live the Vision that You Wish to Fulfill

#7 Build Reproduction into Every Believer & Church

#8 Train All Believers to Evangelize, Disciple & Plant
     Churches

#9 Model, Assist, Watch, and Leave

#10 Discover What *God* is Doing and Join Him

By now you've probably come up with some questions of your own. Let's turn our attention to some of the most frequently asked questions about Church Planting Movements.

15

Frequently Asked Questions

YOU HAVE BEEN patient. Now it's time to open the question drawer. Here are some of the most frequently asked questions concerning Church Planting Movements.

1. What are you calling a church?

That is a good question. If you're thinking cross-crowned steeples, then you're not thinking Church Planting Movements. But if you're thinking two guys in a room studying the Bible, you've also missed it. Jesus made it clear that the church is a new covenant community. Recalling the twelve tribes of Israel, he chose twelve disciples signifying the creation of a 'new Israel.' Then Jesus placed himself in the center of that community with the words, "Wherever two or more are gathered in my name, there am I in the midst of them." Paul seized on this truth when he referred to the church as the body of Christ. The body of Christ is alive and well in today's Church Planting Movements.

Just as all churches around the world are unique, so it is with Church Planting Movements. However, there are some basic elements that we find in every Church Planting Movement church, and there are other elements that are quite diverse.

Common to all CPM Churches
- All observe baptism and the Lord's supper (though the frequency ranges from weekly to quarterly to annually)
- All meet regularly (though some on Sunday, some on Friday and some every night of the week)

- All have some kind of organization (though it varies, see below)All exhibit the five purposes of a church (evangelism, ministry, fellowship, discipleship and worship)
- All exhibited the *Ten Universal Elements* described in chapter 11.

Differences in each CPM church

- Types of leadership organization vary (e.g. Cambodia's seven-member central committee; China's multiple leaders; Jedidistan's Imams; Latin America's pastors)
- Average church size varies (Bhojpuri's 85 members; Jedidistan's 30 members; Cambodia's 45 members; Madhya Pradesh's 10 adults)

While central elements of baptism, the Lord's Supper and the five purposes are found in each of the churches, other elements have been contextualized, informed by Scripture, then adapted to each unique environment. This is what we saw as the Cambodian church blended the seven deacons of Acts 6:5 with the Communist notion of a "Central Committee" to produce a pastoral leadership team called the "Seven-Member Central Committee." In the same manner, the Muslim background believers of Jedidistan met on Friday mornings seated in a circle under the leadership of a pastor whom they called their *Imam*. Meeting in homes, the church size typically remains small and intimate, but ranges widely from the average 85 members in the Bhojpuri movement to 30 in Jedidistan to the 40-50 that we observed in Cambodia. In Madhya Pradesh, church planter Victor Choudhrie found what he called the "optimal" church size.

Optimal Church Size?

In an interview, Dr. Victor Choudhrie commented that ten adult members were the *optimal* size for a CPM church.

"You mean the average church size?" I asked.

"No," he said, "the optimal church size."

"And why is that?"

"Because of what the Bible says."

My empty stare prompted his explanation.

"You remember when Father Abraham met the two angels on the road. They were headed to Sodom to destroy it. Abraham bargained with them saying, 'For 50 righteous men would you destroy this city?' When they relented, he said, 'And for 40? For 30? For 20? For 10?' At last the angels agreed, 'For ten righteous men, we would not destroy this city.'"

"And so," Dr. Choudhrie continued, "we tell our new believers, when they reach ten adult church members, 'Now you have enough to reach this village for Christ, but what about the next village down the road? They have no believers. Surely two of you can go and visit that village and share with them the gospel.'"

Whether 10 members or 10,000, the church is best characterized—not by its size or forms—but by its passionate commitment to the Lordship of Jesus Christ and the fulfillment of his Great Commission. These twin passions are evident across Church Planting Movements.

2. What is the role of volunteers in Church Planting Movements?

The very name *volunteer* connotes someone who is not a professional, and in our highly professional society, this sometimes carries a negative image. But in the economy of Church Planting Movements amateurism is anything but negative. We must remember that the word "amateur" literally means "one who does it out of love," as opposed to one who does it for pay. Let's look at some of the reasons volunteers are so valuable to Church Planting Movements:

1) Volunteers are important because they model self-sacrificing love for, and obedience to, the Great Commission. They are not only unpaid, they actually pay for the privilege of serving God. It is vitally important for new Christians in Church Planting Movements to recognize that not everyone who serves God is on salary. This conveys a powerful message to the new believers.

2) Volunteers come from the *real* world. They are secretaries, farmers, teachers, builders, doctors, lawyers, and numerous other professions—secular professions that exist in the societies of lost people groups all over the world. Many volunteers are now using the Internet to locate the clubs, unions, and civic organizations that correspond to their own profession before they go overseas. Often they are able to arrange meetings with their professional counterparts in the cities where they are visiting. What a tremendous inroad to sharing the gospel and developing an ongoing relationship with a key member of a lost community.

3) Volunteers are God's people, and as God's people they possess the same vibrant Holy Spirit that enlivened the apostle Paul. When they connect with new believers they transfer an awareness that it is the Holy Spirit who makes one a useful servant of Christ, not one's profession or educational training.

There are many ways that volunteers can actively contribute to Church Planting Movements. Consider the following ways God is using volunteers today.

1) Prayer
Long before missionaries venture into contact with unreached people groups with the gospel, God is hearing the prayers of diligent prayer warriors ringing out on behalf of the lost. With new possibilities afforded by international air travel, many

prayer warriors are taking the battle to the field. In 1997 there were two churches with about 40 believers in a North African country of nearly 9 million persons. In 1998 missionaries called on the worldwide body of Christ to pray for the nation's lost. In addition to the many churches that covenanted to pray for the nation, several prayer walking teams arrived in the country to pray "on site with insight."[243]

A year after the prayer emphasis, the number of believers increased 500 percent and 13 new churches were formed. When a local missionary was asked what was the turning point, he said without hesitation, "Prayer."

Prayer-walking teams are now combing the globe, into the Himalayas, across the Sahara, over the Great Wall of China, and into the very seminaries of Islam. A Muslim background believer from Mauritania expressed her gratitude for the prayers of Christians that, she believes, drew her and her family to faith in Christ. "For many years," she said, "you all prayed for my country. And these prayers rose up to heaven where they gathered and gathered like great clouds forming over the desert. Today, these prayers are raining down miracles all across my country. Mauritania has become the land of miracles."

2) Evangelism

As volunteers expand their vision of what is possible, they are making important contributions to evangelism among unreached people groups. Each year, hundreds of Christian volunteers journey to Europe's Mediterranean seaports where they distribute New Testaments, gospel tracts, and *Jesus Film* videocassettes in Arabic to hundreds of thousands of Muslims from North Africa boarding ferries to return to their homeland.

In Asia's Communist countries, Christian tourists are able to venture into restricted areas and distribute Bibles and gospel

[243] See the book by Randy Sprinkle, *Follow Me: Lessons for Becoming a Prayerwalker,* (Birmingham: New Hope Publishers, 2001).

cassettes to villagers. These fearless trekkers for Jesus have played a vital role in the Church Planting Movements that God is unfolding in places where missionaries have little hope of gaining residence.

Church members in the English-speaking world naturally question how effective in evangelism they can be without knowing the local language. God seems to have heard their concerns and filled the world with English speakers! So prolific is the spread of English that in many Asian countries one can find an "English corner" in every major town or city.

An English corner is a place where students of English relax over a cup of coffee and watch for Westerners to pass by. When they see a likely prospect, they call out (in English) something like, "Hello Mister!" The friendly greeting is an invitation to come and "practice English with me." It is also a remarkable opportunity to share the Good News of Jesus Christ.

Another growing international language is the Internet. Listen to what a team of high school students did in a Middle Eastern Muslim country. Traveling around a major Middle Eastern city, the students and their team leader mapped out the location of every Internet café in the city. Most Middle Easterners don't have their own computer and Internet connections. Instead, they welcome the relatively inexpensive and anonymous ability to log-on to the cyber world through public Internet cafes.

The students spent the next few days visiting dozens of these cafes, logging onto the computers and resetting all of the Internet bookmarks and favorite settings from the usual pornography, news, and commerce to sites where the gospel, testimonies, and even streaming video of the *Jesus Film* could be found in the Arabic language.

Later, they visited the city's many video rental kiosks. These are typically one-man video rental stands. They show the owner their *Jesus Film* video and tell him that they are leaving the city at the end of the week and would rather not take the video with them. If he would like to have it and rent it out, they will be happy to give it to him. Very few video renters are unwilling to receive and distribute a video about the life of the Prophet Jesus. And the gospel goes forth.

3) Discipleship

"How can I possibly disciple others if I don't know their language?" Once again, the global spread of English can help. But more important is an improved definition of discipleship. Among Church Planting Movement practitioners, discipleship is increasingly being described as *teaching others to love Jesus as much as you do.*

Following the 222 principle of walking with a new believer there is no reason why anyone can't do this kind of discipleship. Walking with a new believer, listening to his testimony, praying with him, and expanding his vision for reaching a lost world— these are some of the many simple ways that you can help to disciple a new believer in the direction of a Church Planting Movement. Today, with the advent of Internet communications, you can continue to nurture and disciple these believers even after you've returned home.

4) Church Planting

Volunteers are becoming increasingly bold in their aspirations to be on mission with God. As this happens they are leaving groups of house churches in their wake.

In the summer of 2000, a group of volunteers worked with a Strategy Coordinator to conduct a summer ESL (English as a Second Language) Institute on a local college campus.

While each volunteer faithfully and diligently fulfilled all of his or her teaching responsibilities, they were able to do much more. The setting was ideally suited for them to talk about their own lives and—with Jesus at the center of their lives—the conversation naturally turned to him. With the university's encouragement, the teachers hosted students in their apartment for tea, cookies, and conversation.

These afternoon meetings became natural opportunities for modeling a house church, complete with evangelism, discipleship, worship, and training. And they became so popular with the students that the volunteers soon found the need to conduct model house church meetings several times each day just to keep up with the student interest.

Because the work was steeped in prayer, the students were hungry to learn about Jesus and to know more about how they could become churches themselves. By the end of the summer, these *amateurs* had seen more than 90 new house churches spin out of these apartment meetings.

The results far exceeded the expectations of the strategist who requested the volunteer teachers. "It is a God thing," he said.

When we pressed him for details, he continued, "We know that, of the 90 house churches that were begun this summer, about 30 of them later dissolved. But we also know that several of the house churches have already multiplied into additional house churches."

May God bless these *amateurs*.

3. What is the role of foreign funding in Church Planting Movements?

Money isn't evil. Foreign money isn't evil. But if it creates dependency on outside resources, causing local church leaders to turn their attention overseas before they start another church, then it becomes a drag on the movement.

Two years ago, traveling in a South American country with a Christian worker, we observed that the area was quite responsive to the gospel. Later that day, we met with the executive secretary of the denominational church work in the province. We asked him how many new churches he anticipated starting over the next twelve months. "That's easy," he said, "Brother So-and-So (an American volunteer church builder) has assured us that his teams will be able to construct 25 new churches this year. So," he proudly concluded, "we should see 25 new churches this next year."

Church Planting Movements thrive on indigeneity. They must have internal momentum if they are to rapidly multiply through a people group. One of the surest ways to cripple a Church Planting Movement is to link church reproduction to foreign resources. Whenever pastors look beyond their own membership and local resources for salaries or buildings, they bleed the life out of their movement.

So is there a place for foreign funding? Most definitely. Though Church Planting Movements must develop with internal, indigenous momentum, they cannot begin that way. They must receive the gospel from the outside. This is why funding for primary (or initial) evangelization is so important—the lost will not pay for their own evangelization!

What sorts of things fit into the category of primary evangelization? Missionaries to unreached people groups, Bible translation and distribution, gospel literature production and distribution, radio broadcasts and other evangelistic media ministries, church planter training centers and materials, and new leadership development programs all require external funding to get underway.

Foreign funds are also appropriate as demonstrations of Christian compassion to the poor and needy. When a disaster strikes, war breaks out, or famine grips a country, it is very appropriate for foreign Christians to demonstrate their compassion through gifts of charity and relief. So long as they don't create an unending measure of dependency, these mercy ministries are a powerful testimony to Christ's compassion for those in need.

To determine when foreign funds are needed, ask the question, "Is this something that will benefit the movement, something that the locals cannot provide for themselves?"

Correctly answering that question may mark the difference between a Church Planting Movement and a welfare state.

4. What is the role of missionaries in Church Planting Movements?

Given the obvious power of God in these Church Planting Movements, some have questioned whether the role of missionaries has diminished in this new reality. Nothing could be farther from the truth.

What is required of missionaries in a Church Planting Movement is not a *new* role, but rather a return to an *old* role. Roland Allen's classic book *Missionary Methods: St. Paul's or Ours*[244] makes the case well, that somewhere along the way, missionaries stopped following a Pauline model and shifted to a colonial model.

The Pauline missionary role raises up local indigenous leadership and then moves on to places where the gospel has not yet been sown.[245] The colonial model stays to rule over the conquered territory rather than transferring the responsibility, vision, and momentum to new Christians who don't understand why the same Holy Spirit living in their hearts is unable to equip them for leadership.

Great missionaries always understood the transitional nature of their role. John the Baptist initiated this spirit when he said, "He (Jesus) must become more and more, while I become less and less."[246]

Every Church Planting Movement practitioner recognizes that the success of the movement requires everything he has to give when he faces a people group devoid of gospel witness.

---

[244] Roland Allen, *Missionary Methods: St. Paul's or Ours?* (Grand Rapids: Eerdmans, 1962).

[245] Romans 15:20

[246] John 3:30

However, as the gospel takes root among the people, it may require even more effort for the missionary to resist leadership roles and take a backseat to the emerging leaders.

5. What is the role of theological education?

Upon hearing case studies of Church Planting Movements at a conference of seminary presidents, academic deans, and professsors, one of the seminary presidents was invited to respond. "A heretical movement," he said, "is still heretical!" His point was all too clear; he believed seminaries were required to prevent Church Planting Movements from becoming heretical movements.

Are Church Planting Movements capable of conveying heresy? Absolutely. Are they inherently heretical? Absolutely *not*.

Church Planting Movements are rapidly multiplying movements of people. People can multiply truth or error. The secret to keeping them on track is not to slow them down long enough to indoctrinate all of their leaders before they are allowed to reproduce. The secret to keeping them on track is to build fidelity to Scripture into the DNA of the earliest reproducing church models.

Infidelity to God's word—not education or non-education—is what leads to heresy. Christian history teaches us all too well that many of history's most notorious heretics had impeccable theological training and credentials from the finest seminaries.

Putting obedience to God's word into the church's DNA is indispensable to keeping a Church Planting Movement on track, but is not the end of the story. Anyone who's been in the ministry for even a few weeks knows that there are endless questions that come up which require counsel, study, and training.

The need for theological education and ministry training is not in question. Both are sorely needed. The issue is how best to do it? In the past, missionaries relied heavily on seminary institutions that were located in centralized urban settings. For a pastor to get this seminary education might mean years of residence far from his home and village.

Around the world, institutional seminaries have long been eclipsed by decentralized theological education through extension centers and correspondence courses. Church Planting Movements are pushing this distance learning paradigm even farther as missionaries scramble to find new innovative ways to make theological education available for all Christians at all times.

Like a country that has mobilized for war, CPM practitioners are exploiting every means possible for theological training to keep pace with the rapidly multiplying new churches. Among the means being used are radio broadcasts, video and audiocassettes, compact audio and videodisks, and the Internet. When possible, missionaries are organizing mobile training centers that offer two and three week training modules that can be disbanded and relocated wherever they are needed. In several restricted countries there is a steady, discrete influx of pastor's study Bibles pouring into regional distribution centers where they can be reproduced and disseminated throughout the country.

The fear of heresy has been one of the reasons many Western evangelicals opted for the creation of cell church networks rather than independent house churches. Many of these cell church movements are highly structured with complete Bible lessons cascading from a central teaching authority. However, the very structure that prevents heresy can also convey heresy; it simply does so more efficiently. In short, the quest for theological orthodoxy is a never-ending challenge. Wherever people are involved the outcome will remain uncertain.

6. What is the difference between cell churches and house churches, and how is each related to Church Planting Movements?

House churches and cell churches share many common features, but are fundamentally different in their relation to

Church Planting Movements. The masses who are coming to Christ in the world's burgeoning cell-based megachurches are evidence of God's handiwork. However, they do not constitute multiplying indigenous churches. They are as related as classical and jazz music. Both types of music use the same instruments, but while classical music is tightly structured (like cell churches), jazz enjoys the freedom to flow across the range of musical possibilities (like house churches). While cell churches enjoy many of the initial qualities of Church Planting Movements, they tend to reach a plateau owing to the internal controls associated with centralized leadership.

House churches are stand-alone churches that happen to be small enough to meet in homes. After filling their limited space, they grow through multiplication rather than increasing their membership. Each house church has its own leadership and derives its authority directly from Christ, rather than through a church hierarchy, and functions in every way as a church.

Cell churches, on the other hand, are actually large churches that have organized their membership into small cell groups that are not self-consciously functioning as independent churches. Cell churches derive their authority from a senior pastor whose teaching cascades down to each cell group leader. Like house churches, cell churches may grow through multiplication, but they never break ties with the centralized leadership.

Cell churches share many of the qualities that we see in the multiplying house churches of other Church Planting Movements around the world. They are led by laypersons, but they require a well trained visionary leader behind the scenes shepherding the movement. This need for a strong, visionary leader is a key distinctive of cell churches and one of the reasons that, unlike the house church movement, cell churches are self-limiting—i.e. there simply aren't enough well trained visionary leaders around to create enough massive cell churches to reach the whole world.

As with house churches, cell churches also tend to be homo-
geneous in nature, but rarely embrace a vision to reach an entire
people group. This is because the vision driving a cell church is
to grow larger rather than to reach the entire people group or city
through new church multiplication.

7. Why is it not happening here?

The remarkable stories of Church Planting Movements have
left more than a few Christians frustrated. They say, "It's exciting to read about what God is doing in these distant lands, but
why is it not happening here?"

This question reveals a yearning for God's best for a lost
world. If prayer is *a protest against the status quo,* then we
should all be crying out, "Why not here, O Lord?"

Sometimes we find that God is all too willing, but that the
uncooperative partner is us. How many of the universal elements
of Church Planting Movements are currently at play in our own
ministry setting? How many of the common characteristics can
be found? Are there any of the seven deadly sins that we can
identify and remove?

At the end of the day, Church Planting Movements require
the cooperation of three partners: God, ourselves, and our community. Only one of these participants is under our control.
Many great church planters have labored a lifetime without
seeing a movement. They shouldn't feel guilty or exasperated.

At the same time, we are gaining new understanding of these
movements with each passing year. This book reflects a growing
body of insight into how God is at work in these movements.
Just because it's not happening where you are now, doesn't
mean you won't see breakthroughs in the days ahead. Never stop
learning. Never give up. Never stop protesting against the way
things are.

8. If I connect all the dots, can I make it happen?

We've spoken to this issue before, but it bears repeating. Following every step in this book won't guarantee that a movement will occur. God's work isn't mechanical or magical.

God welcomes our participation in his mighty acts, but we must participate on his terms. We should never deceive ourselves into thinking we can ignore the ways he is at work and still expect his blessings.

The best analogy to Church Planting Movements is probably the challenge of winning a lost friend to Christ. As with Church Planting Movements, God has already done the most important work through Jesus, but we have a vital role to play. The ways we relate to our friend and share our faith can be critical to how he or she will respond. In the end, though, it is a person's response to that gospel that closes the circle. The same is true of a Church Planting Movement.

9. But will they last?

This question grows out of a concern that we not be like the man who quickly built his house on the sand, only to find himself with nothing when the storms arose. The same line of thought leads church builders to construct buildings out of stone. There is a sense that the tangible bricks and mortar will somehow assure the permanence of the work.

The body of Christ doesn't depend on the permanence of our physical structures but on its spiritual vitality. The greatest evidence of this is the vitality and endurance of the early church. For three centuries it flourished and spread throughout the known world, without so much as a single cathedral or permanent dedicated building.

Christians living in hostile settings credit the fluid nature of house churches with helping them survive the ravages of persecution. Staying small, decentralized, and mobile allows them to remain a step ahead of their persecutors. House churches are forever adapting to meet the changes that life brings. Some house churches rotate their location from week to week to stay ahead of their opponents. Others disband altogether with changes in migrant work patterns only to resurface later in another part of the country.

Part Four

Launch Pad

16

Practical Handles

Y OU HAVE NOW seen Church Planting Movements around the world and witnessed both the uniqueness of each one and the common elements they share. Hopefully you've been reassured to learn that Church Planting Movements have their roots in the life and teachings of Jesus and are, in fact, 21st century expressions of the same movement that swept through the New Testament world.

So now you are wondering how you too can participate in a Church Planting Movement in your own community. You've been patient as we suspended our value judgments and weighed all the evidence. But now the evidence is in, and it's time to turn our insights into action.

In this chapter, we will give you some practical tools to help fix your vision, assess where your community is, and move you and your team down the road toward a Church Planting Movement.

Making Room

If you are going to see a Church Planting Movement, you're going to have to make some room for it. One of the toughest things for good people to do is to give up the many good things they are already doing in order to embrace the best. Perhaps this describes you. You are excited about a new vision of possibilities but hate the thought of leaving behind the many good things you are already doing.

But if what you are doing now hasn't led you to a Church Planting Movement, then perhaps it is time for a change. If you keep doing what you've been doing, you'll keep getting what you've been getting. So, if you're not already seeing a Church Planting Movement with what you're doing now, you should stop, clear some space, and try something new. Remember, *a good definition of insanity is to keep doing what you've been doing, while expecting different results.* [247]

Begin at the End

The best place to begin your efforts is at the end, with the vision God has given you. Evaluate all that you do in light of that vision. Don't be afraid to change your plans as often as needed. Remember, it's better to change your plans to fit your vision than to compromise your vision just so you can retain your plans.

On July 20, 1969 Neil Armstrong landed on the moon, the final step in a long collaborative effort by thousands of men and women. But the whole enterprise actually began eight years earlier, on May 25, 1961, when John F. Kennedy launched the Apollo space program with these words: "I believe that this nation should commit itself to achieving the goal, before this decade is out, of landing a man on the moon and returning him safely to the earth."[248]

In essence, Kennedy was challenging America's scientific community to answer the question, "What's it going to take to realize this vision?" He didn't ask them to simply improve on their current performance or see how much they could accomplish in a decade. Instead, he pointed to the end vision.

What you hope to accomplish is no less significant than landing a man on the moon. And it must begin at the same place: *with the end vision.* Beginning where you are and committing to

[247] The definition of insanity is commonly used in Strategy Coordinator Training workshops in Southeast Asia.

[248] President John F. Kennedy, "Special Message to the Congress on Urgent National Needs." Delivered before a joint session of Congress. May 25, 1961.

work harder or do more will only lead to frustration and exhaustion. Instead, do what NASA did. Begin with an image of the completed vision (a Church Planting Movement) and then work your way backward step by step. This will help you see just what it's going to take to realize your dream.

Asking the WIGTake Question

The Watsons used this approach when they viewed the enormity of the 90 million lost Bhojpuri-speaking people of India. David called his exercise a generational formula. Beginning with the *WIGTake* question, "What's it going to take to reach 90 million Bhojpuri in <u>this</u> (20-year) generation?"[249] From that beginning point, he devised the following calculations.

Among the Bhojpuri, 90 million individuals live in 172,000 villages. Each village needs at least one church. To reach all 172,000 Bhojpuri villages in 20 years would require the planting of 8,600 village churches each year. Of course no single church planter or Strategy Coordinator could accomplish such a feat, but the work doesn't belong to a single Strategy Coordinator or church planter. The body of Christ is up to the challenge. With this in mind, the Watsons devised a plan to establish church planter training centers that would equip the body of Christ to reach all 90 million Bhojpuri people. Each training center could train 40 Bhojpuri church planters per year.

Now the vision was coming into focus, moving from the impossible to the possible. To plant 8,600 churches per year would require 215 training centers annually equipping 40 church planters. In 20 years the vision of 172,000 churches would be reached. In fact, they should reach the goal much sooner, since they were planting churches that also planted churches. Suddenly the goal of 172,000 village churches didn't seem so farfetched.

---

[249] *WIGTake* is shorthand for the question, *"What's it going to take?"* More than any other question, this one triggers missionaries from the limitations of *"What can I do?"* to the more important question of whatever it takes.

Today, there are nearly a million Bhojpuri believers pursuing the same vision; what once seemed impossible is becoming a reality.

Try it Yourself

Ask God to give you his completed end vision for your people, city, or community. Then begin working backwards from that point. Ask yourself these questions.

1. What is God's vision for this people, city, or community?

2. How many churches will it take?

3. What will those churches look like?

4. Where will their leaders come from?

5. What will these leaders need to know?

6. How will these leaders get the training they need?

7. How long will this training take?

8. How many leaders and churches are there now?

9. How rapidly are new leaders being trained and new churches being planted now?

10. At your current rate, how long will it take to produce the number of churches needed to fulfill God's vision for your people, city, or community?

Living the Vision

Once you have established what it's going to take, you can begin living and modeling the end vision yourself. How do you do this? By forming and participating in the kind of multiplying house church that you hope to see when your movement reaches full bloom. Appendix Two offers some guidelines for forming the kind of POUCH church that we visited in chapter 4 above.

By living the vision yourself, you'll better understand the subtleties and nuances of what you're trying to communicate to others. And you'll find that your own house church moves you one step closer to realizing the vision of multiplying house churches sweeping across your community.

Practicing house church puts you squarely aligned with your God-given vision for a Church Planting Movement, but what about your community? How can you move them from where they are now to where they need to be in relation to a Church Planting Movement? In the next few pages we'll show you how to: 1) assess where they are now, 2) identify the gaps between where they are now and where they need to be, and then 3) devise strategies to close those gaps.

Where Are They Now?

If you don't know how far your community is from a Church Planting Movement, how can you lead them there? Let's take a moment to locate the precise distance between where your community is now and where they need to be to realize a Church Planting Movement. How do we do this? By returning to the essential elements and characteristics that we've already identified.

10 UNIVERSAL ELEMENTS	1	2	3	4	5	6	7	8	9	10
Extraordinary Prayer										
Abundant Evangelism										
Intentional Church Planting										
Authority of Bible										
Local Leadership										
Lay Leadership										
House Churches										
Churches Planting Churches										
Rapid Reproduction										
Healthy Churches										

Assess your community in light of the ten universal elements, ten common characteristics, and seven deadly sins. On a scale of one to ten, with ten being the highest, how would you rate the status of each of these elements in your community? After you've done this exercise, ask your teammates or local partners to do the same thing. Then compare the results.

10 COMMON ELEMENTS	1	2	3	4	5	6	7	8	9	0
Climate of Uncertainty										
Insulation from Outside										
High Cost for Following										
Bold Fearless Faith										
Family Conversions										
Rapid Assimilation of Believers										
Heart Language Worship										
Divine Signs & Wonders										
On-the-Job Training										
Missionaries Suffering										

Not all of the ten common characteristics are within your power to influence. For example, you shouldn't promote a *climate of uncertainty* or try to manufacture *divine signs and wonders*. But you can affect many of these characteristics, such as *evangelism, prayer*, and *intentional church planting*. By doing so you will better align your community with the ways God is at work in Church Planting Movements.

Finally, look at the seven deadly sins. You may want to revisit these seven obstacles in chapter 14, and then assess their status in your community. Invite your teammates to join you in this exercise of identifying which barriers may be preventing the fulfillment of your vision.

7 DEADLY SINS	1	2	3	4	5	6	7	8	9	10
Blurred Vision										
Improving the Bible										
Sequentialism										
Unsavory Salt										
The Devil's Candy										
Alien Abduction										
Blaming God										

In order to remain consistent in the way our graphing instrument appears, we're going to mark these seven deadly sins *opposite* to the way we marked the first twenty elements. For example, marking one of the seven deadly sins low indicates that the obstacle is having a significant negative impact in your community, while a high score means it is not much of a factor. The higher the mark you give, the fewer barriers to a Church Planting Movement in your community.

The result of this exercise will be to provide you, in a single snapshot, a picture of your community through the lens of Church Planting Movements. Let's look at a sample.

IDENTIFYING THE GAPS	1	2	3	4	5	6	7	8	9	10
Extraordinary Prayer										
Abundant Evangelism										
Intentional Church Planting										
Bible Authority										
Local Leadership							G	A	P	S
Lay Leadership										
House Churches										
Churches Planting Churches										
Rapid Reproduction						G	A	P	S	
Healthy Churches										
Climate of Uncertainty										
Insulation from Outsiders						G	A	P	S	
High Cost for Following										
Bold Fearless Faith										
Family Conversions										
Rapid Assimilation Believers										
Heart Language Worship										
Divine Signs & Wonders										
On-the-Job Training					G	A	P	S		
Missionaries Suffering										
Blurred Vision										
Improving the Bible						G	A	P	S	
Sequentialism										
Unsavory Salt										
The Devil's Candy										
Alien Abduction										
Blaming God				G	A	P	S			

In this sample, you can see how one community looks in relation to a Church Planting Movement. *Extraordinary Prayer* is well underway at 40 percent of ideal, but *abundant evangelism* and *intentional church planting* are barely begun with scores of only one out of ten or 10 percent of the ideal.

Closing the Gap

After you and your team have assessed your community and identified the gaps, you are ready to take action. The gaps reveal where you need to concentrate your attention. This is important; without gap identification we tend toward whatever ministry appeals to us most, or else we gravitate toward our talents and gifts. Gap identification lets *your community speak to you*, and tells you where change needs to occur in order to align with Church Planting Movement principles.

Once the gaps have been identified, creating alignment is a simple matter of devising plans of action to close the gap between where the community is now and God's vision for them.

Strategies to Bridge the GAP

What strategies would strengthen and lengthen the bridges (prayer, evangelism, etc.) to vision fulfillment? What strategies

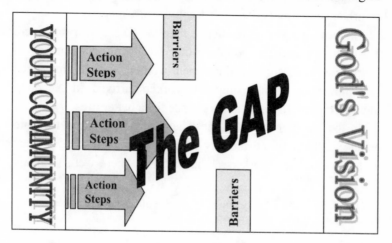

would overcome the obstacles (i.e. *seven deadly sins*) you face? Since each community is unique, each strategist will have to answer these questions for himself. Gap-closing strategies take shape in the form of a good team plan that will provide a dated, measurable course of action toward vision fulfillment.

Let's review what we've done so far. We have clarified our end vision, begun practicing that end vision ourselves, assessed the gaps to fulfilling that vision and begun developing a master plan to close those gaps. Now let's take a look at an actual example of how God used one servant couple to stimulate one of the largest Church Planting Movements in history.

The Story of the Chens[250]

John Chen was born in Taiwan, the son of a Baptist pastor. His father set an example for him of trying to start a new church every year of his ministry. The lesson wasn't lost on young John. When he became a pastor himself he followed the same productive pattern, starting a new chapel each year and personally leading 50-60 people to Christ.

After two decades of pastoring and church planting that took him and his family from Taiwan to Hong Kong and finally the United States, in 1995, he became a missionary. Then, in 2000 John answered God's call to become a Strategy Coordinator to an urban center in the People's Republic of China.

China was a greater challenge than the Chens ever imagined. The urban center he adopted, that we'll call Nandong, was teeming with nearly 20 million men, women, and children. Each day thousands of new migrant workers arrived in Nandong looking for employment and a chance for a better life.

In the summer of 2000, the Chens made their first trip into Nandong. They found the city filled with factories and choked with thousands of workers. John recalls, "There were so many

---

[250] Everything in Chen's story is true. The names of persons and places have been obscured to protect the ministry.

people. There is no time to do the work slowly. But we didn't know how to do it differently."

Then, in October 2000 John and his wife Hope entered Strategy Coordinator training and began to learn about how God was at work in Church Planting Movements. John realized then that he couldn't do it all himself, nor could he simply rely on a group of church planters. John took the principles of Church Planting Movements and asked himself these questions:

"What is better than planting a church?"

Answer: Training others to plant churches

"And what is better than training others to plant churches?"

Answer: Training trainers to train church planters to plant even more churches!

With this exponential formula, John the pastor, John the church planter, became John the trainer and instrument of a Church Planting Movement.

John knew that not everyone was suited to be a church planter, but at the same time he knew that God *could* use anyone. So how do you determine who will and won't be an effective church planter? Rather than try to sort this out in advance, John decided to train *everybody* to be a church planter and a church planter trainer. Those who implemented the training would become his Church Planting Movement co-laborers, those who didn't would simply fall behind.

John picks up the story from here:

"I knew that my wife and I could each bring about 30 people to Christ in one year, but only if every Christian brought someone to Christ could we hope to reach Nandong's millions." In November 2000 John began his work.

Training Trainers

Initially, John found only three towns in Nandong district with any churches, and these had a total membership of 250 persons. John adopted what he thought was an ambitious goal of seeing a church planted in every town in the district. That would mean starting more than 200 new churches! When John shared his goal with one of the local pastors, the pastor shook his head and said, "You should go back to Hong Kong!" After some persuasion, the pastor agreed to let John teach a class on church planting to any members who were interested. The church members were mostly farmers who worked in the fields all day, so the classes were held at night. At the first session, 30 members attended.

The Chens began the class by sharing their vision challenge, but most of the trainees were skeptical. John discovered that there were two obstacles preventing each of them from being effective evangelists. First, they didn't know what to say, and second, they didn't know who to say it to. John tackled the second obstacle by having them list all the lost people they knew who were lost, and then identify the five that God wanted them to share with first.

Then he turned his attention to the first obstacle. John taught the trainees that each of them had a unique story to tell. A person's story is simple consisting of three parts: 1) what you were like before Jesus, 2) how you met Jesus, and 3) what your life has been like since Jesus. Then John instructed them to remove religious vocabulary from their story.

"We don't even call it a testimony," John explained, "A testimony is for Christians. Non-Christians don't know what a testimony is, so we call it 'our story.'" John had each trainee write his testimony on a single sheet of paper.

At first, everyone was a little nervous about telling their story, so John had them read it out loud five times and then tell it to one another in groups of three. By the end of the first class, the farmer trainees were excited and confident.

In the weeks that followed, John taught the little band of trainees six follow-up lessons designed to ground their new converts in the fundamentals of the faith.[251] As he sent them out, he said, "Go this week and share your story with the five people on your list. If you're unable to share with those five people, go to the next five on your list! When you return next week, we'll see what God has done."

After the first class John found that only 17 of the 30 in his class had shared with anyone, but one farmer had shared with 11 persons. To build up their faith, John had each trainee tell the group about their experiences. In this way, they drew insights and encouragement from one another. After the second lesson John inserted a dose of accountability as he told the trainees, "If you choose not to share with anyone this week, you should not come to the class next week." This kept the trainees focused on doing and not just hearing the word. The results surprised even the Chens.

By January 2001 (two months after beginning), they had already started 20 small groups that were becoming churches. By May there were 327 small groups and 4,000 newly baptized believers, and churches were scattered across 17 towns. By the end of 2001, there were 908 house churches with more than 12,000 new Christians.

They Returned with Joy

As with Jesus' disciples in Luke 10, the trainees discovered that in every village they visited God had already prepared a person of peace who was waiting to hear their gospel story. One old farmer who had never before planted a church started 12 house churches in two months, and 110 in a year.

The old man's lifestyle was the foundation for his effectiveness. He began everyday at 5 a.m. reading his Bible till 7 a.m., and then worked in the fields until 5 p.m. when he went home for dinner and family time. At 7 p.m. he went back out again where he "worked in God's fields until midnight."

---

[251] See Appendix One.

The old farmer is not unusual in what has become the largest Church Planting Movement in history. In another town a 67-year old woman became a Christian, and in one year had led more than 60 families to become believers.

"I asked her to take me out and show me how she does it," John said. "She tells people how she was weak and then Jesus saved her. Then she invites them to a Bible study at her house. Clearly she has the anointing of the Holy Spirit upon her."

"We teach new believers how to have a Bible study and daily quiet time. So they can do this forever. Then we teach them what a church is about and how to organize into a church so that they can grow together in Christ."

"Once," John said, "we lost a Christian factory worker that we had trained. After six months, we found him again; he had been transferred to another large factory with 10,000 workers in it. During those 6 months, he had started 70 small groups and seen 10 generations of reproduction (churches planting churches)."

If you ask John the secret of this powerful movement, he will pull up his pants legs and show you the calluses on his knees. "You must spend at least two hours every day in prayer," he says.

John teaches his trainees to pray for the Holy Spirit's anointing, to put on the whole armor of God, to pray for the lost all around them, to pray as they go into each witnessing situation, and to pray for the blood of Jesus to protect them from everything Satan will throw against them.

After two hours of morning prayer, John goes out into the harvest fields. He witnesses faithfully every day with his simple story, all the while seeking those God has called out. John continues to train others to do the same.

By the year 2003, John was regularly training 3-400 church planters each month. "You never know who God is going to use," he smiles, "so we keep training everybody!" John's passionate commitment to train everyone is one reason the movement has exploded past his original vision of 200 churches. Today, the movement is spreading across several districts and shows little sign of slowing.

In fact, by all indications the Nandong movement is still building momentum. In the year 2001, 908 churches were started with 12,000 baptized believers. The following year, the Chens saw 3,535 new churches planted with more than 53,430 baptisms. Then in the first 6 months of 2003, the movement had produced 9,320 new churches and 104,542 baptisms.[252] Today, John leads 15 deputy trainers in 30 training centers meeting in homes and church buildings as the movement continues to grow.

Leading Your Team

John and Hope Chen's story reveals what is possible when we set our sights high and move far beyond our comfort zone. There is much that we can learn from the Chens' experience,[253] but the fuel and engine of the Nandong Church Planting Movement are not found in curriculum or techniques. Instead, they are hidden in the prayer, vision, passionate obedience of the leader and his team.

Everyone who hopes to see the kind of movement the Chens experienced will face the challenges of developing and leading a team of like-minded co-workers. How do you develop such a team? If you want to align your team for success, then ask yourself if you've provided them with the necessary ingredients: 1) vision, 2) training, 3) passion, 4) co-laborers, and 5) account-

---

[252]These officially reported and confirmed numbers are actually an understatement of what is still happening in the Nandong movement. The Chens' training has been adopted to great effect by other denominations in the Nandong area, and the Chens have chosen not to report these other numbers here. Those additional statistics would have increased the total numbers of churches and baptisms by as much as 40%.

[253]You can find a complete outline of the Chens' training in Appendix One.

ability. If one of these components is missing, you won't get the results you desire. Let's examine how each of these ingredients contributes to a Church Planting Movement.

Key Ingredients

1) **Vision** – A clear end vision of a Church Planting Movement among your people group or community.

2) **Training** – Expertise in evangelism, discipleship, church planting, training, and multiplication needed to accomplish the strategy that will lead to the vision's fulfillment.

3) **Passion** – Mutually reinforcing the vision of a Church Planting Movement. Reminding one another that apart from Christ's salvation, your community is eternally lost.

4) **Co-Laborers** – Unless you can train lots of co-laborers, your dreams will never become a reality. Remember, "The resources are in the harvest." Every lost person is a potential convert and every new believer is a potential co-laborer who needs to be trained.

5) **Accountability** – Build into your team a system of accountability that will ensure that everyone continues to multiply out evangelism, discipleship, church planting, and training.[254]

What happens when one of these ingredients is missing? If your team has training, passion, partners, and accountability, but

---

[254] Variations on this model have been used around the world. The author has learned that one of the seminal thinkers in this area is Dr. Mary B. Lippitt of Enterprise Management Ltd. and author of *The Leadership Spectrum*. Visit their website at: www.enterprisemgt.com or www.leadershipspectrum.com, October 2004.

the vision for a Church Planting Movement is not clear, your team will experience **confusion**!

If your team has a clear vision, shared passion, a growing body of co-laborers, and accountability, but lacks the skills needed to accomplish their vision, your team will be **anxious and uncertain**!

If your team possesses the vision and skills along with co-workers, and accountability, but lacks real passion, change may occur, but it will be **slow at best**.

If your team has the right vision, skills, passion, and accountability, but fails to train a growing number of co-laborers from the harvest, your team will experience great **frustration**.

Finally, if you provide your team with visionary leadership, skills, passion, and co-laborers, but fail to reinforce accountability, the team will experience **mixed results**, some good and some bad.

Let's see all of these components laid out on a single chart.

Check List for Team Leadership: (see how missing elements bring unsatisfactory results)

Vision +	Training +	Passion +	Co-Laborers +	Accountability =	CPM Progress
	Training +	Passion +	Co-Laborers +	Accountability =	Confusion
Vision +		Passion +	Co-Laborers +	Accountability =	Anxiety
Vision +	Training +		Co-Laborers +	Accountability =	Slow Progress
Vision +	Training +	Passion +		Accountability =	Frustration
Vision +	Training +	Passion +	Co-Laborers +	=	Mixed Results

Use this chart as a reminder of what it takes to lead a team. When you begin to see confusion, anxiety, slow action, frustration, or false starts, trace the symptom back to its root causes. Make the changes necessary in your team leadership and you'll see the results you desire.

Now you have the key pieces in place: a firm grasp of your vision, an understanding of how you can participate in that vision, an assessment of your community in relation to that vision, and how to lead your team to achieve that vision. What's stopping you?

17

A Call to Action

Y OU'VE COME TO the end of the book, and what have
you learned? What difference will it make for you, for your
community, for eternity?

We've seen a variety of Church Planting Movements and
Church Planting Movement *wanna-be's* as they are unfolding
around the world. We've traced their characteristics back through
the New Testament church to the very life and teachings of Jesus.
We've identified elements that are essential to every Church
Planting Movement, and explored the context of Church Planting
Movements, breathing in the very air that surrounds them.

Together we've exposed the seven deadly sins that can wither
a Church Planting Movement before it gets a chance to flower.
We've explored some of the most frequently asked questions
about Church Planting Movements and hopefully arrived at some
satisfactory answers. Finally we've translated what we've
learned into practical steps that will lead us faithfully toward a
Church Planting Movement.

Where Do You Go From Here?

The answer depends on where you are now, because we all
begin at different places. You may be a mission-minded
layperson, a pastor, a missionary, or simply a Christian who is
convinced that God's ideal is still yearning to be realized.
Whoever you are or wherever you are, you can join God in
spreading Church Planting Movements to your community and
around the world.

Over the past decade we have seen that most Christians who
share an interest in Church Planting Movements are somewhere

on a spectrum ranging between *rhetoric* and *reality*. There are five stages or sticking points that mark progress along the way. As you examine these five stages of Church Planting Movement advance, try to identify where you and your team are. Then make the steps necessary to move forward.

Stage One: A Rhetorical Embrace

Stage one is "talking the talk, but not yet walking the walk." People are quick to embrace the language of Church Planting Movements. Opposing Church Planting Movements is like criticizing mom or apple pie—it just wouldn't be right. But there is a big difference between those who simply add "Church Planting Movements" to their rhetoric and those who take seriously the need to reshape their lives to contribute to these movements.

Talkers often jump on the bandwagon of the latest happening, but they have little grasp of what it's really all about and certainly no intention of redirecting business as usual to make way for a Church Planting Movement.

Stage Two: A Simmering Vision

And then the talking stops. Somewhere along the way, you catch a real vision for a Church Planting Movement. Perhaps it has come as you've read this book. Or perhaps you've caught the enthusiasm in the voice of someone who is immersed in a movement. Or maybe you've visited a place where a Church Planting Movement has broken out. Whatever the trigger, there is something in this new paradigm of possibilities that rings your bell. And soon the vision becomes an obsession, the marvelous awareness that this just might be possible for your own community.

A vision for a Church Planting Movement is absolutely essential to seeing one materialize, but vision alone is not enough. Persons stuck at the vision stage still lack understanding of what they need to do to help make that vision a reality. They may launch out blindly in pursuit of a Church Planting Movement, clueless as to the direction they should be going. Or they may fall into the condition of divine dismissal—seeing the movement as entirely and exclusively an act of God, and so failing to realize that God wants to use *them* to bring his vision into reality. Whatever the reason for languishing at stage two, the solution is to a simmering vision is to *gain some understanding*.

Stage Three: Faith Seeking Understanding

When vision gives way to understanding an amazing sense of purpose and empowerment starts to occur. As your obsession translates into an understanding of the principles that lead to Church Planting Movements and those obstacles that obstruct them, you begin to see that this is not just a dream, but something that God really wants to do in your community today.

Understanding comes through diligent observation of what God is doing and how he is doing it. It is built on the conviction that God wants to use us to fulfill his vision for a lost world. Understanding Church Planting Movements doesn't guarantee that you will see a Church Planting Movement, but it is an important step along the way.

Stage Four: Passionate Pursuit

The timid may satisfy themselves with understanding Church Planting Movements without ever risking everything to passion- ately pursue one. But those who do take that risk and apply what they have learned have a chance to achieve the greatest reward— *though not always right away.*

One who passionately pursues a Church Planting Movement is like the man who discovered a treasure in a field. His passions compelled him to sell all he had to obtain that field (Matthew 13:44). In the same way, the one who stops short of passionate pursuit is like the rich young ruler who went away sad, because he had great possessions (Matthew 19:16-22). Which one describes you?

There will be many failures on the path to a Church Planting Movement. But one thing is certain, without a passionate commitment to implementing that vision, it will never come to pass.

Stage Five: Riding the Wave

And then it happens. One day the churches you've struggled to plant and patiently filled with vision, passion, and skills begin to realize their God-given potential. They start multiplying—not slowly, but rapidly and with zeal that will not stop until the whole community is filled with the glory of the Lord.

Those who successfully ride a Church Planting Movement never exhibit a smug sense of self-accomplishment. Riding a Church Planting Movement isn't like riding a horse. You never break the will of the movement. It's more like riding a wave.

Those who ride the wave of a Church Planting Movement are filled with an awesome awareness of the power of God flowing through the movement as Christ transforms thousands of lives and gives birth to hundreds of vibrant new churches. They are touched with the realization that their own life has been eclipsed by the movement itself—like a seed planted in the earth that dies in order to transfer the DNA of its passion, vision, and skills into an ever-expanding harvest field.

Those who are riding Church Planting Movements have a joyous exhaustion about them. They have learned that there is still much for them to do in the course of the movement's development, even as they celebrate and worship the God on whom the movement rests.

You *Can* Get There From Here!

A Church Planting Movement may seem to be a distant horizon from where you are now, but you *can* get there. If you share the same vision, the vision of rapidly multiplying churches planting churches across a people group, city, or community, then you can close the gap and see the vision become a reality. Rhetoric, vision, understanding, passionate pursuit, or riding the wave—where do you find yourself?

It can't happen here. This is what they said in Vietnam until they saw it in Cambodia. It's what they said in Cambodia before they saw it in China. It's what they said in Central America before they saw it in Bogotá. It's what they said in Sudan before they saw it in Ethiopia. Perhaps it's what they are saying where you live.

Satan would have us remain silent and skeptical. But Christ would have us shout it from the roof tops, *"Be no longer unbelieving, but believe!"*

Doubt is contagious. But then so is faith. God offers us the chance to believe and join him in something so amazing that *you wouldn't believe it even if you were told.* Well, how about you? Do you believe?

Look to the nations; watch and be utterly amazed for I am going to do something in your days that you would not believe even if you were told.

Epilogue

CHURCH PLANTING MOVEMENTS reveal a new understanding of how God is at work in the world. Despite their deep roots in the New Testament, Church Planting Movements pose a challenge to many of today's conventional church practices. Nonetheless, Church Planting Movements are here to stay. Each year their numbers increase, ushering thousands more lost souls into the Kingdom.

This book has addressed the question of *how* God is at work in Church Planting Movements, and has found clear steps we can take to align ourselves with Him. As with so much in the world, though, God also allows us the freedom to reject his ways. The choice is ours, but his work goes on.

History is full of hinge opportunities, moments when a single decision determines whether we will be players or observers in history's grand unfolding. Among many examples is the early Japanese rejection of firearms.[255] The first guns were introduced to Japan in 1543 by Portuguese travelers. So impressed were the Japanese that they reverse engineered them, carefully dismantling the weapons and analyzing their construction before proceeding to copy them. In the years that followed, the Japanese not only learned to make their own weapons, but greatly improved on gun-making technology, so that by 1600 they manufactured the finest guns in the world.

However, guns soon fell into disrepute in Japan. Japan's warrior caste, the samurai, were numerous and well established in society. They lived and fought by time honored codes of conduct all of which were undermined by guns. With guns, a

---

[255] Jared Diamond, *Guns, Germs and Steel, a short history of everybody for the last 13,000 years* (London: Vintage, 1998), pp. 257-8.

simple washerwoman could instantly fell a mighty samurai—*and where was the honor in that?* So, gradually, guns were eliminated from Japan. By 1650, there were virtually no guns left in the country, a condition that continued until 1853 when Commodore Perry's Pacific Fleet forced open the isolated nation, at gunpoint.

In salvation history, much more is at stake than the acceptance or rejection of firearms. The hinge of history before us concerns the eternal destiny of millions. The question we face is not whether Church Planting Movements are right or wrong, but whether we will be participants or observers—allowing God's movements to pass us by. God's handiwork in these movements is as irrefutable as these movements are inevitable; it is we who are the question mark.

David Garrison
India 2003

Additional Resources

Appendix One

Training for Trainers

NO WRITTEN DESCRIPTION can do justice to the remarkable effectiveness of John and Hope Chen's "Training for Trainers." [256] John has taken the lofty ideals of Church Planting Movements and reduced them to simple actions that anyone can take. Yet no approach has yielded more new believers and new churches than this.

If you find yourself struggling with some of the material, or wishing you had more explanation, don't wait for the answers to all your questions. Instead, follow John's advice: "Just do it!"

Creating a Church Planting Movement Ethos

1. Prayer – John spends two hours a day in prayer and teaches his students to do the same. Modeling prayer in his own life enables him to effectively train others to do the same.
2. Spiritual Warfare – John warns trainees that Satan will try everything he can to defeat them. Their response to Satan's attacks is to watch, fight, and pray.
3. Thankfulness in *All* Things – In keeping with Romans 8:28, John teaches his trainees to be thankful for all things, knowing that "all things work together for good to them that love God and are called according to his purposes." Thankfulness prepares the trainee for the inevitable attacks and calamities that will accompany his or her ministry. Without a spirit of thankfulness in all things,

---

[256] Adapted and abridged from John Chen's (pseudonymous) T4T: Training for Trainers.

Satan will find the one thing that will cause a trainee to stop serving the Lord and return to his passive lifestyle.

4. Church Planting Movement Proverbs – John has filled his training sessions with proverbs, gems of wisdom, that communicate important and often overlooked truths.

    a. Church Planting is <u>not</u> rocket science (so don't leave it for the experts or professionals; everyone should be planting churches).

    b. Just do it (God honors doers of the word and not hearers only)!

    c. It is a great joy to win someone to Jesus; it is a greater joy to start a church; it is the greatest joy of all to train someone else to start a church!

5. Training is different from teaching. Teaching transfers knowledge, training changes behavior. John's workshops emphasize training.

6. You've got to practice what you preach and preach what you practice. John never satisfies himself with simply instructing others. An effective trainer must also be a doer.

7. Everyone you meet is in need of either evangelizing or training. Evangelize the lost and train the Christians.

8. You begin by training any Christian who is willing to be trained. However, training implies action. Trainees who fail to carry out the assignments of sharing their story will be embarrassed when they have nothing to share during accountability time. Before long they may drop out, leaving the 'doers of the word' to carry on.

9. John's Training for Trainers does not replace other effective evangelism approaches. Instead, it complements them. John and his trainees continue to use a range of evangelism tools including the *Jesus Film, Four Spiritual Laws, Evangecube, Evangelism Explosion*, and others.

Training Trainers

1. John begins his training session in any church that will allow him to train its lay members. He begins with a biblical foundation of God's command for every Christian to be involved in sharing the gospel.

    a. The call from above – Mark 16:15; Isaiah 6:8
    b. The call from below – Luke 16:27-28
    c. The call from inside – 1 Corinthians 9:16-17
    d. The call from outside – Acts 16:9

2. John next explains that, according to the Bible, it is God's will for you to extend His salvation to your family.

    a. Noah – Genesis 7:1
    b. Abraham – Genesis 19:12-23
    c. Rahab – Joshua 2:17-20
    d. The Gerasene Demoniac – Mark 5:19
    e. Cornelius – Acts 10:23-27
    f. Lydia – Acts 16:14-15
    g. Philippian Jailer – 16:30-33
    h. God also cares about your family and wants to reach them through you.

3. John then teaches his trainees the character of a man or woman that God can use.

    a. They should exhibit qualities of faithfulness and self-sacrifice, be spiritual warriors, full of praise and thanksgiving.
    b. They must rely on the blood of Jesus every day for their protection

4. Next John talks to them about the nature of church and the types of church that are currently prevalent.

a. Traditional church (with building and professional clergy)
b. Cell church (see chapter 8)
c. G-12 church (see chapter 8)
d. A Church Planting Movement church (only this model has unlimited potential for reproduction)

5. John then addresses the four questions facing every Christian who would become a Church Planting Movement implementer.

The Four Questions

Question 1:   What do I say?

a. You tell them your story. Your story is unique to you. It is not subject to argument or refutation. It consists of three parts: before Jesus, how you met Jesus, since Jesus came into your life.
b. Your story needs to be reduced to a 3-4 minute presentation with as few religious words as possible. Lost people don't know religious words.
c. After writing down your story, you will practice saying it out loud 5-10 times before leaving the training session. First, you say it to the ceiling and the floor, then you break into groups of three and practice saying it to each other. Offer one another suggestions as to how to say it more smoothly.

Question 2:   Who do I say it to?

a. If you don't know exactly who you're going to tell your story to, you probably won't tell it to anyone.
b. Make a list of all the lost people in your family and immediate community.
c. Ask God to reveal to you the five persons you're going to share your story with this week.

d. Leave the training session with a prayerful spirit, asking God to create opportunities for you to tell your story to those five persons this week.

Question 3:   What makes you think I'll do this?

a. Accountability is a part of God's plan. Jesus knows we're inclined to avoid doing uncomfortable things; that's why he sent out his disciples in twos and formed groups of believers.
b. At the next training session we will all relate our experiences of sharing our story with our five select persons.
c. The following week, those who have not shared their story will grow uncomfortable. A self-selection process is now underway. Over time those who are doers of the word will be exemplary and inspire the others to follow their example, while those who fail to act will drift away.

Question 4:   What do I do if they say "Yes?"

a. If they say "Yes" to your offer of Jesus in their life, you should rejoice! Then you can begin them in a simple six lesson series that will ground them in their new life and set them on a course of partnering with you in the pursuit of this Church Planting Movement.
b. The Six Lessons – there's nothing magical in these six lessons. There is no special curriculum. As much as possible, John tries to rely on Scripture alone. These lessons can be taught daily, weekly, or anything in between. It is important to note that at the end of lesson six, the new believer/trainee is now prepared to join the multiplication movement.
c. After the six lessons are completed, the new trainee will be participating in an ongoing POUCH church (see Appendix 2 and chapter 4), that will ensure his

continued growth in Christ and the community of
faith.

The Six Lessons

<u>Lesson One</u>: Assurance of Salvation

a. The new believer's new relationship to God in Christ
    is reconfirmed through Scripture.
b. Key verses to review and memorize: Isaiah 59:2;
    Ephesians 2:8-9; 1 Peter 3:18; John 10:28; 2
    Corinthians 5:17; 1 John 1:9; 1 John 5:13
c. The trainer helps the new believer create a "New Birth
    Certificate" to keep in his or her Bible. It states the
    date when "I received Jesus into my heart as my
    savior. He forgave my sin, became my Lord and took
    control of my life. Now I have become a child of God
    and a new creation." Signed:_____.

<u>Lesson Two</u>: A Life of Prayer

a. The trainer explains why we need to pray, the content
    of prayer, three types of answers to prayer, and new
    attitudes that result from prayer.
b. Why we need to pray: Luke 18:1; Ephesians 6:18; 1
    Peter 5:7; Jeremiah 33:3; Hebrews 4:16; Philippians
    4:6-7.
c. The content of prayer: 1 John 1:9; Philippians 4:6-7;
    Psalms 135:3; 1 Thessalonians 5:18; 1 Timothy 2:1
d. Three answers to prayer – Yes, No, Wait
e. New attitudes resulting from prayer – James 1:6;
    James 4:2-3; Psalm 66:18; 1 John 5:14; Luke 18:1

<u>Lesson Three</u>: Having a Daily Quiet Time

a. The trainer explains: "If we really want to know God,
    we need to have close regular contact with him." Set a
    regular time for daily quiet time with God.

b. What can we learn about devotional time with God from these biblical examples? Genesis 19:27; Psalms 5:3; Daniel 6:10; Mark 1:35; Psalm 42:1-2; Psalm 119:147-148.

c. Suggested tools for quiet time: Bible, pen and notebook, quiet place, set time, a reading plan.

d. Preparation for quiet time: Psalm 119:18

Lesson Four: Understanding and Being Church

a. Church is not a building, but "the household of the living God" (1 Timothy 3:15). Church consists of God's people and can meet in your own home.

b. What do these verses teach us about church? Romans 12:5; Ephesians 1:23; Ephesians 5:23.

c. The church has five purposes: Worship – Psalm 149:1; Fellowship – Hebrews 10:25; Teaching – Matthew 28:20; Evangelism – Acts 1:8; and Ministry – Matthew 22:38-39; Romans 12:9-13.

d. The church has rights and obligations. Baptism – Matthew 3:15; Romans 6:3-4; The Lord's Supper – Matthew 26:26-30; 1 Corinthians 11:23-29; Tithes and Offerings – Leviticus 27:30-31.

Lesson Five: Knowing God

a. God, as revealed in Jesus Christ, may be radically different from the conceptions of God that the new believer held in his or her previous life. Understanding God is a lifelong pursuit, but a good foundation begins here.

b. What can we learn about the nature of God from these passages? Jeremiah 31:3; Ephesians 2:4-5; 1 John 3:1; Luke 15:11-24; 2 Thessalonians 3:3; 2 Kings 6:15-18; Daniel 3; 1 Corinthians 10:13; Philippians 4:19; Matthew 6:31-32; Romans 8:31-39; Hebrews 12:6-7; 2 Timothy 3:16; 1 John 4:4

Lesson Six: **God's Will for You**

  a. At this point the training has come full circle. While the new believer is incorporated into a POUCH church meeting in a home (see Appendix 2), he/she is also ready to join forces with you in spreading the good news of Jesus Christ.

  b. Return to the beginning of this training and walk through it with the new believer. Be sure to answer the four questions that he or she will have.

  c. Remember, new believers make the best evangelizers. All their friends are still lost, and their passion for Christ is fresh.

Appendix Two

POUCH Churches

T HERE ARE A variety of indigenously reproducible church models. One of the easiest to implement is one that we encountered in China (see chapter 4) called the POUCH church. You'll remember that POUCH stands for: Participative Bible Study and Worship, Obedience as the mark of success for every believer and church, Unpaid and multiple leaders in each church, Cell groups of 10-20 believers meeting in Homes or storefronts. A POUCH church can be implemented anywhere.

POUCH churches typically gather in the intimacy of someone's home. They may begin with a shared meal during which the members fellowship together and share what God has been doing in their community. The meal may end with communion or prayer time followed by participative worship and Bible study time.

During worship time, a prayer leader may facilitate the sharing of prayer concerns and then leads the group in prayer. If there are other types of leaders they will share their various ministries aimed at the edification of the church body: words of prophecy, offerings of praise and song, reports on evangelism and ministry. Afterwards the group is ready to join in a participative Bible study.

What Does a Participative Bible Study Look Like?

One person or several persons together can lead a participative Bible study. The key to its success is to involve as many participants as possible. So you'll need some leading questions that will invite lots of input. As much as possible, share the leadership role with others in order to develop future Bible study leaders for future churches.

Here are some questions that will lead to thorough study, personal application and life change. You may choose any or all of these to stimulate a lively study.

I.   **Observation (What does the passage say?)**

> Who?
>   What? .
>   Where?
>   When?
>   How?
>   Why?

II.   **Interpretation (What does the passage mean?)**

What did it mean to the original audience?
What does it mean now?
What is the main idea?
How does this passage relate to the rest of the chapter/book?
What other Scripture passages might shed light on this one?

III.   **Application (What should I do?)**

Teaching: *what we should know.*
Rebuking: *what we should avoid doing or stop doing.*
Correcting: *what we should do differently.*
Training in righteousness: *what we should begin or continue doing.*

IV.   **Discussion (To encourage everyone to engage the Scripture)**

What did you like about the passage?

What did you not like about the passage?
What did you not understand about the passage?
What will you take with you or remember about the passage?
What was the main idea of the passage?
What should you do as a result of knowing this passage?

V.   Developing an application plan (instilling obedience)

Decide what is to be applied from the Bible study.
Agree on when the members will obey.
Discover when it will be difficult to obey.
Discuss where they will be when they obey.
Discuss to whom they will teach what they have learned.
Discuss when and to whom they will report their progress—and then pray about it.

Appendix Three

Qur'anic Bridge

BEFORE YOU BEGIN, spend time praying for Muslims, and realize that God is at already at work in this community. There are already 'persons of peace' among them who are open to the good news of his gospel.

It's better that you not walk into a conversation with a copy of the Qur'an; you are only likely to offend Muslims. Instead, ask them to open their Qur'an and read the passages in question. This will draw them into the conversation while preventing you from offending them.

In your encounter with Muslims, it is better to ask questions and draw the truth out of them than to preach the truth at them. There is not enough light in the Qur'an to bring them to salvation, but there are enough flickers of truth to draw out God's 'man of peace' from among them.

Remember, as long as you stay within the Qur'an and ask questions, they can't blame or attack you for teaching Christianity. However, once you have drawn out the man of peace, you will be able to leave the Qur'an behind and teach him the Bible.

There is a Qur'anic passage in Sura 5, called "The Dinner Table Sura" that bridges Muslims with Christians. "You will certainly find the nearest in friendship to those who believe (to be) those who say: We are Christians; this is because there are priests and monks among them and because they do not behave proudly."(5:82)[257]

---

[257] All Qur'anic citations are from *The Holy Qur'an*, translated by M.H. Shakir and published by Tahrike Tarsile Qur'an, Inc., 1983. Available in electronic searchable format at www.hti.umich.edu/k/koran November, 2003.

It's good to know that Mohammed did not begin with a bias against Christians. With work, perhaps we can build on this foundation.

Make a Vocabulary Translation

If you want to communicate with Muslims, you'll need to adopt language that they will understand. Here are some of the basic terms that are common to Muslims and their equivalent in English.

Jesus = *'Isa* (EE-sah)
God = *Allah*
Church = *Jamaat*
Bible = (see below)
    New Testament = *Injil*
    Old Testament = *Torah*
    Psalms = *Jobur*
        Chapter = *Sura* (Each chapter of the Qur'an has its own name; chapter three, for instance, is called *Imran*.)

When you mention the Qur'an, you should be aware that Muslims believe the only true Qur'an is the Qur'an that is in Arabic. Any translation of the Qur'an, they believe to be a paraphrase or deviation from the original. Some may use this to discount your claim to have read the Qur'an. Should this happen you might try the following:

"I want to give special thanks to King Fahd of Saudi Arabia and the Islamic Foundation for directing the Qur'an to be translated into local languages all over the world for clear understanding."

Then offer the following story:

The American owner of a garment factory wrote a letter in English to the factory workers telling them that they should stop making red shirts and start making yellow shirts. In addition, for their hard work, they will be receiving a bonus at the end of the month. The office manager read the letter in English to the workers (who spoke no English) and then placed the letter on the table in front of the employees. The employees were happy to receive the letter, but did not change from making red shirts to yellow ones. When the factory owner found out that his factory was still making red shirts, he was very upset with the manager and the factor workers. He decided to hire a new factory manager and new workers.

"How fortunate we are that King Fahd has paid to have the Qur'an translated into all the languages of the world." (They will certainly agree.)

Now the way is prepared for you to reference the Qur'an in a local or English language translation.

Step One: Some Opening Statements

After a friendly introduction, there are several ways to begin a fruitful discussion. You can say: "I have been reading the Qur'an and I discovered an amazing truth that has given me hope of eternal life in heaven. Will you read to me Sura Al-Imran 3:42-55?"

Or you can say: "I speak to Christians and Muslims about peace and salvation. May I show you what I have found about peace and salvation in Imran 3:42-55?"

During the Muslim holiday of Qurbani Eid (Feast of the Sacrifice), which occurs 40 days after Ramadan, you can say:

"Do you know the correct prayer that you are to pray before the sacrifice?"

If they don't know, you can answer: "Lay your hands on the animal and say to Allah, 'I know that I am a sinner and that I deserve full punishment for my sins. It is my blood that is required for the sacrifice. Yet, instead of taking my blood for my punishment, substitute the blood of this animal.'"

This opens the door to the importance of blood sacrifice in the atonement of Jesus.

Step Two: What the Camel Knows

Christians are accustomed to leading a prospective new believer down *the Roman Road* of verses from the Book of Romans leading one to salvation (Romans 3:23; 6:23; 10:9-10). When you talk to a Muslim, you'll want to take them down *the Camel Trail*.

Arab Muslims have a saying that Allah has 100 names; man knows 99 of these names, but only the camel knows the 100th name of Allah.

For our purposes, CAMEL is an acronym:

Chosen
Announcement
Miracles
Eternal
Life

Chosen

3:42-43 At a dark moment in the history of the world, Allah did something very unusual. Allah spoke through an angel to a young virgin woman named, Marium (Mary). He told her that he had chosen her for an unusual role.

3:44 The Qur'an says the angels cast lots to see who would be given the privilege to guard over Marium during the time of this assignment that Allah had given to her.

Announcement

3:45 Then Allah sent angels to tell Marium his words. Allah said that he would put his Word inside Marium. "Allah's Word" (Ruhollah, in the Arabic) would become flesh in the form of a baby. Allah told Marium to name the baby 'Isa Masih.' Isa is Jesus, and Masih means 'The Anointed or Promised One.'

Isa would be honored by all people in this world and forever in heaven. Finally, Allah said 'Isa would be one of those nearest to himself.

3:46 Furthermore, Allah said that 'Isa's birth will be a message to the entire world and that 'Isa will be one of the good or righteous ones.

3:47 Marium was shocked at the news that Allah had given her. She said to Allah, "How can I have a baby when no man has ever touched me?" Allah was very patient with Marium. He answered her, "I am God, it is easy for me to do whatever I wish."

Why would Allah have 'Isa born without a father? Has there ever been another prophet born without a father? What does this mean to all Muslims?

Imran 3:59 says that 'Isa is like Adam, and this is true, because both of these prophets were born without a father.

What is the significance of being born without an earthly father?"

The answer is apparent

The Qur'an
Book of Imran 3:42-55

3.42 And when the angels said: O Marium! surely Allah has chosen you and purified you and chosen you above the women of the world.

3.43 O Marium! keep to obedience to your Lord and humble yourself, and bow down with those who bow.

3.44 This is of the announcements relating to the unseen which We reveal to you; and you were not with them when they cast their pens (to decide) which of them should have Marium in his charge, and you were not with them when they contended one with another.

3.45 When the angels said: O Marium, surely Allah gives you good news with a Word from Him (of one) whose name is the '. Messiah, Isa son of Marium, worthy of regard in this world and the hereafter and of those who are made near (to Allah).

3.46 And he shall speak to the people when in the cradle and when of old age, and (he shall be) one of the good ones (righteous ones).

when you realize that Adam, before he committed his sin in the garden and became evil, walked with God in the garden. Adam could walk and live with God because he did not have any sin. Adam, at first, was righteous and holy because he inherited his father's righteous nature. Once Adam committed disobedience to Allah, he and all of his descendants became unholy and could no longer live together with the holy God.

In the Qur'an Sura 20:121 we read "Then they both ate of it, so their evil inclinations became manifest to them, and they both began to cover themselves with leaves of the garden, and Adam disobeyed his Lord, so his life became evil (to him)." Now if Adam was expelled from the garden because of only one sin, how are we ever going to get to heaven with our whole book of sins?

And here's the point: Most certainly all of us are children of Adam, except one, his name is 'Isa Masih. Not all Muslims will agree with the concept of sinfulness from birth, but most will admit that all have sinned. The Qur'an gives us a word of hope! Allah gave a Word to Marium in the form of 'Isa. He is a Word of Hope for the entire world. In the Qur'an Sura 21:91 we read: "And she (Marium) guarded her chastity, so We breathed into her of Our inspiration and made her and her son a sign for the nations."

According to the Qur'an, both Marium and her son received the blessing of Allah. Allah breathed His Spirit into her. Now the Spirit is nothing less than the essence of a person.

Do you understand why I love to read the Qur'an? This discovery has enlightened us. But wait, there's more...

3:48 Allah taught 'Isa all the holy books (what Muslims call *Kitabs*). I have read more about 'Isa in the Torah, and the Injil. These books (*Kitabs*) have been translated directly from the original languages and are trustworthy. A friend of mine said that reading all of the holy books makes him feel like a complete Muslim. How about you? Have you read all the holy books?

Miracles

3:49 Allah demonstrated his power through 'Isa. The Qur'an says that lepers were healed, the blind received sight, the crippled walked again and the dead came back to life.

Once again, the Qur'an fills us with hope. 'Isa had the power to bring the dead back to life. POWER OVER DEATH, this is amazing! Before, I had thought that death was the strongest enemy in the world. But now I realize from the Qur'an that 'Isa has been given power over death. The world has been waiting for a prophet that could conquer our greatest and final enemy, death.

3:50 'Isa said that his life verified or confirmed what the prophets had spoken about him in the 'Before Kitabs (books).' The old prophets spoke much about 'Isa Masih. When I read the 'Before Kitabs,' I found over three hundred prophecies about 'Isa

3.47 She said: My Lord! when shall there be a son (born) to me, and man has not touched me? He said: Even so, Allah creates what He pleases; when He has decreed a matter, He only says to it, Be, and it is.

3.48 And He will teach him the Book and the wisdom and the Taurat and the Injil.

3.49 And (make him) an apostle to the children of Israel: That I have come to you with a sign from your Lord, that I determine for you out of dust like the form of a bird, then I breathe into it and it becomes a bird with Allah's permission and I heal the blind and the leprous, and bring the dead to life with Allah's permission and I inform you of what you should eat and what you should store in your houses; most surely there is a sign in this for you, if you are believers.

3.50 And a verifier of that which is before me of the Taurat and that I may allow you part of that which has been forbidden t you, and I have come to you with a sign from your Lord therefore be careful of (your duty to) Allah and obey me.

spoken by the prophets. For example this one was written 758 years before the birth of 'Isa; it says: "God himself shall give you a sign, 'Behold a virgin shall conceive, and bear a son, and shall call his name, Emanuel.' In the original language, the name 'Emanuel' means, 'God is with us.'"

3:51 'Isa said that the Straight Path is to worship Allah and him alone.

3:52-53 In order to get all of the people of the world to worship Allah alone, 'Isa asked for some helpers. A small group of men came forward and said that they are Muslims and that they will help 'Isa. They said that they believe in Allah's message and the Messenger that he sent down. Down from where? Obviously, down from heaven.

Eternal Life

3:55 It is exciting to read that the Muslims who follow 'Isa and do his work will be lifted above all the unbelievers in the world.

Now that you're drawing near the end of your Camel Trail, you will find this story/application of the truth helpful. "If I wanted to get from here to the capital city, who should I choose to help me, someone who has never been there or someone who knows the way and lives

3.51 Surely Allah is my Lord and your Lord, therefore serve Him; this is the right path.

3.52 But when Isa perceived unbelief on their part, he said Who will be my helpers in Allah's way? The disciples said: We are helpers (in the way) of Allah: We believe in Allah and bear witness that we are submitting ones.

3.53 Our Lord! we believe in what Thou hast revealed and we follow the apostle, so write us down with those who bear witness.

3.54 And they planned and Allah (also) planned, and Allah is the best of planners.

3.55 And when Allah said: O Isa, I am going to terminate the period of your stay (on earth) and cause you to ascend unto Me and purify you of those who disbelieve and make those who follow you above those who disbelieve to the day of resurrection; then to Me shall be your return, so l will decide between you concerning that in which you differed.

there now?" According to the Qur'an 'Isa came down from heaven and is in heaven today.

In closing, I have two questions for you...

"Can this prophet, 'Isa, help you and me get to Allah?"

"Can this prophet show you and me the way to eternal life with Allah in heaven?"

Let's Review What the Qur'an Says About 'Isa

1) 'Isa was born without a father and therefore did not inherit Adam's sinful nature.

2) Allah gave Marium's baby the name 'Isa Masih.'

3) From his childhood, 'Isa lived a righteous and holy life.

4) Allah gave 'Isa tremendous power to heal the sick and raise the dead to life.

5) 'Isa has power over our greatest enemy, death.

6) Allah himself taught 'Isa the Holy Kitabs (Books).

7) If anyone wants to know more about 'Isa, they should read the Holy Kitabs.

8) The men who helped 'Isa in his ministry of telling the unbelievers to worship the one true God were called 'Muslims.'

9) Allah lifted 'Isa to himself. He came from Allah and was raised back to Allah. So, 'Isa knows the way to Allah.

10) Muslims who join in 'Isa's work will receive blessings from Allah and will be more blessed than the unbelievers in this world.

The Last Question You Should Expect

If you reach this point, your Muslim friend is bound to ask you, "What do you say about Mohammed?"

This is a deeply emotional question for Muslims, and the best way to answer it is with their own holy book, the Qur'an.

Answer with a question: "What does the Qur'an say? What does Allah have to say about the Prophet Mohammed? Sura 46:9 reads "Say: I am not the first of the apostles (or prophets), and I do not know what will be done with me or with you: I do not follow anything but that which is revealed to me, and I am nothing but a plain warner."

Allah says that Mohammed is *nothing new* among the prophets. He says that Mohammed doesn't know what will be done with him or his followers. He says that Mohammed is simply a *warner*.

The Qur'an also attests to Mohammed being *a sinner*. The Victory Sura 48:1-2 reads: "We have given you (O Mohammed) a manifest victory. That Allah may forgive you your sins of the past and the future..." [from *The Interpretation of the Meanings of the Noble Qur'an*, transl. by M. Al-Hilali and M. Khan (Saudi Arabia: Islamic Book Service, 2002), p. 693.]

Finally, tell them where they can find you if they want to discuss this further. Give those you're talking with an opportunity to follow up with you alone or in a smaller group for further talk about 'Isa. Many of them will not want to see you again, but God's "man (or woman) of peace" will seek you out later and want to know more about 'Isa Masih.

Using the Bible with Muslims

If all goes well, a "person of peace" will seek you out. When this happens, you may want to show him the Jesus Film or make a simple gospel presentation to him. We don't use the Qur'an for presenting the gospel or discipleship, But here are a couple of verses from the Qur'an to help your Muslim friend to understand that Allah's Truth is perfectly revealed in the "Book that came before (the Qur'an)."

In Sura 10:94 we read "But if you are in doubt as to what We have revealed to you, ask those who read the Book before you; certainly the truth has come to you from your Lord, therefore you should not be of the disputers."

Allah tells Mohammed, if you have doubts, you should question "those who read the Book that was before you," because the Truth is found in those Scriptures. He urges Mohammed not to be among the waverers.

Be sure to point out that the Torah and Injil that you are sharing with your friend has been translated from their original languages and from the oldest manuscripts in existence.

Finally, ask your friend to read what it says in the Qur'an, Sura 4:136:

> O you who believe! Believe in Allah and His messenger and the Scripture which He has revealed unto His messenger, and the Scripture which He revealed aforetime. Whosoever disbelieves in Allah and His angels and His Scriptures and His messengers and the Last day he verily has wandered far astray.

It is common for Muslims to allege that the Book "that came before," or the Old and New Testaments have been changed and corrupted and are therefore unreliable. If this issue arises, refer them to their Qur'an, the Cattle Sura 6:114-115 which reads:

> Who has revealed to you the Book (which is) made plain; and those whom We have given the Book know that it is revealed by your Lord with truth, therefore you should not be of the disputers. And the word of your Lord has been accomplished truly and justly; there is none who can change His words, and He is the Hearing, the Knowing.

So, Allah has assured Mohammed that the Book (the Bible) was given by him; it is perfect and no one can change it.

Now that you have drawn out God's "man (or woman) of peace" you should shift completely from the Qur'an to the Bible. As you have seen, the Qur'an makes an effective bridge for Muslims to the gospel, but you don't want to camp on the bridge!

Biblical Index

The Ten Universal CPM Elements

1. **Extraordinary Prayer**

   Psalm 2:8 Ask of me, and I will make the nations your inheritance, the ends of the earth your possession.

   Matthew 9:38 Ask the Lord of the harvest, therefore, to send out workers into his harvest field.

   Mark 1:35 Very early in the morning, while it was still dark, Jesus got up, left the house and went off to a solitary place, where he prayed.

   Mark 9:29 He replied, "This kind can come out only by prayer."

   Luke 10:2 He told them, "The harvest is plentiful, but the workers are few. Ask the Lord of the harvest, therefore, to send out workers into his harvest field."

   Acts 1:14 They all joined together constantly in prayer....

   Acts 3:1 Peter and John were going up to the temple at the time of prayer....

   1 Thessalonians 5:17 pray continually....

2. **Abundant Evangelism**

   Matthew 28:19 Therefore go and make disciples of all nations....

Mark 1:38-39a Jesus replied, "Let us go somewhere else—to the nearby villages—so that I can preach there also. That is why I have come." So he travelled throughout Galilee, preaching in their synagogues....

Mark 16:15 And He said to them, Go into all the world, proclaim the gospel to all the creation.

Act 1:8 But you shall receive power, after the Holy Spirit comes upon you. And you shall be witnesses to Me both in Jerusalem and in all Judea, and in Samaria, and to *the* ends of the earth.

Act 17:17 So he reasoned in the synagogue with the Jews and the God-fearing Greeks, as well as in the marketplace day by day with those who happened to be there.

Act 19:8, 10 Paul entered the synagogue and spoke boldly there for three months, arguing persuasively about the kingdom of God.... This went on for two years, so that all the Jews and Greeks who lived in the province of Asia heard the word of the Lord.

3. **Intentional Planting of Multiplying Churches**

Matthew 28:18-20 Then Jesus came to them and said, "All authority in heaven and on earth has been given to me. Therefore go and make disciples of all nations, baptizing them in the name of the Father and of the Son and of the Holy Spirit, and teaching them to obey everything I have commanded you. And surely I am with you always, to the very end of the age."

Luke 5:1-11; 9:1; 10:1; 1 Corinthians 15:6; Acts 2:41 Just as Jesus chose Twelve, they themselves multiplied into 72 who then multiplied into 500 who then multiplied into 3,000.

John 15:8 This is to my Father's glory, that you bear much fruit, showing yourselves to be my disciples.

Acts 9:31 Then the church throughout Judea, Galilee and Samaria enjoyed a time of peace. It was strengthened; and encouraged by the Holy Spirit, it grew in numbers, living in the fear of the Lord.

Acts 16:5 So the churches were strengthened in the faith and grew daily in numbers.

4. **The Authority of God's Word**

Matthew 5:18 I tell you the truth, until heaven and earth disappear, not the smallest letter, not the least stroke of a pen, will by any means disappear from the Law until everything is accomplished.

Luke 24:27 And beginning with Moses and all the Prophets, he explained to them what was said in all the Scriptures concerning himself.

Luke 24:45-46 Then he opened their minds so they could understand the Scriptures. He told them, "This is what is written: The Christ will suffer and rise from the dead on the third day,"

Acts 17:11 Now the Bereans were of more noble character than the Thessalonians, for they received the message with great eagerness and examined the Scriptures every day to see if what Paul said was true.

2 Timothy 3:16-17 All Scripture is God-breathed and is useful for teaching, rebuking, correcting and training in righteousness, so that the man of God may be thoroughly equipped for every good work.

Hebrews 4:12 For the word of God is living and active. Sharper than any double-edged sword, it penetrates even to dividing soul and spirit, joints and marrow; it judges the thoughts and attitudes of the heart.

5. Local Leadership

Acts 6:3 Brothers, choose seven men from among you who are known to be full of the Spirit and wisdom. We will turn this responsibility over to them

Acts 14:23 Paul and Barnabas appointed elders for them in each church and, with prayer and fasting, committed them to the Lord, in whom they had put their trust.

1 Corinthians 14:26 When you come together, everyone has a hymn, or a word of instruction, a revelation, a tongue or an interpretation.

Titus 1:5 ...appoint elders in every town, as I directed you.

1 Peter 4:10 Each one should use whatever gift he has received to serve others, faithfully administering God's grace in its various forms.

6. Lay Leadership

Matthew 4:18-20 As Jesus was walking beside the Sea of Galilee, he saw two brothers, Simon called Peter and his brother Andrew. They were casting a net into the lake, for they were fishermen. "Come, follow me," Jesus said, "and I will make you fishers of men." At once they left their nets and followed him.

Mark 3:18 ...Andrew, Philip, Bartholomew, Matthew, Thomas, James son of Alphaeus, Thaddaeus, Simon the Zealot.

Luke 5:30 But the Pharisees and the teachers of the law who belonged to their sect complained to his disciples, "Why do you eat and drink with tax collectors and 'sinners'?"

Acts 4:13 When they saw the courage of Peter and John and realized that they were unschooled, ordinary men, they were astonished and they took note that these men had been with Jesus.

1 Corinthians 1:26 Brothers, think of what you were when you were called. Not many of you were wise by human standards; not many were influential; not many were of noble birth.

2 Corinthians 3:4-6 Such confidence as this is ours through Christ before God. Not that we are competent in ourselves to claim anything for ourselves, but our competence comes from God. He has made us competent as ministers of a new covenant— not of the letter but of the Spirit; for the letter kills, but the Spirit gives life.

7. Home Cell Churches

Jesus brings worship and communion with him into the home. He teaches, does miracles, heals and is worshiped at Peter's house in Capernaum (Mark 2, 9), at the wedding feast in Cana (John 2), in the homes of Zaccheus (Luke 19), and the home of Mary, Martha and Lazarus (John 12).

Mark 2:1-2 A few days later, when Jesus again entered Capernaum, the people heard that he had come home. So many gathered that there was no room left, not even outside the door, and he preached the word to them.

Luke 10:7 Stay in that house, eating and drinking whatever they give you, for the worker deserves his wages. Do not move around from house to house.

Acts 5:42 Day after day, in the temple courts and from house to house, they never stopped teaching and proclaiming the good news that Jesus is the Christ.

Acts 8:3 But Saul began to destroy the church. Going from house to house, he dragged off men and women and put them in prison.

Acts 12:12 When this had dawned on him, he went to the house of Mary the mother of John, also called Mark, where many people had gathered and were praying.

Romans 16:5 Greet also the church that meets at their house.

1 Corinthians 16:19 The churches in the province of Asia send you greetings. Aquila and Priscilla greet you warmly in the Lord, and so does the church that meets at their house.

Colossians 4:15 Give my greetings to the brothers at Laodicea, and to Nympha and the church in her house.

Philemon 1:1-2 Paul, a prisoner of Christ Jesus, and Timothy our brother, To Philemon our dear friend and fellow-worker, to Apphia our sister, to Archippus our fellow-soldier and to the church that meets in your home

8. **Churches Planting Churches**

Jesus expected each of his disciples to bear fruit (Luke 19:13-26; John 15:8). So he sent them out two by two into all the surrounding villages to establish His kingdom (Mark 6, Matthew 10, Luke 10).

In the same way, He equipped the early church to spread the gospel and establish churches wherever they went.

Acts 8:4 Those who had been scattered preached the word wherever they went.

Ephesians 4:11-12 It was he who gave some to be apostles, some to be prophets, some to be evangelists, and some to be pastors and teachers, to prepare God's people for works of service, so that the body of Christ may be built up

1 Thessalonians 1:8 The Lord's message rang out from you not only in Macedonia and Achaia—your faith in God has become known everywhere. Therefore we do not need to say anything about it,

9. **Rapid Reproduction**

Jesus summoned disciples to follow Him immediately and they did.

Mark 1:18 At once they left their nets and followed him.

Mark 1:20 Without delay he called them, and they left their father Zebedee in the boat with the hired men and followed him.

Jesus drew enormous crowds of followers from the earliest days of His ministry.

Mark 2:2 So many gathered that there was no room left, not even outside the door, and he preached the word to them.

Acts 2:47 praising God and enjoying the favor of all the people. And the Lord added to their number daily those who were being saved.

Acts 14:21-23 They preached the good news in that city and won a large number of disciples. Then they returned to Lystra, Iconium and Antioch, strengthening the disciples and encouraging them to remain true to the faith. "We must go through many hardships to enter the kingdom of God," they said. Paul and Barnabas appointed elders for them in each church and, with prayer and fasting, committed them to the Lord, in whom they had put their trust.

Acts 16:5 So the churches were strengthened in the faith and grew daily in numbers.

Acts 19:20 In this way the word of the Lord spread widely and grew in power.

10. Healthy Churches

Jesus defined church in relation to Himself, as His body. It was built, not of bricks and mortar, but of His Spirit and the fellowship of His saints.

Matthew 18:20 In this way the word of the Lord spread widely and grew in power.

Likewise in the early church, church buildings as we know them today appear nowhere. Instead, the believers worshiped wherever they were—home, synagogue, temple, riverside. What mattered was the vitality of the body of Christ.

Acts 2:41-47 Those who accepted his message were baptized, and about three thousand were added to their number that day. They devoted themselves to the apostles' teaching and to the fellowship, to the breaking of bread and to prayer. Everyone was filled with awe, and many wonders and miraculous signs were done by the apostles. All the believers were together and had everything in common. Selling their possessions and goods, they gave to anyone as he had need. Every day they continued to meet together in the temple courts. They broke bread in their homes and ate together with glad and sincere hearts, praising God and enjoying the favor of all the people. And the Lord added to their number daily those who were being saved.

1 Corinthians 12:27 Now you are the body of Christ, and each one of you is a part of it.

Ephesians 4:12 to prepare God's people for works of service, so that the body of Christ may be built up

Additional CPM Characteristics in the Bible

All Peoples Will Be Reached
Psalm 2:8 Ask of me and I will make the nations your inheritence
Psalm 67 Let all the peoples praise you.
Matthew 24:3, 14 ...and this gospel shall be preached to all peoples.
Revelation 5:9 . you purchased men for God from every tribe and language and people and nation.
Revelation 7:9 a great multitude that no one could count, from every nation, tribe, people and language, standing before the throne and in front of the Lamb.
Revelation 15:4 All nations will come and worship before you

Bold Response to Persecution
Luke 21:12-15 But before all this, they will lay hands on you and persecute you. They will deliver you to synagogues and prisons, and you will be brought before kings and governors, and all on account of my name. This will result in your being witnesses to them. But make up your mind not to worry beforehand how you will defend yourselves. For I will give you words and wisdom that none of your adversaries will be able to resist or contradict.
Acts 4:13 When they saw the courage of Peter and John
Acts 4:29 Now, Lord, consider their threats and enable your servants to speak your word with great boldness.

Acts 4:31 And they were all filled with the Holy Spirit and spoke the word of God boldly.
Acts 5: 41 The apostles left the Sanhedrin, rejoicing because they had been counted worthy of suffering disgrace for the Name.

God Himself Will Do It
Habakkuk 1:5 For I am going to do something in your days that you would not believe, even if you were told.
Philippians 1:6 he who began a good work in you will carry it on to completion until the day of Christ Jesus.
1 Peter 4:11 If anyone speaks, he should do it as one speaking the very words of God. If anyone serves, he should do it with the strength God provides

Indigenous Leadership (Model, Assist, Watch & Leave)
2 Timothy 2:2 And the things you have heard me say in the presence of many witnesses entrust to reliable men who will also be qualified to teach others.
Titus 1:5 appoint elders in every town, as I directed you.

Multiple Church Leaders
1 Corinthians 12:7 Now to each one the manifestation of the Spirit is given for the common good.
1 Corinthians 14:26 (…everyone has a hymn, or a word…a revelation…)
Ephesians 4:11 gave some to be apostles, some to be prophets, some to be evangelists, and some to be pastors and teachers
1 Peter 4:10-11 Each one should use whatever gift he has received to serve others, faithfully administering God's grace in its various forms.

Family-Based Conversion Patterns
Acts 16:15 When she and the members of her household were baptized

Acts 16:31 Believe in the Lord Jesus, and you will be saved—you and your household.

Paradigm Shift

Jonah 1-4, the reluctant missionary

Habakkuk 1:5 ...you would not believe even if you were told.

Matthew 9:17 they pour new wine into new wineskins

Romans 12:2 Do not conform any longer to the pattern of this world, but be transformed by the renewing of your mind.

Persecution and Suffering

Matthew 10:17-25 they will hand you over to the local councils and flog you in their synagogues.

2 Corinthians 11:23-29 I have...been in prison more frequently, been flogged more severely, and been exposed to death again and again.

1 Peter 4:12-13 do not be surprised at the painful trial you are suffering

Revelation 6:9-11 How long, Sovereign Lord, holy and true, until you judge the inhabitants of the earth and avenge our blood?

Revelation 12:10-12 "the devil has gone down to you! He is filled with fury, because he knows that his time is short."

Rapid Spread of the gospel

Acts 2:47 the Lord added to their number daily those who were being saved.

Acts 19:20 the word of the Lord spread widely and grew in power.

Rapid Assimilation of New Believers

Acts 2:41 about three thousand were added to their number that day.

Acts 8:26-39 "Look, here is water. Why shouldn't I be baptized?"

Acts 16:5 the churches were strengthened in the faith and grew daily in numbers.

Remove Obstacles

Matthew 13:44 The kingdom of heaven is like treasure hidden in a field. When a man found it, he hid it again, and then in his joy went and sold all he had and bought that field.

Mark 2:4-5 Since they could not get him to Jesus because of the crowd, they made an opening in the roof

Luke 3:4-6 Prepare the way for the Lord, make straight paths for him. Every valley shall be filled in, every mountain and hill made low. The crooked roads shall become straight, the rough ways smooth.

The Man of Peace, Opening New Work

Matthew 10:5-15 Whatever town or village you enter, search for some worthy person there and stay at his house until you leave.

Luke 10:1-18 If a man of peace is there, your peace will rest on him;

John 4:7-42 When a Samaritan woman came to draw water, Jesus said to her

Acts 10:1-31 At Caesarea there was a man named Cornelius....He and all his family were devout and God-fearing

Acts 16:14-40 ...a woman named Lydia... who was a worshipper of God. The Lord opened her heart to respond....

Unreached People Groups

Matthew 18:12-13 will he not leave the ninety-nine on the hills and go to look for the one

Acts 1:8 ...you will be my witnesses...to the ends of the earth.

Romans 15:20-23 It has always been my ambition to preach the gospel where Christ was not known...

Glossary of Terms

alien abduction – when foreigners dominate Christianity among a people group, sapping local initiative for a Church Planting Movement.

Bhojpuri – a language spoken by several people groups residing primarily in the northern Indian states of Uttar Pradesh and Bihar, and southern Nepal.

Bible storying – using stories from the Bible, without written texts, for evangelism, discipleship, and leadership development. Begun as a means of evangelizing nonliterate peoples, it has subsequently expanded into broader audiences.

CAMEL training – Muslim evangelism training that uses the Qur'an as a bridge. CAMEL is an acronym for Chosen, Announcement, Miracles, and Eternal Life. This is a mnemonic device to help remember key verses in the Qur'an that speak of Jesus.

cell churches – small church-like groups that meet in homes, but are linked together under the leadership of a single church pastor.

chronological Bible storying – relating the Bible's great themes through stories that culminate in the gospel.

Church Growth Movement – school of missiology and church growth begun in the 1960s at Fuller Theological Seminary by Donald McGavran aimed at growing more dynamic churches.

Church Planting Movement – a rapid multiplication of indigenous churches planting churches that sweeps through a people group or population segment.

contextualization – missionary efforts to eliminate Western cultural forms of Christianity by adapting the faith to non-Christian cultures.

devil's candy – Something that initially seems positive, but is ultimately destructive. In the case of Church Planting Movements, the devil's candy can be any Christian virtue that consumes one's energies at the expense of pursuing multiplying indigenous churches.

evangelized – having heard the gospel in an intelligible manner so that response can be made.

house churches – churches that meet in homes, generally smaller than 30 members with unpaid lay leaders.

indigenous – literally, generated from within. Refers to churches or movements that have their driving force from within the group itself rather than from outside funds or outside direction.

Khmer- The majority people group of Cambodia.

Khmer Rouge – literally "Red Khmer," the Communists of Cambodia under Pol Pot in the 1970s.

Kui – Tribal people group located in the Khond Hills of Orissa, India.

MAWL - Model, Assist, Watch and Leave. The mantra of the CPM practitioner. Model evangelism and church, Assist local believers to do the same, Watch to ensure that they are able to do it, and then Leave to go start the cycle elsewhere.

people group – More specifically an *ethnolinguistic* people group. Refers to a people having a shared sense of ethnic identity (the *us*-ness) and a common language.

people movements – A movement of an ethnolinguistic people or community into the Christian faith.

population segment – A subset of an ethnolinguistic people, such as a youth-subset of a given people group, or an urban subset of a given people group.

POUCH churches – POUCH is an acronym for a type of church frequently found in Church Planting Movements. The acronym stands for **P**articipative Bible study worship groups, **O**bedience to God's Word as the mark of successful life and belief, **U**npaid church leaders, clustered in small **C**ell groups, meeting in **H**omes or other non-religious settings.

precision harvesting – a process of evangelism that begins with broad proclamation of the gospel followed by careful follow up with those who respond positively to the message.

Qur'anic bridge – using the Qur'an as a bridge to introduce Muslims to Jesus Christ.

RLTC – Rural Leadership Training Centers developed and used to train leaders and church planters in the Cambodia Church Planting Movement.

Strategy Coordinator – a missionary who takes responsibility for developing and implementing a Church Planting Movement strategy for a people group or population segment.

training for trainers – also called T4T, the training program developed by John Chen that led to the largest Church Planting Movement in history.

two-by-two principle – the principle of leadership development through one-on-one modeling and mentoring. It is built on and named after the 2 Timothy 2:2.

unreached-people group – a people group that is less than 2% Christian and lacking the internal evangelization momentum to reach the remaining 98% who are lost, thus necessitating missionary assistance.

WIGTake – An acronym for What's It Gonna Take? This is the trigger question that challenges a Christian to ask God what it will take for an entire people to come to faith in Christ.

Selected Bibliography

Adeney, David. *"Springtime for the Church in China?"* Christianity Today. (June 18, 1982) 28-31.

Allen, Donald R. *Barefoot in the Church*, Richmond: John Knox, 1972.

Alexander, Gary. *"House Churches: Your Hope for the Future"* Christian Life Vol. 43:9 (January 1982) 32.

Allen, Roland. *Missionary Methods: St. Paul's or Ours?* Grand Rapids: Eerdmans, 1962.

Allen, Roland. *Spontaneous Expansion of the Church.* Grand Rapids, Michigan: Eerdmans, 1962.

Anderson, Philip, and Anderson, Phoebe. *The House Church*, Nashville: Abingdon, 1975.

Armstrong, Heyward, ed. *Church Planting Movements Workbook*. Richmond: ICEL, 2001.

"Around 25,000 Gypsies gather in France." Agence France Presse. (August 24, 2000).

Baker, Robert A., *The Southern Baptist Convention and Its People*. Nashville: Broadman Press, 1974.

Banks, Robert. *Paul's Idea of Community: The Early House Churches in Their Historical Setting*. Grand Rapids: Eerdmans, 1980.

Barrett, David. *Schism & Renewal in Africa, an analysis of six thousand contemporary religious movements.* Nairobi: Oxford University Press, 1968.

Barrett, David. *World Christian Encyclopedia, 2nd Edition, Vol. 1.* London: Oxford University Press, 2001.

Barrett, Lois. *Building the House Church.* Scottdale: Herald Press, 1986.

Benko, S., and J. I. O'Rourke, eds. *Early Church History: The Roman Empire as the Setting of Primitive Christianity.* London: Oliphants, 1971.

Berger, Peter L. *A Rumor of Angels: Modern Society and the Rediscovery of the Supernatural.* Garden City: Doubleday, 1967.

Bird, Warren. *"The Great Small-Group Takeover."* Christianity Today Vol. 38:2 (February 7, 1994)25-29.

Branick. V. *The House Church in the Writings of Paul.* Wilmington, Del.: Michael Glazier, 1989.

Campenhausen, H. von. *Tradition and Life in the Church.* London: Collins, 1968.

Carlton, Bruce. *Acts 29, practical training in facilitating church-planting movements among the neglected harvest fields.* Singapore: Radical Obedience Publishing, 2003.

Carlton, Bruce. *Amazing Grace, lessons on Church Planting Movements from Cambodia.* Chennai: Mission Educational Books, 2000.s

Cho, David Yonggi. *Successful Home Cell Groups,* New Brunswick, NJ: Bridge-Logos Publishers, 1981.

Choudhrie, Victor. *"House Church: A Bible Study."* House2House (March 2001). On-line at www.house2house.net

Creswell, Mike. *"The Netherlands: Providing an anchor."* The Commission (November 1997).

Collins, Travis. *The Baptist Mission of Nigeria, 1850-1993.* Ibadan, Nigeria: Associated Book-Makers Nigeria Limited, 1993.

Comiskey, Joel. *Home Cell Group Explosion.* Houston: Touch Publications, 1999.

Comiskey, Joel. *Groups of 12.* Houston: Touch Publications, 1999.

Cosby, Gordon. *Handbook for Mission Groups.* Waco: Word, 1975.

Crider, Stephanie P. *"The Evangelical Movement Among Spanish Gypsies."* Senior honors thesis submitted to the faculty of the Department of History and the Honors Council at Samford University, Birmingham, Alabama [1989].

Cullmann, 0. *Early Christian Worship.* London: SCM, 1953.

Diamond, Jared. *Guns, Germs and Steel: the fates of human societies.* New York: WW Norton & Co., 1999.

Darnton, John. *"Europe's Gypsies Hear the Call of the Evangelicals."* The New York Times. Late City Final Edition, Section A (August 25, 1983), 2.

Dulles, Avery. *Models of the Church.* Garden City: Doubleday, 1978.

Dumbaugh, Donald F. *The Believers' Church: The History and Character of Radical Protestantism.* New York: Macmillan, 1968; Scottdale, Pa.: Herald Press, 1985.

Eller, Vernard. *The Outward Bound: Caravaning as the Style of the Church.* Grand Rapids: Eerdmans, 1980,

"Evangelical Leaders Assess Home Churches." Christian Life Vol. 43:9 (January 1982) 32-44.

Filson, Floyd V. *"The Significance of the Early House Churches."* Journal of Biblical Literature 58 (1939): 109-I 12.

Foster, Arthur L., ed. *The House Church Evolving.* Chicago: Exploration, 1976.

Gager, I. G. *Kingdom and Community: The Social World of Early Christianity.* Englewood Cliffs, N.J.: Prentice-Hall, 1975.

Garmo, John. *Lifestyle Worship* Nashville: Nelson. 1993.

Garrison, David. *Church Planting Movements.* Richmond: International Mission Board, 1999.

Gerber, Michael. *The E-Myth Revisited: why small businesses don't work.* London: HarperBusiness, 1995.

Getz, Gene. *Building Up One Another.* Wheaton: Victor, 1976.

Getz, Gene. *Sharpening the Focus of the Church.* Chicago: Moody, 1974.

Gillmor, Verla. *"Community is Their Middle Name."* Christianity Today (November 23, 2000) 50.

Gladwell, Malcolm. *The Tipping Point: how little things can make a big difference.* London: Little Brown and Co., 2000.

Green, M. *Evangelism in the Early Church*. London: Hodder & Stoughton, 1970.

Griffin, E. *Getting Together: A Guide for Good Groups*. Downers Grove: Inter-Varsity, 1982.

Grimes, Barbara. *Ethnologue, 14th Edition Vol. 1: Languages of the World*. Dallas: Summer Institute of Linguistics, 2002.

Hinton, Keith. *Growing Churches Singapore Style*. Singapore: OMF, 1985.

Hobbs, Andrew. *"Gypsies take to highway to heaven."* The Observer (August 1, 1993) 20.

Icenogle, Gareth Weldon. *Biblical Foundations for Small Group Ministry, An Integrational Approach*. Downers Grove: InterVarsity Press, 1994.

"India: 3,000 House Churches Planted in Madhya Pradesh Since 1994" on-line at www.youtharise.com/news/14feb2000/story8.htm

Johnston, Patrick. *Operation World*. Grand Rapids: Zondervan, 1993.

Judge, E. A. *The Social Pattern of Christian Groups in the First Century*. London: Tyndale Press, 1960.

Kraus, C. Norman, ed. *Evangelicalism and Anabaptism*. Scottdale: Herald Press, 1979.

Kreider, Larry. *House to House*. Houston: TOUCH Publications, 1995.

Lambert, Tony. *China's Christian Millions: the costly revival*. Singapore: OMF, 1999.

Latourette, Kenneth Scott. *A History of the Expansion of Christianity*. New York: Harper, 1937-1945.

Leatherwood, Rick. *"Mongolia: As a People Movement to Christ Emerges, What Lessons Can We Learn?"* Mission Frontiers (July/August 1998).

L'Engle, Madeline. *A Wrinkle in Time*. New York: Bantam, 1976.

Lewis, Bernard. *Race and Slavery in the Middle East, an historical enquiry*. London: Oxford University Press, 1990.

Liégeois, Jean-Pierre. *Roma, Gypsies, Travellers*, transl. by Sinéad ní Shuinéar. Strasbourg: Council of Europe, 1994. Originally published in French as *Roma, Tsiganes, Voyageurs*, in 1992.

Lindner, Eileen W. ed. *Yearbook of American and Canadian Churches, 2001*. Nashville: Abingdon Press, 2001.

Martin, Ralph P. *The Family and the Fellowship*. Grand Rapids: Eerdmans, 1979.

Martin, Ralph P. *Worship in the Early Church*. Westwood: Revell, 1964.

McGavran, Donald. *"House Churches: A Key Factor For Growth"* South Korea Global Church Growth Bulletin 29:5-6 Jan 1992.

McGavran, Donald. *Understanding Church Growth*. Grand Rapids: Eerdmans, 1970.

Minear, Paul S. *Images of the Church in the New Testament*. Philadelphia: Westminster, 1960.

Mir, Tariq. *"It's Conversion Time in the Valley."* in The Indian Express. Srinagar, India, April 5, 2003.

Morey, Robert A. *Worship is all of Life*. Camp Hill: Christian Publications, 1984.

Neill, Stephen. *A History of Christian Missions*. New York: Penguin, 1964.

Parshall, Phil. *New Paths in Muslim Evangelism: evangelical approaches to Contextualization*. Grand Rapids: Baker Books, 1981.

Perry, Tobin. *"Reaching a city, reaching the world."* The Commission. Richmond: International Mission Board. September 1999.

Peterson, Jim. *Church without Walls, Moving Beyond Traditional Boundaries*. Colorado Springs: Navpress, 1992.

"Revival in Inner Mongolia- 500,000 Saved in Past 12 Months." Voice of China, the official voice of the house churches in China. Vol. 1:1 (Summer edition).

Sauder, Brian. and Kreider, Larry. *Helping you build Cell Churches*. Ephrata: House to House Publications, 1998.

Schaller, Lyle E. *Assimilating New Members*. Nashville: Abingdon, 1978.

Shurden, Walter. *"The Southern Baptist Synthesis: Is it Cracking?"* in A Baptist History and Heritage, Vol. 16:2 (April 1981).

Simson, Wolfgang. *Houses that Change the World*. Carlisle, U.K.: Paternoster Publishing, 2001.

Singh, Manpreet. *"Harassed Kashmiri Christians Reach out to Discrete Muslims."* Christianity Today. Vol. 46:10 (September 9, 2002) 26.

Skoglund, John E. *Worship in the Free Churches.* Valley Forge: Judson, 1965.

Smith, Elliott. *The Advance of Baptist Associations Across America.* Nashville: Broadman Press, 1979.

Sng, Bobby E.K. *In His Good Time: the story of the church in Singapore, 1819-1992, 2ND edition.* Singapore: Singapore: Graduates' Christian Fellowship, 1993.

Snowden, Mark. ed., *Toward Church Planting Movements*, Richmond: International Mission Board, 1997.

Snyder, Graydon F. *Ante Pacem: Archaeological Evidence of Church Life Before Constantine.* Macon: Mercer University, 1985.

Snyder, Howard A. *Liberating the Church. The Ecology of Church and Kingdom.* Downers Grove: InterVarsity, 1983.

Snyder, Howard A. *The Radical Wesley and Patterns for Church Renewal.* Downers Grove: InterVarsity, 1980.

Snyder, Howard A. *The Problem of Wineskins.* Downers Grove: InterVarsity, 1977.

Sprinkle, Randy *Follow Me: Lessons for Becoming a Prayerwalker,* Birmingham: New Hope Publishers, 2001.

Trueblood, Elton. *The Company of the Committed.* New York: Harper and Row, 1961.

Trueblood, Elton. *The Incendiary Fellowship*. New York: Harper and Row, 1967.

Viola, Frank. *Rethinking the Wineskin: The Practice of the New Testament Church*, Jacksonville: Present Testimony Ministry, 1998.

Warren, Rick. *The Purpose-Driven Church*. Grand Rapids: Zondervan, 1995.

Weber, Hans-Ruedi. *"The Church in the House."* Concern. (June, 1958) 7-28.

Webster, Justin. *"Gypsies for Jesus."* The Independent, *Features* Section. London (February 11, 1995) 30.

Wuthnow, Robert. *"How Small Groups are Transforming Our Lives."* Christianity Today Vol. 38:2 (February 7, 1994) 20-24.

Zdero, Rad. *The House Church Manifesto: a guidebook for the global house church movement*. Pasadena: William Carey Library, 2003.

Zoba, Wendy Murray. *"The Gypsy Reformation."* Christianity Today (February 8, 1999) 50-54.

General Index

222, 234, 282, 284, 294, 334, 340

Order additional copies of *Church Planting Movements* and
Kevin Greeson's *Camel Training Manual* at:

U.S. Toll free phone: (866) 698-7564 or (806) 853-8068
U.S. Fax number: (806) 853-8076
Or visit us on the web at:

www.ChurchPlantingMovements.com

Church Planting Movements is also available from
Fresh Wind Distributing at: www.FreshWindDistributing.com

Single copies $ 18.95 each*

10-49 @ $ 17.95 each*

50 copies or more @ $ 15.95 each*

(*plus shipping & handling)

- - - - - - - - - - - - - - - cut here -

Number of copies_____

Mail book(s) to:
Name   _____
Address   _____
City/State   _____
Country & Postal Code _____

Credit Card Information: ___ MasterCard
                            ___ Visa
                            ___ American Express

Name as it appears on the card: _____
Expiration date: _____
Credit Card Number: _____
(Allow 2 weeks for delivery)

Church Planting Movements
Fresh Wind Distributing
P.O. Box 94182
Lubbock, TX 79493-4182